India's Economic Growth

Also by Jati Sengupta

COMPETITION AND GROWTH

LA TEORIA DE LA POLITICA ECONOMICA CUANTITATIVA (*with K. Fox and E. Thorbecke*)

India's Economic Growth

A Strategy for the New Economy

Jati Sengupta

University of California
Santa Barbara, USA

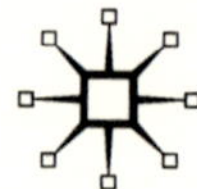

First published 2005 by
PALGRAVE MACMILLAN
Houndmills, Basingstoke, Hampshire RG21 6XS and
175 Fifth Avenue, New York, N.Y. 10010
Companies and representatives throughout the world

PALGRAVE MACMILLAN is the global academic imprint of the Palgrave
Macmillan division of St. Martin's Press, LLC and of Palgrave Macmillan Ltd.
Macmillan® is a registered trademark in the United States, United Kingdom
and other countries. Palgrave is a registered trademark in the European
Union and other countries.

ISBN-13: 978–1–4039–9617–6
ISBN-10: 1–4039–9617–2

This book is printed on paper suitable for recycling and made from fully
managed and sustained forest sources.

A catalogue record for this book is available from the British Library.

Library of Congress Cataloging-in-Publication Data

Sengupta, Jatikumar.
    India's economic growth : a strategy for the new economy / Jati K. Sengupta.
        p.   cm.
    Includes bibliographical references and index.
    ISBN 1–4039–9617–2
    1. India—Economic conditions—21st century.   2. Information
technology—Economic aspects—India.   3. Information services
industry—India.   4. India—Economic policy—21st century.
    5. Asia—Economic conditions—21st century.   I. Title.

    HC435.3.S46 2005
    330.954—dc22   2005048778

10   9   8   7   6   5   4   3   2   1
14   13   12   11   10   09   08   07   06   05

Transferred to digital printing in 2006.

To my wife, who impressed me with her vision of India – her promise and potential

Contents

List of Tables

Preface

A new paradigm of growth and development is the focus of this volume. This is based on the New Economy and its growth. Information technology (IT) and its diffusion throughout India and the world is the key to the new economy and its growth. It holds all the promise and potential.

This new economy is characterized by three Is: innovation, interdependence and investment in knowledge capital. Innovation takes many forms besides new technological inventions and designs. It includes new areas of applied research, new methods of learning by doing and new organizational methods. Interdependence means the interaction between sectors through knowledge diffusion, trade and commerce and externality effects. This interaction helps other sectors grow by forward and backward linkages through cost efficiency and demand expansion respectively. The IT services act as a catalyst, improving the productivity of other sectors using IT services. They also expand markets through e-trade and e-commerce. In China and Taiwan this force has played a dominant role in raising national growth rates and revitalizing rural and agricultural sectors. Finally, the investment in human and physical capital has helped speed up the growth miracle in Southeast Asian countries. Investment in skill development for the IT sector helps to build the information infrastructure, which is so crucial to the growth of the new economy.

The growth strategy for the new economy is based on three Cs: core competence, competition efficiency and comparative advantage. Core competence involves productivity improvements, which entail cost efficiency. This cost efficiency enhances the market, both domestic and foreign. Economies of scale and scope can then be readily captured in this elastic market. Competition efficiency exploits the income elasticity in world markets and price elasticity in the domestic markets. India has much to gain from following competitive strategies in the world markets for its IT services. Finally, the comparative advantage principle suggests that India has to restructure its export trade particularly in the IT services: from body shopping to software package development, from the agency system to new start-ups and from old ways to new. This is the transition that is urgently needed and which should be based on market research studies of the world market and a continuous monitoring of strategic policies. This should be the new model of policymaking for India.

The old economy was based mainly on a zero-sum set of strategies. The net growth dividend was nil to negligible. The new economy must develop new strategies for an expanding positive-sum game, where the public and private sectors forge effective cooperative links, so that the net payoff could be an increasing-sum game. This volume presents a list of such growth enhancing strategies for India.

Growth strategies for the new economy in India are based on three sources: the successful experiences of the newly industrializing countries (NICs) in Asia, the lessons of new growth theory and the catalytic role of the IT sector growth in India over the last decade.

It is my conviction that India will attain her potential within the next two decades. It is only necessary to follow the growth strategies for the new economy. As Vivekananda declared: "Already before my mind rises one of the marvelous verses of Rig-Veda Samhita which says, 'Be thou all of one mind, be thou all of one thought'. Being of one mind is the secret of society. For mark you, the future India depends entirely on that. That is the secret – accumulation of will-power, coordination, bringing them all, as it were into one focus."

I take this opportunity to record my deep appreciation to the two people who helped me most as I was writing this volume: to my daughter who is marketing director of a large international company in Silicon Valley, and to my wife. My daughter helped me with my thoughts about the IT service sector in India, and my wife insisted that I write about India, her strength and potential. I hope I have succeeded in fulfilling their expectations.

JATI SENGUPTA

1
Growth Synergy in India: a Challenge

India, today, is facing a challenge: her history versus her expectations. India's past history with its regulations and lack of openness in trade has faced the challenge of policy reform. The information technology (IT) sector of today has given India a jolt. It has catapulted the country to a new economy. Economic reforms have set up new expectations: more openness, more liberalization and a new demand for growth like the NICs (newly industrializing countries) in Asia.

The history of economic growth in India is marked by several striking features and contrasts. First, its growth potential is very high, much higher than is observed. The recent growth of the IT sector and its cumulative impact is one evidence of this. The global contributions of non-resident Indians (NRIs) provide another. Yet India presents a contrast with the rapidly growing newly industrializing countries (NICs) of Southeast Asia. The NICs have grown at a much faster rate and countries like South Korea have shown remarkable success in world markets for high technology products. Second, India has a huge potential market due to a large population base with a strong middle class. Yet foreign investment has been very low, lower than for the NICs. It is much lower than in China, where totalitarian controls are more pervasive.

The population base provides a growth synergy when it combines skills and creativity. Human capital, learning by doing and knowledge spillover emphasize this growth synergy. Synergism is at the heart of India's growth potential; its total effect is much greater than the sum of individual effects taken independently of one another.

Third, compared to the NICs India has followed a very slow process of transition from regulation and control to an open market system of competition and outward orientation. Even countries like China and Vietnam with their long history of communism and centralist planning have adopted a more rapid transition. Economic reforms in India have been slow, unsteady and at times clouded by the uncertainty of the political climate. The growth success of the NICs in Asia has evidenced four major components:

(a) outward-looking orientation in trade with a strong emphasis on export strategies;
(b) transparency in policy hospitable to private foreign investment;
(c) keeping stable monetary and fiscal policy with realistic exchange rates and favorable input prices, and;
(d) providing incentives and support for the "knowledge capital" so that the IT sector can compete in international markets more efficiently.

In some NIC countries like Taiwan high growth rates have maintained a more equitable distribution of income and less concentration of heavy industries. The Taiwan model exhibits the hypothesis that rapid economic growth may foster equity in distribution of personal and sectoral incomes. Low inflation rates and high state support for the primary and secondary education sector have helped the strategy of "growth with equity".

Finally, India has a large potential of managerial talents and leadership skills. But much of these were stifled due to bureaucratic controls and government regulations. For too long the five-year plans in India continued the license raj: import controls, strict restrictions on foreign technology and defunct political interventions which created significant economic inefficiency. But look at the success story of the NRIs who migrated to the US in the 1970s and 1980s. They are the Silicon Valley entrepreneurs from India. Their story has been told most succinctly by Gurcharan Das (2001) in his *India Unbound*. As he noted, the Vedic adage "Knowledge is wealth" sums up the Indian opportunity in the new century. For the world has changed from an industrial to a knowledge economy. Now the knowledge sectors of the economy are the most important. The contributions of other NRIs in the professional sectors of the US like education, health and technical research have also been quite remarkable. This success story has two major implications for India's growth strategy today. "From brain drain to brain gain" should be the motto. The talent and skill of Indian entrepreneurs in Silicon Valley in the US have to be actively sought after in stepping up the growth process in the knowledge sectors of the Indian economy. Already the Silicon Valley IT entrepreneurs of Indian origin have formed a network called the Indus Entrepreneurs ($T_i E$), which finance Indian students in the US in engineering and professional fields and fund new start-ups in India and by Indians in the US. As *Business World* says, their brains are in Silicon Valley but their hearts are in India. Growth synergy should put the two together, the brain and the heart for activating industrial growth in India. For this to happen both the state and private entrepreneurs in India have to take active steps in the process of growth synergy. So far the efforts in this direction have been slow, weak and even disorganized.

The success story of NRIs in US research and education fields has a second implication for India's growth. India should encourage more active collaboration in research ventures through universities and industrial research enterprises. Already the computer-oriented companies in the US like Microsoft, Oracle, HP and IBM have opened networks in Bangalore and other major cities of India, but the Indian universities, Institutes of Management and Institutes of Technology have not actively pursued the road to effective collaboration. The steps taken by the Indian government have been slow and disorganized.

Our objective here is to analyze the potential sources of India's growth: her growth synergy, i.e., the why and how of India's economic growth in the future. We attempt here a broad overview of growth synergy and of its problems and implications by drawing lessons from three fronts: modern growth theory, empirical evidence in the growth of NICs in Asia and the principles of managerial efficiency as emphasized in modern theories of industrial organization.

1.1   Growth synergy: processes and problems

The term "synergy" has three interrelated meanings. First, it means the joint action of several agents. In this sense growth synergy means that economic growth is multidimensional. The "jointness" implies cooperation and "action" implies that the potential is realizable. Second, synergism refers to the doctrine that the total effect is greater than the sum of two or more effects taken independently. Sometimes this doctrine is applied in theology, where it means that in regeneration there is active cooperation of divine grace and human activity. In economic terms synergism implies that increasing returns fosters economic growth through increasing productivity. Classical economists stressed this aspect of growth very strongly. Modern growth theorists in economics also emphasize this aspect through learning curve effects of human capital, e.g., skill formation, R&D externalities and learning by doing. Finally, a synergistic policy is to apply energy on a cumulative basis so that a self-sustained phase can continue over time. This is very close to the concept of total factor productivity (TFP) growth used by Robert Solow to measure *growth efficiency as opposed to* level efficiency. TFP is usually estimated in a neoclassical framework by subtracting from output growth the portion of growth due to physical capital accumulation and to labor force growth. TFP change can then be found as the residual of growth of output per worker after deducting the contributions of human and physical capital. The World Bank estimates of TFP growth for the period 1960–89 for the East-Asian economy comprising 23 economies showed that this region grew faster than any other region in the history of the world. Most of this growth was due to the stellar performance of the eight high-performing Asian economies (HPAEs), Japan, the "four tigers" Hong Kong, South Korea, Singapore and Taiwan, and the three newly industrializing economies (NIEs) of Southeast Asia: Indonesia, Malaysia and Thailand. The most spectacular TFP growth rates are 3.6470 for Hong Kong, 3.4776 for Japan, 3.1021 for South Korea and 3.7604 for Taiwan. By contrast the figures are 0.1274 for Latin America and –0.9978 for Africa. It is no wonder that economists have turned to these HPAEs for clues that might explain their success. The case of India has to be judged against this background. One careful estimate of the sources of economic growth in India over the period 1950–2000 by Sivasubramonian (2004) is as follows:

	Average annual compound growth rate			
	1950–65	*1965–1981*	*1981–2000*	*1950–2000*
GDP growth	4.15	3.13	5.67	4.40
TFP	1.80	0.41	2.01	1.42

These estimates of TFP refer to the nonresidential sector. It is clear that TFP growth has declined by 1.39 over the period 1950–65 to 1965–1981 and has accelerated by 1.60 from 1965–81 to 1981–2000. His estimates for the shorter periods show that in the 1950s, 45.5% of GDP growth was realized through TFGP growth, followed by labor contributing 28.1% and capital 21.3%. During the next two decades when GDP was decelerating, the contribution to TFP declined to 32.1% in the 1960s and a mere 5.2% in the 1970s. Two other points emerge from his calculations. The labor input played a more important role than the capital input during the deceleration phase of GDP growth and the reverse was seen during the acceleration phase. Secondly, the contributions of education have not yet become very important as in the NICs in Asia. For example the relative contribution of education exhibited the following trend in terms of the growth rate of GDP.

	1950–65	*1965–1981*	*1981–2000*	*1950–2000*
Education	3.61	4.04	3.35	3.64

The contributions of other dynamic sources to GDP growth in the non-residential sector in percentage terms have also been very low.

	1970–80	*1980–90*	*1990–2000*
Output per unit of output	0.16	2.02	2.01
(a) structural change	0.33	0.37	0.30
(b) economies of scale	0.09	0.16	0.18
(c) foreign trade effect	0.04	0.04	0.10
(d) advances in knowledge as a residual	0.06	1.25	1.64

Here structural change refers to the productivity effect of reallocation of resources from sectors with low productivity to sectors with high productivity. Percentage gains in output due to reallocation of resources from the agricultural to the industrial sector at 1993–94 prices have been estimated as follows:

1970–80	*1980–90*	*1990–2000*	*1950–2000*
3.32	3.76	2.70	12.82

The role of scale economies in the industrial sector and the foreign trade effect have also been very insignificant for a growing economy. By comparison the estimates for South Korea during 1963–82 by Enos and Park (1988) are shown in Table 1.1.

Table 1.1   Sources of output growth

	South Korea *1963–82 (%)*	*Japan* *1953–72 (%)*
Labor	35.8	17.1
Capital	21.4	23.8
Scale economies	18.0	22.0
Technological advance	11.8	22.4
Others	13.0	14.7
Total	100.0	100.0

In this comparative framework one has to agree with the conclusions derived by Sivasubramonian that the contributions of education and advances in knowledge, which reflect the possible improvements in the qualities of labor and capital input and the adoption of modern technology have not yet become as important as they should be in a rapidly growing economy. Not only has the adoption of modern imported technology been very slow, its diffusion has been nonexistent. Clearly one has to examine in some detail the role of these important sources of growth in the growth synergy of India.

Growth synergy can be analyzed in two ways: the macroscopic and the microscopic. These two aspects are closely interrelated. Whereas the macro aspect emphasizes the overall sources of economic growth in terms of aggregate saving, investment and productivity changes through structural transformation of the economy, the micro aspect deals with the expansion of firms, households and other enterprises, e.g., how they grow and decay over time and affect the evolution of industry. Whenever constraints are imposed on the expansion of firms and enterprises, their growth is stifled. The whole economy suffers.

Look at the growth process in South Korea. It has no natural resources, no specific international aid. Yet it has been able to maintain an extremely high rate of growth of 7.7% a year over the period 1970–89 and this growth has been sustained by significant structural change. This structural change involved reallocation of resources, in both physical and human capital, from low to high productivity sectors.

Two microeconomic forces played a critical role in this dynamic of structural change. One is the policy of "keeping prices right" by which trade theorists imply a relatively low real price of labor, a relatively high real rate of interest and "realistic" exchange rates. The second is the incentives offered by the state so as to maintain the outward-looking orientation of the economy. In particular it meant a very hospitable climate for private foreign investment and an environment for private domestic firms to compete successfully in the competitive world market. The Korean success story in the microeconomic front is very similar to other NICs in Southeast Asia. Taiwan's success has two other distinct features. One is that high growth rates involved more equitable distribution of per capita incomes: a reversal of the "Kuznets hypothesis". This has occurred through more emphasis on smaller firm sizes, small-scale industries and less emphasis on heavy industry compared with Korea. Secondly, the state involvement in guiding economic reforms has been mostly in the form of incentives to foreign capital and in keeping prices right in factor markets. As one close student of Korea's development experience has put it: "Korea's success has been due to investment running ahead of domestic saving, along with an ability to reduce the capital–output ratio at the margin, thereby succeeding in increasing its competitiveness and securing greater market penetration into the countries of the West and Japan" (Chakravarty, 1987).

The growth episode of the high-performing Asian economies may be simply told in terms of the profile of a typical country. Let us call it Korwan: a mix of Korea and Taiwan. We start in the decade of 1960. The economy of Korwan is decomposed into three sectors: primary, secondary and tertiary. The primary sector mainly comprises agriculture, the secondary includes mainly manufacturing and the tertiary comprises all kinds of services including banking, trade, communications and knowledge-based information technology (IT). Add to this scenario a new kind of human capital specializing in software skills in the IT sector and the emergence of a global market which is highly price elastic and also subject to increasing returns to scale on the demand side. If Korwan could develop this human capital in the 1960s, it would achieve stellar economic performance in several directions. First, this type of human capital provides a complementary input, so that its interaction with other inputs improves the productivity of all inputs. As a result the TFP growth is positive whenever this type of human capital is active in a production function. Second, increasing returns to scale are more likely to prevail and if exploited properly would contribute to a faster rate of growth of the overall economy. For the Korean manufacturing industry Sengupta and Okamura (1993) estimated the intensity of scale economies as given in Table 1.2.

This shows very clearly that the scale economies have been very significant. Since the data for each variable is in terms of its permanent component the degree of scale economies may be said to be persistent and not transitory. For the whole period the degree of scale economies is the reciprocal of cost elasticity of output, i.e., $1.134 = 1/0.882$ and for the two periods it changed from 0.175 to 1.050 thus implying exploitation of scale economies over time. Note that the cost elasticity with

Table 1.2   Cost elasticity of Korean manufacturing output with respect to total output and the wage rate

	Output	*Wage rate*
1961–74	0.851	–0.465
1975–90	0.952	0.259
1961–90	0.882	0.351

respect to the labor input was consistent with the neoclassical principle of keeping prices right.

Finally, the stellar growth performance of the Korwan economy was realized due to the globalization of the export market. Outward orientation implies that the manufacturing and the tertiary sectors have to face world competition and its technology-intensive products and services. To circumvent the huge technology gap the state adopted a three-pronged strategy: it offered liberal incentives for direct foreign investment, intensified the education policy and offered subsidies to entrepreneurs who were willing to compete in the international market. Major economic reforms followed the twin principles of comparative advantage and competitive advantage. The former policy involved improving labor productivity so that foreign firms would have added incentives to invest on a self-sustained basis. The latter policy adopted the method of competitive efficiency in industries such as microelectronics, computers and software technology.

Rapid growth in exports helped on two other fronts. One was the diffusion of the growth process to other sectors, both in terms of employment and productivity improvement. This helped improve agriculture and the related infrastructure. Here also the principle of demand creating its own supply worked, i.e., investment tended to exceed saving. For example in the Korean economy during the period 1961–90 the compound rate of growth of exports was around 22, which is almost three times the 8.5% rate of growth of total output; manufacturing output grew at a rate of 16.5%, more than twice the 7.4% growth rate of non-manufacturing. Over the period 1961–90 the GDP share of the manufacturing sector rose from 5.6 to 30%. The structural change implied by this resulted in raising the overall efficiency of the economy, as the aggregate productivity of the economy as a whole moved closer to the higher productivity levels prevailing in manufacturing. The linkages between manufacturing and other sectors were most active and flexible in this rapid phase of growth. Both forward and backward linkages through demand and cost efficiency respectively were considerably helped by an outward-oriented flexible state policy.

The second important aspect of the rapid growth in exports is the change in the character of the export mix. The technological intensity of the export mix has changed considerably from less to more sophisticated goods and services. In both Japan and Korea the state played a very active role in this transition to a more competitive efficiency level in world trade. According to the estimate of Sengupta and España

(1994) the percentage share of high-technology exports in total exports changed as follows for the NICs and other countries in Asia:

Korea	1960–87	0.0 to 33.7
Taiwan	1961–87	1.3 to 32.3
Japan	1960–85	22.9 to 62.3
Thailand	1961–87	1.3 to 10.5
Philippines	1960–87	0.0 to 10.5

The recent trend shows a further increase in high-technology exports (HTX) for Korea, Taiwan, Singapore and Hong Kong. This process is particularly pronounced in the case of Japan and virtually nonexistent in the cases of Thailand and Philippines. The case of India during this period of 1960–87 falls even behind Thailand and Philippines.

The remarkable thing about the phenomenal export growth in Korea and Taiwan is the widespread diffusion of export growth to other sectors. The immediate impact of this diffusion is the externality effect of growth in the export sector. For example in Korea this effect is roughly three to seven times larger than the reverse effect. For Taiwan the effect of diffusion on other sectors was transformed into more investment in the small and medium scale industries catering to the export sector. In India the growth of the IT sector in recent years has not accentuated this diffusion process either as an externality effect or as an endogenous source of growth. Why? What are the reasons for nondiffusion? For an answer we have to analyze in more detail the pattern of export growth of the software technology in India and its dynamic changes. Sengupta (2003) has analyzed this question and found two major reasons. One is the lack of core competence of the enterprises in the Indian software companies. The second is inadequate diversification for the changing world market.

As one practitioner who worked in the USA as a consultant to Tata Consultancy Services (TCS) has put it:

Till now most of the Indian software companies are doing body shopping and do not have many products/designs to offer. While in the US I was working on the design and development of hospital information systems for a US company. I knew that TCS is earning about $1 million from the project but when the product was ready, it was selling for $5 million. But when the US company started selling it in US and world markets it was expected to earn $500m. The lesson is clear. Indian IT managers and entrepreneurs should develop software packages like SAP/Oracle and BAAN but at a much cheaper cost and sell internationally. For this we need a well rounded marketing and distribution network. It is precisely here that the Indian government and the Indian expatriates of Silicon Valley can form partnerships and help the core competence of the IT entrepreneurs in India. It is true that many US companies have set up collaborative arrangements with Indian economies, e.g., Texas Instruments, Citibank, Siemens and Hewlett Packard but most of the collaborations involve an Indian company acting as a local agent for a foreign supplier's software packages and undertaking sales, marketing and training support. This is much like the old managing agency system, where Indian firms acted as local agents for British industries. By 1996 most of the largest US hardware manufacturers in computers had some form of agency linkup with an Indian software company. It is only very recently during the last four years that top-notch global IT companies like Microsoft, Oracle, Cisco and others have invested in Indian laboratories to develop their next generation products. IBM has also indicated its plan for heavy investment in India in 2004 and thereafter.

This appears to be the most opportune moment for economic policy reform so that the diffusion of gains in the IT sector to other sectors may be activated. One aspect of this reform should deal with providing incentives through state subsidies so that the small and medium sized firms could carry on the diffusion process as in Taiwan. The second aspect is the state developing a support program for training skills in the knowledge sector. Partnership with the private sector and foreign investment firms would appear to be very useful in this framework. The example of Motorola in India is worth pursuing. As Dutta (2003) has noted: "Motorola has enhanced its software excellence globally and has created a series of offshore software centers across the world to leverage the successful Indian experience. It has shown the way for other firms to make the most of their centers in India." It is for the Indian firms to take up the challenge and follow up the Motorola experience. Tata Consultancy Services which provided IT support to the US for more than two decades is ideally suited to take up such challenges.

It is necessary however to stress some caution with these new technology-oriented reform policies. One is the need for prudence in the monetary and fiscal management so that the inflationary pressures are under proper control. Stability in the foreign exchange market is essential. The so-called market mania of deregulation and privatization without analyzing the pros and cons should be avoided at all costs. Secondly, India has to realize that it can develop its talent pool in the knowledge economy by a significant margin. Compared to China, Korea and Taiwan, it has more capability and core competence. But the policy need is to speed up the investment spending in R&D in the IT sector both public and private. The managerial challenge is much more on the private sector, since it can reap the gains more directly by raising the export drive to higher products in the value chain. According to the estimate by Lall (1999) the average real rate of growth of inhouse R&D expenditure during the post-reform period 1992–95 is 5.05% per year in the public and 10.28% in the private sector. For the crisis year 1991–92 it was 1.81 and 0.91 respectively. By comparison the private sector figures for the same period 1992–95 exceed 18% for both Taiwan, Korea and Japan.

Here there is ample scope for the Indian expatriates of Silicon Valley to set up training and research institutes in India, training Indian students how to embark on new ventures in software markets in India and the world. Surely this strategy would directly compete with the recruitment and training strategies of Microsoft and Intel in India in recent years but the principle of competitive advantage would benefit the Indian companies in the long run, since the Indian companies need not concentrate only in cities like Bangalore and Hyderabad to speed up its talent drive.

1.2   Korea and India

In many ways it is instructive to compare India with South Korea. The lessons of stellar growth performance in Korea are worth examining in some detail. Its export growth of 22.9% followed the average annual growth rate of per capita income of 6.4% over the 1965–87 period. Unlike China, Korea did not follow a totalitarian regime of political and economic control. The World Bank study of the Asian miracle by Page (1994) provides ample empirical evidence to show that governments in the high performing Asian economies (HPAEs) made systematic efforts to alter industrial structure for the purpose of accelerating productivity change. Two policy lessons can be derived from this record. One is that export promotion was at the heart of HPAE's spectacular productivity performance. Secondly, one of the keys to success of the export push, for example in Korea and Japan, was the government's ability to combine cooperation with competition. Competent and honest civil servants could successfully join private firms to improve efficiency in the export sector. As Page has put it:

> Export targets provided a consistent yardstick to measure the success of market interventions. When protected sectors interfered with the

exports of other sectors, the latter could seek redress and were successful. Even where domestic content rules were imposed, e.g., on foreign direct investment in Taiwan, they were suspended if they interfered with exports. The emphasis on export competitiveness gave businesses and bureaucrats a transparent and objective system to gauge the desirability of specific actions. Interventions could not be made arbitrarily, because these could be appealed at a higher level of government if they interfered with exports. The more recent export push efforts of the Southeast Asian NIEs have relied less on highly specific incentives and more on gradual reductions in import protection, coupled with institutional support of exporters and a duty-free regime for inputs into exports. These "GATT friendly" export promotion strategies offer substantial scope for adoption by other developing economies.

Two key elements of this policy recommendation are worth noting in the Indian context. One is to develop a duty-free regime for all inputs into the export sector, particularly those which have long run implications for the export sector's performance, for example R&D inputs which can be outsourced from US and Japan and also the technology intensive inputs into the IT sector. The second is to foster a climate of cooperation with competition.

Competition has a static and a dynamic aspect. In its static aspect it requires firms to be cost effective, so that prices tend to equal the minimum level of average cost. In the world market this is a very critical yardstick. Many jobs in the US and Europe today in the IT sector get outsourced in India and the Southeast Asian NIEs, because of this competitive pressure. But the dynamic aspect of competition is to ensure dynamic efficiency through increased R&D investment. This is the area of innovations efficiency. The complexity of the innovations process in the IT sector raises two critical issues for the modern IT sector companies. It raises the development costs both internally and externally; internally because the firms may not have all the necessary strongholds and externally because the firms may not be able to appropriate or internalize all the spillovers in knowledge capital. Secondly, the technology strategy and its economic aspects, for example how to choose between fixed and flexible technology have strongly influenced the risk in developing these firms. To reduce these twin costs, the incentives for collaboration and/or networking in R&D have increased significantly in modern times. Theorists have argued that if competitors are not allowed to collaborate in R&D, then they may not invest enough because of the free-rider problem associated with spillover externalities. Competition policymakers have been increasingly aware of these circumstances and recognized the fact that most firms do not have all the necessary capital, both physical and human for developing the latest technologies. This is also true for India. Over the last decade many countries have explicitly adopted policy reforms which provide direct incentives and organizational support for firms forming joint ventures and collaborative R&D activities. In Europe, Japan and the US companies are allowed to form R&D collaborations in some form, which are collusive in nature, but such collusions are forbidden in product markets. The NICs in Southeast Asia have explicitly encouraged the formation of collaboration in R&D investments and provided significant incentives by the state in their fiscal and monetary policies. The latter have made significant contributions to the rapid growth in exports of technology-intensive products in the last two decades.

1.3   Growth synergy in India

In order to assess the export contribution of the software industry in India one has to adopt a broader perspective. Four types of criticism have been made about the development of the PC industry and the software sector in India. One is that it has not helped the masses at all, neither has it contributed much to raise the average level of living, since it is mostly urban centered and geared to world export market. Secondly, the impact of software industry growth on other businesses and other sectors of the economy has been nil or almost negligible. It has not helped investment to grow in other sectors. Thirdly, it has accentuated the so-called "brain-drain" movement resulting in large-scale exodus of skilled talents from engineering and management institutes. This has resulted in significant costs to the national economy, since the engineering and management graduates migrating abroad receive large subsidies in their education and training. Finally, very few expatriates who make it big in the Silicon Valley return to India or invest heavily to improve the export earnings for India.

To assess the effect of the growth of software and hardware industry on the average level of living one has to look at the history of the computer industry in India. Though India was initiated into using mainframes and data machines as early as the 1960s, the Indian software industry only took off in the mid-1980s. Its phenomenal growth can be seen from the fact that the total industry output increased from Rs. 500 million in 1988–89 to 159,000 million in 1998–99. This is more than 300 times the initial output level. Heeks (1996) estimated the Indian software export growth rates as follows.

	Growth in exports (%)	Growth in US market share (%)
1988–89	29	–5
1990–91	24	9
1991–92	33	18
1992–93	26	10
1993–94	43	25
1994–95	53	28
1998–99	60	35

Thus export growth rates for the Indian software industry are impressive, though Indian software exports formed less than 0.15% of the total world computer services and the software market in 1994–95. This shows two things. One is that the Indian software industry has great scope in increasing its share of the world market and the domestic multiplier and accelerator effects of such increase in export volumes would be considerable. Secondly the volume of domestic employment creation consequent on such export-led growth is likely to be very significant. The latest software developments are attracting increasingly large interest and investment in IT has enabled teleworking services like call conferencing, medical and legal transcriptions, managing large data bases, web content creation, animation and visual imaging. Companies like Swissair, GE, Bechtel, US insurance companies, the US fashion industry and Hollywood studios have outsourcing arrangements with Indian companies. Currently these subcontracting arrangements employ more than 25,000 people and over the next eight years it is expected to create at least a million jobs. The Indian software companies have demonstrated their economic and technical strength in the main domains of (a) banking and financial services, (b) insurance, (c) manufacturing and (d) internet and e-commerce. Three other areas that may be successfully explored are (e) video games and electronic toys, (f) herbal medicines and related pharmaceutical products, and (g) outsourcing in publishing and accounting areas.

The impact of the software sector on the rest of the economy is also changing very rapidly. For the years 1998 and 1999 for example, Indian software companies sold $3.9 billion worth of software, of which almost 70% was exported according to the estimates by India's NASSCOM (National Association of Software and Services Companies). Their estimates further show that during the 6-month period April–September

1999, Indian software exports amounted to \$1.87 billion or about 10.5% of the country's total exports. The major problem before the industry is how to change from the lowest component in value chain, e.g., offering on-site professional services or body shopping at the client's location overseas, to higher components in the value chain such as packaged products and superior consultancy services and turnkey projects.

The brain-drain argument has several flaws on the economic side. Certainly it is true that engineering and management graduates in India are trained at the Indian taxpayers' expense, which is mostly unrecovered if they seek employment abroad. However if the domestic industry provides no scope of employment, these graduates would contribute at a very low level. There are two possible remedies: develop privately sponsored engineering and management institutes, and foster the growth of software firms so that the tempo of employment creation can move at a fast rate. This calls for more investment in the software industry sector and active government support to encourage such investment. One area where more investment is urgently called for is the R&D field. According to an estimate by *The Economist* (1994) US software companies spend an average of 14% of sales on R&D. In India the figure is 3% and most of it is due to government support. A recent estimate by Mani (1998) exhibits the following pattern (see Table 1.3).

One effective way to utilize the talent pool in India is to speed up the research-spending investment in both the public and private sectors. The managerial challenge is much more on the private sector, since it can gain more directly from such investments which will raise the export drive to higher products in the value chain. For its part the national government in India can help found a "Brain Trust," where the Indian expatriates of Silicon Valley may contribute along with the private sector. This trust could set up new training and research institutes in India, training students in how to embark on new ventures in software markets in India and the world. This would counteract the steps adopted by Microsoft and Intel for decades to drain India of its brains and talents. One has to mention in this connection the recent

Table 1.3   Average real rate of growth of inhouse R&D expenditure (in % per year)

	Public sector	*Private sector*
Average of the pre-reform period 1987–91	6.07	7.99
Average during the post-reform period 1992–95	5.05	10.28
Year 1991–92 of monetary crisis	1.81	0.91

drive by the CEO Azim Premji of the info-tech giant Wipro to bridge the huge digital divide between the technology-capable and the illiterate poor in India. It is time that the other software industries participated in this innovative venture. Such an effort offers great hope of creating the social and economic infrastructure needed in the twenty-first century.

The criticism that few expatriates and nonresident Indians in the US return to India or set up investments in the software industry is not appropriate or valid. For one thing recent times have seen collaborative arrangements between these two partners: one in Silicon Valley and the other in Mumbai and Bangalore. The main culprit seems to be the lack of a clear focus in the liberalization and industrial policy reform by the Indian government. The openness in trade required for export-led growth is much less compared to Singapore, Korea, Taiwan and even China. Estimates by Lall (1999) (Table 1.4) reveal the overall pattern of export growth.

Note that recent Indian growth is much lower than for China or Latin America. The contrast with China – the most similar to India in terms of market size and industrial structure, historic inward-orientation and aversion to foreign investment is particularly noteworthy. China went through several stages of "combining plan with the market" before adopting the current goal of "socialist market economy." No one has attempted to quantify the contribution of the expansion of foreign trade and foreign capital inflows to China's economic growth, although it is known to be substantial, e.g., its GDP growth was 9.9 and 10.5% during 1985–89 and 1990–94 respectively and it has sustained its export growth along with GDP growth maintaining a huge balance of trade surplus with the US. Since 1978 China was increasingly able to import the most up to date capital equipment produced in Japan, the US and Europe. The increase in the quality of capital more than offsets the slight reduction in the rate of increase in the quantity of capital. The pressure to export more and more manufactures and also software products led Chinese enterprises in these sectors to rapidly upgrade the quality of products and reduce costs. These improvements spread quickly to the

Table 1.4   Annual growth rate of manufactured exports, current US $(%)

	1980–85	*1985–90*	*1990–95*	*1997*
India	4.9	18.2	12.8	3.0
Mature NICs	7.3	17.9	12.4	2.4
China	3.1	23.1	22.4	21.0
Latin America	2.1	4.5	20.6	12.5

production of items for both domestic and foreign consumption. Thus according to World Bank estimates the growth of total factor productivity (TFP) which measures technological progress attained a value of 2.9% per year on the average during 1990–94, when it was only 2.2% during 1985–94. This is a remarkable rate of progress far exceeding that of the US and NICs in Asia. One has to note that the major contribution of market reforms in China was not to the large state-owned sector. It was the small and medium scale enterprises owned collectively or privately that benefited the most. This remarkable success record is also shared by Taiwan, where small and medium enterprises spearheaded the growth and high levels of education and skill fueled the rapid growth process. For Taiwan the decentralized reforms have helped reduce corruption at the government level and generated an egalitarian income distribution.

The rapid growth episode of China is largely due to the growth of its export trade, where software industry has contributed to a significant degree. Today the Chinese economy looks very different. As Zerega (2000) points out: "Once almost as common as bicycles, Communist Party billboards in Shanghai are being replaced by catchy dot-com advertisements urging the nation of more than 1.2 billion inhabitants to get online." "Sister, get on the Web!" screams a billboard sponsored by a portal and e-commerce company named pAsia. "Unity is power" declares another. China developed the conviction and the determination that its future depends on its successful entry into the technology-intensive global economy.

India needs this determination. It is the greatest challenge before Indian management. They have to realize that success in today's world comes from good and innovative management and careful investment of capital and not the sudden flash of a brilliant idea.

The greatest challenge before India today is how efficiently to enter into the software markets of the world. New paradigms of hypercompetition demand that Indian businesses follow the three Cs of economic efficiency, culminating in core competence. India has all the requisite resources: a talent pool, appropriate contact with modern technology, facility in English language and communication and a democratic form of government. It only needs will and determination. The rest should follow.

1.4   Global challenge in software markets

The new economic order emerging today, sometimes called the *new economy*, is spreading all over the world. This is nothing short of an industrial revolution. It is a revolution in information explosion and in knowledge capital. Three key elements of this revolution are: increasing efficiency of the microcomputer industry, intra-firm and inter-industry diffusion of knowledge and new innovations in the Schumpeterian sense, and the global expansion of trade through network externalities. It is of some importance to analyze the impact of these key elements on the rapid and steady development of the US economy over the last decade. According to the recent estimate by Jorgenson and Stiroh (2000) the price decline for computers has accelerated in recent times, reaching nearly 28% per year from 1995 to 1998. Exploitation of significant scale economies has been the key to this rapid price decline. In response, investment in computers has exploded in the US and the overall national growth contribution of computer hardware has increased more than fivefold, to 0.46 percentage points per year in the late 1990s. Software and communications equipment contributed an additional 0.30 percentage points. More recent estimates until 2000 reveal further increases. The following analysis of the new paradigm in economic policy has been made by Sengupta (2003).

As the production of computers improves and becomes more efficient, more computing power is being produced from the same inputs, i.e., learning by doing. This increases the overall productivity in the computer-producing industry and contributes to growth in total factor productivity (also called technological progress) for the economy as a whole. Labor and R&D productivity also grow at a faster rate. Secondly, the computer using industries are now using skilled labor who are working with more and better computer equipment and this investment increases labor productivity in these industries further. Thus the computer industry has experienced a sustained increase in returns to scale (RTS) and in technological progress. In their empirical estimate Norsworthy and Jang (1992) found for the US computer industry as a whole the level of RTS as 1.400 for the period 1973–80 and even higher in recent years. The productivity growth (technological progress) for the electronic equipment industry (which includes the computer industry) over the period 1958–96 was 2.0% per year on the average. For the more recent period 1992–98 the comparable figure for the computer industry (mainframe and microcomputer) exceeds 2.5% per year. The major source of productivity growth has been the growth in demand over the last two decades, which has exceeded 12% per year on the average.

The rapid growth episodes of NICs in Southeast Asia exhibit the impact of openness in international trade and demand growth on the high growth rate of these countries. For example the average annual growth rate of real national income in Korea over the period 1970–73 was 16%, of which export expansion contributed 55.7% and domestic demand expansion 51.9%. By comparison Mexico contributed about 5.9% in export expansion to the annual growth rate of 6.1%. India's contribution is much lower than that of Mexico.

Recently Kraemer and Dedrick (1994) analyzed the pattern of investment in information technology (IT) industries of 11 countries of the Asia–Pacific region over the years 1984–90, where the spending on computer hardware and software services was used as a measure of IT investment. They found the average growth in IT investment over 1984–90 has been very high for Korea (24.49%), Taiwan (21.64%), Singapore (18.06%) and Hong Kong (15.22%), whereas for slower growth countries it has been much lower, e.g., Malaysia (10.77%) or Philippines (12.21%). The infrastructure investment in Korea, Taiwan and Singapore has considerably helped the growth of IT investment in the higher performer countries of Asia. As Dahlman and Nelson (1995) have shown, the four East Asian high performers Singapore, Taiwan, Hong Kong and Korea have consistently used the following strategies to capture the international diffusion of technical knowhow, for example extensive use of technology licensing and links with foreign subsidiary firms, large scale contact with foreign buyers and the development of strong high-tech industries embodying the latest technical knowhow from the US. Taiwan's growth followed a different pattern from Korea or Japan. While Japan and Korea followed a policy of increasing the average size of firms and thus increasing the degree of industrial concentration, Taiwan increased the number of firms or establishments in the manufacturing sector, including the software and microelectronic industries.

The growth of IT investment in the US has been most rapid over the last two decades, exceeding on the average 15% per year. It has outpaced the growth of demand. As a result the average rate of return on all assets for the computer industry as a whole has increased from an annual rate of 31.1% to 34.5% over the period 1975–84, according to Norsworthy and Jang's estimate. For the years 1985–98 it has increased still higher. The diffusion of impact of investment in the computer industry to other sectors, e.g., bioengineering, telecommunications and consumer electronics has been most spectacular in the current decade. The basic trend of this impact has been an all around increase in industrial productivity, leading to a growth rate of the US economy of 4% or higher per year over the last decade. The new paradigm fueling this rapid growth process can be summed up by the three letters IDI. The first I refers to the stream of new innovations in the computer industry including the software development sector. The second letter is D for demand, reflecting the impact of new innovation on the increase of demand and national income. This generates a further round of innovations. The term innovations (I) is used here in a broad Schumpeterian sense; it includes new processes, new forms of knowledge creation and application and new products such as the development of new and industry-specific software. All IT investments are for innovative goods and services and it augments the demand flow in three ways: one is B to B trade (i.e., business to business transactions), the others are the domestic and international trade. Shapiro and Varian (1999) have emphasized very strongly this point about the increased demand flow in today's Internet economy fueled by the personal computer network. They have characterized it as the economies of scale in demand. This means that any new innovative investment in the computer industry generates a multiplier effect on demand, both specific and more general, and this growth in demand affects the next flow of innovations through new capacity creation, replacement of old technology and utilization of scale economies. Thus the cycle goes on.

Note that the IDI process is a mere restatement of Adam Smith's thesis that the division of labor is limited by the size of the market. For Adam Smith this is an evolutionary and growth perspective. Dividing the production process into increasingly simpler elements is a *continuous discovery process*, yielding new knowledge with both internal and external effects. Current innovations in the microelectronic industry has expanded the market size in all computer-using industries and this trend is unlikely to slow down. This is because the continuous discovery process emphasized by Adam Smith is going on in all other traditional fields and industries. This framework has often been called a state of hypercompetition, which has two aspects: static and dynamic. The static aspect stresses the destructive aspect in the sense that only the fittest survive, i.e., only the cost efficient firms remain, others exit. This occurs in a world of fixed and limited demand, where profits are driven to their lowest levels. The dynamic aspect of hypercompetition assumes interactive and increasing demand due to market expansion and here competition between firms improves the innovative efficiency of all firms. This has sometimes been called Metcalfe's law, which states that the value of a network or process goes up as the square of the number of users or suppliers.

What makes a firm grow? What causes an industry to rise? What causes a country to prosper? From a very broad standpoint two types of answers have been given to these questions. One is managerial, the other economic. The managerial perspective is based on organization theory, which focuses on the core competence or dynamic capabilities as the primary sources of growth of firms, industries and organizations. The economic perspective emphasizes national productivity and efficiency as the basic source of growth. Adam Smith's inquiry into the causes of the wealth of nations identified the market or demand as the prime mover of productivity increase across nations. Economic efficiency in both physical and human capital and innovations through improvements in skill and technologies have been considered as the key sources of economic growth by the modern theory of endogenous growth, also called the new growth theory.

These three major sources of growth start at the microeconomic level of a firm (enterprise) or organization and spread over the industries across the national economy. These growth sources serve to emphasize the following three principles: the three C's:

1   the principle of competitive advantage
2   the principle of comparative advantage
3   the principle of core competence.

Each of the three principles characterizes the broad framework of strategies for a firm, an industry or the whole economy. Together they form a growth synergy: a cumulative process of sustained growth through a complementary set of principles of action.

The heart of the competitiveness principle is how to improve national productivity. Sustained growth in productivity requires that a nation's firms continually improve productivity in existing industries in several different ways, for example by raising product quality, improving technology, reducing costs and prices and increasing production and access efficiency. Recently Porter (1990) and Prahalad and Hamel (1994) have emphasized the point that in today's global market competitive advantage may emerge in many forms. For example, firms may gain competitive advantage from conceiving new ways to conduct activities, developing new procedures and technologies and improving productivity levels. Thus Makita in Japan emerged as a leading competitor in power tools, because it was the first to develop standardized models in a single plant which it sold worldwide. Samsung in Korea rose to prominence in the consumer electronics market in the US by pioneering new products and clones at cost-efficient prices. Volvo of Sweden maintained a steady share of the highly competitive automobile market in the US by sustaining product quality, product safety and improving servicing standards.

The principle of competitive advantage emphasizes the network of opportunities that exist in a given environment and the dynamic strategies that may be adopted to exploit them. This is essentially the Schumpeterian notion of innovations, which continually shift the strength of competitive advantages from one firm or industry to another, or from one nation to another. Porter (1990) has identified two major sources of competitive advantage as innovations, which firms can employ to develop viable and successful business strategies in today's global markets: these apply specifically to software markets.

1 Moving early to exploit structural change in the market. Early movers gain advantages by reaping substantial economies of scale, reducing costs through learning curve effects and establishing reliable customer channels through brand loyalty.
2 Perceiving and pursuing innovation. Information technology (IT) today has reached a phase where companies which innovate are frequently not established leaders or even large firms. Even when the innovators are large firms, they are often invaded by new entrants. The software development and related R&D activities provide classic examples. Today's Silicon Valley in the US saw many small software development and start-up companies make big in the success arena, e.g., Junglee, a small start-up company with a capital of less than $40 thousand started by four engineering graduates from IIT in India was sold to Amazon.com for more than $10 million after a few years. Similar success stories of Indian multimillionaires in Silicon Valley are plentiful. Many of the successful strategies owe their origin to the relentless pursuit of innovation in the software development area. One has to note that firms like Microsoft, Intel, Sun Systems and others arose as small start-up firms and proved their role in the hypercompetitive world.

Attempts to improve product quality and upgrade it constantly are the major sources of sustaining competitive advantage. For Indian business to compete in the world software market today this is one of the most important strategies to be considered. Some international examples may help in setting the appropriate strategies. Consider the consumer electronics industry in the US and the world today. Sanyo, Sharp and other Japanese companies competed initially on costs and prices in selling portable TV sets. As they penetrated the US and other foreign markets, they gained substantial economies of scale and reduced costs and prices further by exploiting the learning curve effects. Today the Korean competitors such as Samsung, Gold Star, etc. are following the same route and competing on costs and price. There is no reason why Indian companies cannot follow the Japanese and Korean style in the field of software markets.

The current trend of Indian software exports is less than 3% of the US software market. In 1981 it was barely 0.18%, rose to 0.82% in 1990–91, then to 1.70% in 1994–95. By contrast the NICs in Asia, e.g., Korea, Singapore, Thailand and Hong Kong (China) have outperformed the Indian record significantly. Three characteristics of the Indian software exports sector are important to note, as they would determine the power of sustaining competitive advantage in the future. The first is the export profile. Dividing the exports into three categories, software services, software packages and data entry, India's exports have mainly concentrated on software services, which were as high as 90% in 1992 by the World Bank's estimate. Singapore and even China concentrated on software packages to the extent of 58 and 56% respectively. This shows that India is valnerable to stiff and increasing competition in the future, in particular from Singapore and China. Secondly, the Indian software export market has been dominated by the two largest exporters, Tata Consultancy Services (TCS) and Tata Unisys Limited (TUL), so that no other Indian company managed to gain more than a 5% share in the 1990s. Those companies which make up the next six largest exporters after the Tatas were the strongest at the start but failed to sustain their competitive advantage. Table 1.5 from Heeks (1996) shows this very clearly.

The third characteristic of the software export market in India is the significant loss of skilled manpower. The impact of brain-drain to overseas competitors in the US and Europe is quite significant and increasing

Table 1.5   Major Indian software exporters

Rank	1985/86	1989/90	1994/95
3rd	PCS	COSL	Wipro
4rd	Hinditron	Datamatics	Pentafour
5rd	Infosys	TI	Infosys
6rd	Datamatics	DEIL	Silverline
7rd	DCM DP	PCS	Fujitsu
8rd	COSL	Mahindra-BT	DEIL

over time. Oracle, Microsoft and other US companies are actively "head hunting" in India for skilled software engineers and technicians. According to one estimate about 13% of Indian software developers working on exports have been leaving their Indian companies every year to go abroad permanently or semi-permanently.

It is clear that Indian software developers must forge a dynamic global strategy in order to develop and sustain their competitive advantage. The government has to play a more active role here as in Korea and Taiwan. Taiwan's example is noteworthy in that it has many electronic firms in software development which started small but shared access to the R&D results from the government-affiliated laboratories in the Industrial Technological Research Institute (ITRI). Very often research team members of ITRI leave to set up businesses on their own, or join private companies in their R&D department. Thus Acer of Taiwan sells under its own brand because it has its own PC sets and is hence able to offer new products and services directly competing with major US and Japanese rivals. Indian companies have yet to set up any close links with US technology institutes and research centers. Also private firms in India scarcely contribute to R&D activity in software development in government research laboratories.

Strategic alliances between Indian software developing companies and global partners in the US, Europe or Japan offer substantial advantages in forming a global strategy. These alliances usually take the form of long term agreements between firms operating in the world market which attempt to exploit the benefits of network externalities, economies of scale through cooperation in component production, assembly of particular models and reducing costs of marketing. The most important benefit from alliances of Indian software developers with their US counterparts is to spread risks in developing new software and make them suitable for international markets. A classic example occurs in the pharmaceutical industry, where firms have successfully entered into cross-licensing agreements on new drug discoveries in order to hedge the risks that their own research may prove to be unsuccessful. Indian software companies have two unique roles in this global strategic alliance. Trial runs, simulations and product profiling of software packages developed in the US may be attempted in India at a substantial cost advantage due to the skilled manpower advantage in India. Secondly, Indian developers may use the global alliance to develop their own R&D sector in both hardware and software production. Most of India's computer exports today have been basic PC units, which are assembled in India and have a very high import content.

However such exports make very little positive contribution to India's balance of trade or its overall GNP growth. On the negative side such exports tend to hinder the efficiency of technological capability in developing both software and hardware production in India. Another point: the majority of India's hardware exports went to Russia and other former East European bloc countries under bilateral trade agreements that were paid for in Indian currency. But the Indian companies had to pay for the components in foreign exchange, thus these exports caused India a substantial foreign exchange loss.

Clearly India has to modernize its export strategy in two major directions. One is to develop an effective system of alliances with US counterparts so that appropriate market niches can be set up, and where Indian skills have a comparative advantage. This calls for moving away from selling manpower services to developing software packages, so that trial experiments can be performed on the latter in India and unit costs can be lowered. Secondly, the alliance must not be viewed as a short term measure to boost exports through lower labor costs, nor should they be looked on as a subsidiary of a foreign partner or as their managing agent, since these arrangements hinder the efficiency of the local industrial structure suitable for competition in world software markets. Too often Indian companies have opted for the easier route of agency or overseas subsidiary, e.g. the HCL–HP subsidiary and shifted away from developing the R&D sector and the component parts of the hardware production. Clearly the government has a very important role here in helping the software companies in India, as the very successful examples of Korea, Singapore and China show.

The principle of comparative advantage has three facets of application. In the economic theory of international trade a country has a comparative advantage in the good that is relatively intensive in the country's relatively abundant factor. Hence if labor is relatively abundant in a country relative to capital, then it should export labor-intensive goods to other countries which are either capital-intensive or less labor intensive. Similarly a country has a comparative disadvantage in the good that is relatively intensive in the country's relatively scarce factor. This means that a country should not export goods which are intensive in the scarce factor, e.g., capital. Finally, the theory of comparative advantage has a dynamic counterpart, which may sometimes run counter to the static aspect of the theory. As we mentioned before, software exports from India take three forms: (a) export of software services through consultancy, overseas assignment or temporary brain-drains, (b) software packages through developing and testing software of different forms in India for US and other overseas companies, and (c) electronic bookkeeping, data entry and storage services. All these forms of software exports are highly labor-intensive information services and India faces stiff competition from the eight countries identified by the *World Bank Development Report* (1992) in Table 1.6.

It is clear that India's competitors rely more on software packages than services. Since software package exports provide more stable, long term and greater earnings than software services, India's skewed pattern of software exports exposes its vulnerability in the future due to its nondiversification. The relative efficiency in software diversification in exports may be measured by the percentage decline in software services and the increase in software package development. Measured by this efficiency India's performance has been below average. Over a decade India's dependence on software package exports has been less than 3%, where even China and Mexico performed much better. However compared to China and Mexico, India has several points of comparative advantage, i.e., more educated engineers, proficiency in English language and links with computer and software firms in Silicon Valley through entrepreneurs of Indian origin.

Due to its dependence on software services in exports India will face increasing competition in the international software market, unless new

Table 1.6   Pattern of software exports from India and its competitors (1990)

	Proportion of exports (%) in			*Total*
	Software services	*Software packages*	*Data entry and storage*	
India	90	5	5	100
	(88)	(7)	5	100
China	17	56	27	100
	(12)	(60)	(28)	(100)
Singapore	25	58	17	100
	(20)	(62)	(18)	(100)
Ireland	65	21	14	100
Mexico	53	32	15	100
	(50)	(35)	(15)	100
Hungary	40	59	1	100
Philippines	39	20	41	100
Israel	19	76	5	100
	(15)	(81)	(4)	(100)

Note: The numbers in parentheses denote the percentage for 1997.
Source: World Bank (1992).

strategies are forged by India. The relative success of Taiwan may provide some examples along this line. First of all, Taiwan has attempted to exploit the licensed clone market in different niches of the computer software market by entering into alliances and joint ventures with other international firms, for example Umax Data Systems in Taiwan working for Apple Mac OS, Mosel-Vitelic in joint venture with Siemens AG of Germany. Secondly, Taiwanese computer and software industries are highly decentralized into the network of small firms, each being free to work for any client. Taiwanese software and PC industries have a success rate comparable to the successful NICs in Southeast Asia. With respect to foreign investment Taiwan offers some mild selective inducement offering up to 2.5% subsidy. Also it fosters active participation of small electronic and software firms into the R&D network of government-affiliated laboratories in the Industrial Technological Research Institute (ITRI). This two-way interaction is most helpful for the continued success of Taiwan in its export diversification strategy. India has much to learn from this experience. The link between the research laboratories and private sector firms in the computer and software development fields is almost negligible in India. A similar state of affairs prevails in the field of technical and management education in India. Support from the private sector companies for the technical and managerial research in ITTs and IIMs in India has been almost insignificant. It is no wonder that the graduates from these institutions to the extent of 70% or more migrate to US and other overseas countries including Korea and Singapore. Clearly this highlights the need for a modern outlook for a new education policy at the national and state levels.

1.5   Core competence as global strategy

Core competence rather than market power has been identified by Prahalad and Hamel (1994) as the basic cornerstone of success in the hypercompetitive world of technology-intensive industries today. Core competence has been defined as the collective learning in the organization, especially in learning how to coordinate diverse production skills and integrate multiple streams of technologies. Four basic elements of core competence are: learn, coordinate, integrate and innovate. One has to assess within this framework the Indian software industry and the network of hardware, software and web development. Dynamic strategies need to be developed in each of these areas in order to achieve success and sustain it in today's technology-based world.

Learning has three components: intrinsic, extrinsic and teamwork. Intrinsic learning is internal to the organization, it helps intra-firm growth of knowledge and competence. Company R&D, on-the-job training, and incentive systems to explore technical knowhow available in the industry as a whole comprise intrinsic learning. On a rating schedule of low, medium and high, Indian software companies fare very low in this rating scale. Extrinsic learning involves learning from the experiences of other firms and the trends of technology in the computer field. Alliances, collaborations and joint ventures provide direct access to this form of extrinsic learning. India's rating is somewhere below the medium. It is true that many US companies have set up some collaborative arrangements with Indian companies, e.g., Texas Instruments, Citibank, Siemens and Unisys have helped create many of the smaller Indian software companies to facilitate exports, but most of the collaborations involve an Indian company acting as a local agent for a foreign supplier's software packages and undertaking sales, marketing and training support. This is much like the old managing agency system acting as local agents for the British industries in the colonial era. By 1996 most of the largest US hardware manufactures had some form of agency linkup with an Indian software company, but apart from Novell and Oracle no major software product company from the US or Europe had made a direct production investment in India. It is only very recently that top-notch global IT majors like Microsoft, Motorola, Oracle, Cisco, Texas Instruments, Alcatel and others have invested in Indian laboratories to develop their next-generation products. Similarly, out of a dozen top software labs across the world rated at level 5 (i.e., the highest) by SEI-CMM standards, five are in India with nearly ten at level four. More than 200 of Fortune 1000 companies outsource their software needs from India for their core operations. However few of these are joint ventures. In most cases the foreign companies use the Indian firm as a source of software labor to service its own needs or those of its customers. Hence the learning process for Indian companies does not involve any teamwork, nor does it help the Indian software companies develop their own packages and market them abroad.

Coordination of diverse production skills and various innovative expertise related to the knowledge capital is central to software development and affects every branch of the modern industrial age. Every new software has to be adapted to the needs of specific industries, which may range from the Internet, three dimensional graphics, telecommunications, banking and manufacturing to video games, special effects imaging, and so on. Coordination essentially involves finding appropriate niches for Indian companies, where they may have dynamic comparative advantage and gather the requisite talents from India to develop new software packages suitable for international markets. Consider how the US companies pressure the government to satisfy their coordination goal. The "21st century Technology Resources and Commercial Leadership Act" which Senator John McCain brought to the US Senate in late 1999 is designed to keep the US high-tech industry on top by filling the need for skilled technology manpower. There is a clear need for an Indian government policy attempt to modernize the Indian economy so as to recreate Silicon Valley's business culture in India. Recently the Securities and Exchange Board of India (SEBI), India's equivalent of the US Securities and Exchange Commission has recommended a number of progressive steps for the government of India: (a) establish government-sponsored incubators; (b) allow a wider array of financial institutions to attract venture capital (VC) from abroad, and (c) liberalize the complex regulations and tax laws that hinder the growth of the VC industry. Currently the Indian tax laws are friendlier towards foreign venture capital than Indian counterparts, hence the proliferation of VC firms that are registered in Mauritius with whom India has a tax treaty. However these steps are yet to be implemented in practice.

One of India's great attractions is the talent pool of engineers and skilled manpower. Skilled entrepreneurs can leverage this relatively inexpensive talent pool to build business whose market is the whole world. Here comes the need for coordination and upgrading, the other two key elements of core competence. To find the appropriate niche in the world software market and then integrate the available talent pool so as to upgrade the software packages for the world market should be the goal of Indian software companies in the world markets today. Two recent examples offer hopeful signs for the future. One is the Infosys Technologies which is the first Indian IPO (initial public offering) in the US NYSE market. Infosys develops software, turnkey projects and software services for the banking, telecommunications and manufacturing industries. Its shares were priced initially at $34 each but soared to $179.50 on 11 October 1999 and the successful record continues. Another example is Satyam Infoway, India's second largest internet service provider. Satyam launched in November 1998, after the deregulation of the ISP market in India. The company offers dial-up internet access, email and webpage hosting to consumers in India through online registration and user-friendly software. The most important thing is that Satyam has formed strategic partnerships with US companies such as America Online's Compuserve Network Services, Sterling Commerce and Open Market. Through these partnerships Infosys can offer all relevant business information and content sites tailored to Indian interest worldwide.

These examples need to be multiplied in view of India's talent pool in the PC and software sector today and the high rate of success of Indian entrepreneurs and venture capitalists in Silicon Valley in the US. The example of Japan may provide a pointer. Japan not only borrowed US technology but improved it significantly and then competed very successfully in the US market. This is as true in the automobile market as in computer and related industries in the world today. In may ways India has a superior resource base, and needs to develop core competence. And the time is now. All that is needed is will and determination – the will of the people and of Indian entrepreneurs and the determination of government policymakers. As Peter Drucker (1999) points out, in developed countries today the central challenge is no longer to make manual work productive. The central challenge is to make knowledge workers productive. Knowledge workers are rapidly becoming the largest single group in the workforce of every developed country. They already comprise 40% of the US workforce. It is on their productivity above all that the future prosperity and indeed the future survival of the developed economies will increasingly depend. India has a comparative advantage in the talent pool of knowledge workers. They provide the most valuable asset to build core competence. This is the greatest managerial challenge before India and its policymakers.

1.6   Recent policy trends

Economic reforms initiated in 1991 abolished industrial licensing and import licensing except for most consumer goods. Entry requirements for foreign direct investment were relaxed and some forms of privatization of public sector enterprises were given a green signal. While assessing the privatization policy in internationally tradable goods, a close student of Indian economic development has noted:

> The most important consideration in privatizing an enterprise is that once privatized it will perform more efficiently. For this to come about it is essential that a privatized enterprise will face adequate competition from other domestic and foreign enterprises. In fact private firms had been insulated from import competition through

import quotas and licensing and from international competition through industrial licensing. This insulation led to their being inefficient as well and also to the underestimation if not outright disbelief, by the public of efficiency gains from privatization of public sector enterprises. After all competition is the most effective means for efficiency improvement and for ensuring that the resources employed can earn the maximum returns. (Srinivasan 2000: 7)

The actual impact of these reforms for the period 1991–1996 was marginal at best. Improving economic efficiency is the basis of core competence and the experience of rapid growth episodes in Southeast Asian NICs has highlighted the importance of core competence in world competition. As we have noted in our analysis of Korean growth experience two types of policy reforms are most instrumental. One is "keeping prices right." The other is "keeping investment demand competitive and outward oriented." On both fronts the economic reforms in India have negligible impacts. The estimates reported by Athukorala and Sen (2002) show the following trend for private corporate investment and public investment as a percentage of GDP.

Private corporate investment		*Public investment*
1990	4.3	9.7
1992	6.7	8.9
1994	7.1	9.0
1996	8.2	7.4

For this period there has not been any noticeable increase in the share of net foreign capital inflow in the domestic investment rate. Hence the trend of outward orientation is insignificant.

A recent econometric study by UNCTAD (1999) of 52 countries suggests that there is a significant positive correlation between FDI (foreign direct investment) and manufactured export performance. For example in China the foreign share in total exports rose from 17% in 1991 to 41% in 1997. In India FDI accounted for only 2.9% of gross fixed capital accumulation in 1996 against China's 17%. The clear implication is that India has lost out on potential labor-intensive and related exports which would have generated greater employment.

The liberalization policy improved after the BJP government came to power in October 1999. The World Bank (2000) country study on India summarized the trend of reforms till 2000 as follows.

> Although investment remained fairly high after 1996–97 exports slowed as cuts in protection stopped and world trade slowed. In 1997 India lost its share of world markets for the first time since 1991. Without further reallocation of resources, growth in total productivity slowed. Added to this explanation is the slowing of agriculture in 1997–98 and the development of excess capacity in industries like steel, cement and autos reflecting large new investments and a slowing of financial loans from non-bank financial corporation. This excess capacity could not be utilized to increase exports because overseas sales had become unprofitable. (79–80)

This explanation suggests that a second phase of reforms will be needed to restimulate growth which attained a rate of 7.5% for GDP growth at 1980–81 prices during 1994–95 to 1996–97.

The economic reform policy pursued by the BJP government over the period October 1999 through May 2004 can be broadly classified as follows:

1 A continuation of the policy of privatization of public sector enterprises, which had some success in telecommunications, banking and financial sectors like insurance.
2 More positive steps undertaken to invite foreign direct investment in IT sectors including automobiles, telecommunications and some consumer goods in pharmaceuticals and consumer electronics.
3 Special strategies undertaken for the software sectors in cities like Bangalore and Hyderabad. The IT sector helped to increase the export share by a significant amount. The export growth rate for the IT sector exceeded that of Singapore and Taiwan.
4 Liberalization of rules for investment by NRIs (nonresident Indian) helped step up the foreign exchange reserves by a significant amount, even exceeding that of Singapore and other NICs in Asia.

However the impact of the liberalization policy had some adverse implications. Although India's GDP growth during 2000–03 was 6 to 7% per year due mostly to growth in IT exports, overall employment growth fell from 22.2% to 1.5% per annum. The phenomenal performance of the software industry and the related IT sector in augmenting the export markets failed miserably on two fronts: one is its failure to spread the benefits of IT sector growth to other sectors like domestic trade and agriculture and other services like tourism and infrastructure development. The second is the failure of Indian entrepreneurs to anticipate the growth in world demand for such technical services as cell phones and international communications, and to undertake new investment in these areas.

The failure of transmission of growth impetus from the software industry to other sectors of the Indian economy may be traced to the education policy pursued by various federal and state systems. Under-use of computers and IT-related knowledge in the overall education system of the country is most striking. Even in the IITs and IIMs and the elite colleges where computer usage is available, its use in research and R&D purposes is very limited. Even today there exists political opposition in some states for any favorable IT-related education policies. For example in West Bengal where the literacy rate is higher than the national average there was open and deliberate opposition till 1997. Recently this attitude has changed somewhat but not within the CPM party which controls the state government. By contrast Chinese economic policy has adopted an IT-based education policy for over a decade and a half, along with outward export orientation. Public education policy in China has made systematic attempts to spread the technical knowhow about computer usage across all sectors, so that no child is left out.

There is a similar policy trend within NICs in Asia, including Japan. By contrast the Indian experience is very disappointing. It is interesting to note in this context the conclusions of a noted economist, who analyzed the growth miracles of countries like Korea and Taiwan.

The main engine of growth is the accumulation of human capital – of knowledge – and the main source of differences in living standards among nations is differences in human capital. Physical capital accumulation plays an essential but decidedly subsidiary role. Human capital accumulation takes place in schools, in research organizations and in the course of producing goods and engaging in trade. Little is known about the relative importance of these different modes of accumulation but for understanding periods of very rapid growth in a single economy, learning on the job seems to be by far the most central. For such learning to occur on a sustained basis, it is necessary that workers and managers continue to take on tasks that are new to them, to continue to move up what Grossman and Helpman call the "quality ladder". For this to be done on a large scale, the economy must be a large scale exporter.

This picture has the virtue of being consistent with the recent experience of both the Philippines and Korea. It would be equally consistent with post-1960 history with the roles of these economies switched. It is a picture that is consistent with any individual small economy following the East Asian example producing a very different mix of goods from the mix it consumes. (Lucas 1993)

Failure to spread the gains of export growth of software and IT products to other sectors of the economy had a political fallout for the BJP government. It lost power and the UPA (United Progressive Alliance) government led by National Congress and its allies such as DMK, RJP and RPI took power in May 2004 with Manmohan Singh as prime minister. The UPA government announced a common minimum program with six basic principles of governance, which include the following steps for the industrial sector:

1 The Government will immediately enact a National Employment Guarantee Act to provide a legal guarantee for at least 100 days of employment, to begin with, on public works programs.
2 The Government will ensure that the services industry is given all support to fulfill its true growth and employment potential. This includes software and all IT-enabled services, trade, distribution, transport, telecommunications, finance and tourism.
3 It will take immediate steps to reverse the trend of communalization of education that had set in over the past five years. It will also ensure that all institutions of higher learning and professional education retain their autonomy. Academic excellence and professional competence will be the sole criteria for all appointments to national apex institutions overlooking education and research in technical, managerial and general education at college and university levels.
4 The UPA government pledges to raise public spending in education to at least 6% of GDP with at least half allocated to primary and secondary education.

Clearly this is a ambitious agenda. Much depends on the will and determination of the UPA government and the cooperation of the different state governments, who are primarily responsible for implementing the educational goals.

1.7   Concluding remarks

The growth of the software and IT sector has helped the stellar export performance of India over the last decade. Two new trends have began since 2003. One is the sharp increase in FDI in sectors like telecommunications, electronics, automobiles and trade services. Liberalization of equity participation rules and the realization of the vast potential market in India have helped this process. Companies like IBM have started joint ventures with Indian companies like Tata Consultancy so as to develop international call centers and consultancy services. As the Director General of CSIR in India recently announced: India is on its way to become "the innovative hub of the world." Inforsys Technologies of Bangalore, which has become India's second-largest software maker thanks largely to outsourced work from the US and Europe is investing $20 million to create nearly 500 consulting jobs in the US. Recently Keijian Corporation of China launched mobile phone products in India. Other NIC countries like Korea, Singapore and Taiwan also approached India in order to start joint ventures.

The second trend is that the masses have never felt the gains in this stellar industrial growth in the export sector. Hence there is suspicion and apathy. Since this impression is based on empirical facts, India should adopt a three-pronged strategy. One is to develop a sequencing policy centered around the leading sector industries which today comprise software and related industries. This has happened to other industrial countries. For example industrial policy in Japan has been centered around promoting industry after industry: textiles and toys, steel, chemicals and high-tech industries. Due to the required sophistication the Japanese government was aware of the importance of sequencing industries from low-tech to mid-tech and so on. In India the developments in software and computer technology should adopt a common policy of sequencing. Secondly, the R&D side should be actively pursued in the IT sector. Look at the trend: India has received only $4 billion in foreign direct investment (FDI) from the OECD countries in 2003, while China received $53 billion. The technology transfer and enhanced job opportunities associated with FDI have helped China sustain its growth, while India is still limping. Moreover the R&D aspect of FDI has a great potential for India but the current record is almost insignificant compared with China or Korea. Recently a study by Yussof and Ismail (2002) estimated a knowledge-based development index based on spending on human capital through higher education and professional training which improve a country's competitiveness in the world. They also estimated the four components of this knowledge-based development index: (a) computer infrastructure, (b) information structure, (c) education and training, and (d) R&D and technology improvement.

Table 1.7   Knowledge-based development index in 2000 and its components

Country	Knowledge index	(a) Computer infrastructure index	(b) Infostructure index	(c) Education & training index	(d) R&D etc. index
US	1	1	10	8	3
Japan	2	8	3	10	1
Korea	15	16	11	16	13
Singapore	16	14	16	19	6
China	19	18	19	18	20
Philippines	20	22	18	20	18
Indonesia	21	21	20	21	21
Malaysia	17	17	17	17	16
India	22	20	22	22	22

In Table 1.7 the computer infrastructure index is measured through the share of worldwide computer use in the form of computer power per capita and connections to the Internet. The infostructure index includes investment in telecommunications, TV sets and newspaper circulation. The education and training index is based on total expenditure on education per capita, literacy rate, student–teacher ratio in primary and secondary education and higher education enrollment. Finally, the R&D etc. index includes high-technology exports as a proportion of manufacturing sectors, number of scientists and engineers in R&D, total expenditure on R&D as percentage of GDP and average annual number of patents.

It is no doubt true that these indices are not always very exact, due to different weightage on the components and the cultural variations across countries. The definition of R&D and related expenditures also varies significantly across countries. In spite of these deficiencies two aspects stand out very clearly: India is at the bottom of the countries listed. Korea and China fare much better than India. Secondly, countries like Singapore and Malaysia perform much better in R&D intensity than India. Some recent estimates project the trend that the R&D outsourcing market in information technology in India is expected to grow from $1.3 billion in 2004 to over $8 billion by 2010. For this expectation to be realized India has to step-up high-technology exports and the proportion of R&D investments. More incentives are needed for the private sector to accelerate their R&D investment.

Finally, there is urgent need for transmission of growth in the IT sector to other sectors of the economy like trade, communication, banking and rural financial structure. According to an estimate by Sengupta (1998) the externality or transmission effect of the export sector on the rest of the economy is roughly three to seven times larger than the reverse effect for Korea over the period 1964–86. For Taiwan it is much higher. Much of this transmission of the externality effect was due to deliberate incentive and other policies pursued by the state. As of October 2004 many US software companies are opening up strategic alliances with Indian companies. For example one of the major IT firms, Polaris Software Laboratory in India entered into a strategic alliance in September 2004 with the US-based IT services firm CTG to provide outsourcing services to banking, financial services and insurance clients in the US and Europe. The US company Nucleus Software Exports announced plans in September 2004 to expand R&D activity and add 60 professionals to its R&D unit in Chennai by the end of 2004. Clearly many of these outsourcing jobs and related software activities can be transmitted to other sectors of the economy. Also this should lead to an expansion of the infostructure of IT-related services, which would transmit the gains of the IT sector to other parts of the economy. This is a challenge for the new economy. It is up to the leaders of business and managers to take up the challenge. Only then can growth synergy in India can be achieved.

References

Athukorala, P. and Sen, J. (2002) *Saving, Investment and Growth in India*. New Delhi: Oxford University Press.

Chakravarty, S. (1987) Marxist economics and contemporary developing economies. *Cambridge Journal of Economics* 11, 3–22.

Dahlman, C. and Nelson, R. (1995) Social absorption capability, national innovation systems and economic development. In: B. Koo and D.H. Perkins, (eds) *Social Capability and Long Term Economic Growth*. New York: St. Martin's Press.

Das, Gurcharan (2001) *India Unbound*. New York: Alfred Knopf.

Drucker, P. (1999) *Management Challenges for the Twenty-first Century*. New York: Harper Collins.

Dutta, S. (2003) Using offshore software development to drive value: the experience of Motorola in India. In: F. Richter and P. Banerjee (eds) *The Knowledge Economy in India*. New York: Palgrave Macmillan.

Enos, J.L. and Park. W.H. (1988) *The Adoption and Diffusion of Imported Technology*. London: Croom Helm.

Heeks, R. (1996) *India's Software Industry*. New Delhi: Sage Publications.

Jorgenson, D.W. and Stiroh, K.J. (2000) Raising the speed limit: US economic growth in the information age. In: W.C. Brainard and G.L. Perry (eds) Brookings *Papers on Economic Activity*. Washington, DC: Brookings Institution.

Kraemer, K. and Dedrick, J. (1994) Payoffs from investment in information technology. *World Development* 22, 1921–31.

Lall, S. (1999) India's manufactured exports: comparative structure and prospects. *World Development* 22, 1921–31.

Lucas, R. (1993) Making a miracle. *Econometrica* 61, 251–72.

Mani, S. (1998) A curmudgeon's guide to economic reforms in India's manufacturing sector. *Economic and Political Weekly* 33(50), 3257–72.

Norsworthy, J.R. and Jang, S.L. (1992) *Empirical Measurement and Analysis of Productivity and Technological Change*. Amsterdam: North Holland.

Page, J. (1994) The East Asian miracle: four lessons of development policy, in NBER: *Macroeconomics Annual 1994*. Cambridge: MIT Press.

Porter, M.E. (1990) *The Competitive Advantage of Nations*. New York: Free Press.

Prahalad, C.K. and Hamel, G. (1994) *Competing for the Future*. Cambridge: Harvard Business School Press.

Sengupta, J.K. (1998) *New Growth Theory: an Applied Perspective*. Cheltenham: Edward Elgar.

Sengupta, J.K. (2003) Facing hypercompetition in world software markets: global strategies for India. In: F. Richter and P. Banerjee (eds) *The Knowledge Economy in India*. New York: Palgrave Macmillan.

Sengupta, J.K. and España, J.R. (1994) Exports and economic growth in Asian NICs. *Applied Economics* 26, 41–51.

Sengupta, J.K. and Okamura, K. (1993) Scale economies in manufacturing. *Empirical Economics* 18, 469–80.

Shapiro, C. and Varian, H. (1999) *Information Rules: a Strategic Guide to the Network Economy*. Cambridge: Harvard Business School Press.

Sivasubramonian, S. (2004) *The Sources of Economic Growth in India 1950–1 to 1999–2000*. New Delhi: Oxford University Press.

Srinivasan, T.N. (2000) *Eight Lectures on India's Economic Reforms*. New Delhi: Oxford University Press.

UNCTAD (1999) *Report on UN Conference on Trade and Development*. New York: Oxford University Press.

World Bank (1992) *World Bank Development Report*. New York: Oxford University Press.

World Bank (2000) *India: Reducing Poverty, Accelerating Development*. New Delhi: Oxford University Press.

Yussof, I. and Ismail, R. (2002) Human resource competitiveness and the inflow of foreign direct investment to the Asian region. *Asian Pacific Development Journal* 9, 89–107.

Zerega, S. (2000) What would Mao think? *Red Herring* 83, 120–32.

2
Lessons of Growth Experience

The economic growth experience of other countries provides two important tests for the development process. One is the historical test showing why some countries succeeded in growing. The other is the empirical test of the most prevalent theory of economic growth. The historical test is more comprehensive, since it includes economic policies and also institutional and political decision making that affect the growth process. The empirical test is more econometric in that it seeks to test specific hypotheses, for example how does export substitution accentuate the growth process? How does "knowledge capital" improve the externality effect, where the latter measures the impact of information technology (IT) and the related knowledge from the base sector to other sectors of the economy?

Our object here is twofold. One is to analyze the successful growth experiences of selected countries in terms of both historical and empirical tests to see if there are economic lessons for growth for India today. The second object is to explore the state of world competition today and the future prospect of US–India links through trade and investment in the IT sectors of both countries.

Four countries have been selected for study in view of their growth experiences, either because of their successful performance or their economic importance. China, the NICs (newly industrializing countries) in Southeast Asia, Japan and the US are the selected countries.

2.1   The Chinese growth experience

China's growth experience is important for India today for several reasons. Over the last two decades China has maintained a very high growth rate of its GDP and competed very successfully in the world market. It has enjoyed a trade surplus with the US exceeding $100 billion. A World Bank country study has summarized its progress thus:

> Consider the period 1985 to 1994, when average GDP growth in China was 10.2 percent. Two-thirds of the growth was the result of capital accumulation, supported by an extraordinarily high savings rate that has come to depend increasingly on China's thrifty households. Less important but significant nonetheless have been increasing labor force participation rates. One third of growth was the result of productivity improvements in the use of inputs, due to structural change across sectors and efficiency improvements within production units.... The most striking feature of structural change in industry is the extraordinary growth of "private" firms, i.e., privately and individually owned enterprises, foreign joint ventures and foreign funded enterprises. This group increased its share of industrial value added from 1% in 1984 to 24% in 1994, much of it in the past five years. (World Bank 1996: 89)

The empirical estimates for GDP growth of 10.2% during 1985–94 can be decomposed by the four major sources as: (1) factor accumulation: 6.6%, (2) agricultural reallocation: 1.0%, (3) ownership reallocation: 0.4%, and (4) TFP growth 2.2%. For the recent period 1990–94 the GDP growth rate of 10.5% has the following breakdown: (1) factor accumulation 6.1%, (2) agricultural reallocation 0.6%, (3) ownership reallocation 0.9%, and (4) TFP growth 2.9%.

The most striking feature is the TFP growth resulting in significant productivity gains. To achieve these productivity gains and maintain this speed over 2004 and beyond, the Chinese government accelerated reforms in three strategic directions. The first is to accelerate the role of the competitive market forces, especially for activating state enterprises and the financial services sectors. Despite tremendous opposition and bureaucratic resistance the government continued this market reform and placed economic efficiency under competition as the sole criterion of industrial performance in both the public and private sectors. The second strategy is to set up active links of market reforms with the export sector, which culminated in China's membership of the WTO (World Trade Organization) in 2000, with a bilateral agreement with the US in November 1999 and the European Union in May 2000. As a result of WTO accession China has agreed to make specific commitments to reduce protection for merchandise and services. The reductions in tariff protection, quotas and licenses are some of the significant steps China has to take. Thus the average tariff on manufactures is to be reduced to 9.44% from the high level of 17.4%. China has also made comprehensive commitments on telecommunications, banking, insurance and other professional services thus creating transparency and openness in the distribution network. As Martin et al. (2003) have concluded:

> It is clear that China's accession to the WTO will require a very large number of reforms both in legislation and in the way business is conducted. The need for reform is particularly acute in areas such as the financial sector and telecommunications, where substantial reforms in the regulatory structure, as well as international trade policies, are likely to be required. Agricultural policy will be unable to take the inward-looking approach that has characterized agricultural policy in other East Asian "miracle" economies. (Martin et al. in Hope, Yang and Li 2003)

The rapid increase in China's openness is evidence of the rapid increase in China's share of world exports which rose from 1.0% in 1982 to 3.0 in 1998 and is still rising. The share of exports of goods and nonfactor services increased from 7% in 1982 to more than 16% in 1998. Along with this openness came the policy of complete duty exemptions for inputs used in the production of export goods. This clearly boosted the development of export processing industries which rely heavily on imported intermediate goods or inputs. As a result there was a dramatic change. For example manufactures comprised about 50% of exports in 1984 but rose to 87% in 1998. In the current period 1999–2003 this share has exceeded 90%. The estimates by Martin et al. (in Hope, Yang and Li 2003) of the impact of WTO accession are self-revealing (see Table 2.1).

Table 2.1   Output and exports as a share of the world economy (%)

	Output 2005			*Exports 2005*		
	1995	*Without accession*	*With accession*	*1995*	*Without accession*	*With accession*
Meat & livestock	6.70	11.62	12.09	3.51	0.51	0.43
Textiles	10.79	13.88	13.54	8.43	8.84	10.15
Wearing apparel	7.02	8.84	19.09	19.58	18.54	45.14
Electronics	2.63	1.34	1.32	1.92	2.50	2.58
Business & finance	0.89	1.34	1.32	1.92	2.50	2.58

The third strategic direction of economic reform in China was to keep prices and costs in balance: prudence in fiscal reform, good management of the exchange rate system and transforming the economy of state-owned enterprises (SOEs). Before 1994 a two-tier approach was followed for foreign exchange markets: an official rate and a market rate. On 1 January 1994 the two tiers were merged into a single market rate. In December 1996 China went a step further in adopting current account convertibility. This may be one important reason why China was able to handle the Asian financial crisis which so badly affected the NICs in East Asia. Following this exchange rate reform both exports and FDI increased dramatically, reaching about US $45 billion in 1997 and 1998, and went still higher to 2003.

Reforming the SOEs was another gigantic task handled with much success. Prior to 1992 China did not privatize any SOEs. These SOEs were dominated by small and medium sized enterprises under government supervision. Most of these were not economically viable or were overwhelmed with excess workers. Three new policies were adopted by the state in September 1999 to transform the SOEs so as to achieve economic efficiency. The first and perhaps most important policy was to narrow the scope of SOEs dramatically by which the state decided to concentrate its control over SOEs in some specific areas such as industries related to national security, and backbone industries in high-tech and new-tech industries. The state decided to withdraw from all other areas. Thus Qian and Wu (2003) estimated that the ownership composition of industrial output changed as shown in Table 2.2.

In the retail sales of consumer foods private enterprises rose from 2.1% in 1978 to 40.9% in 1995 and 62.7% in 1998 and is still rising, although in telecommunications, banking and insurance services its share is less than 3%. The development of new private enterprises rather than privatization of existing SOEs has provided a strong boost to export growth. China's experience of this type of privatization shows very clearly that the spreading of growth impetus across sectors comes mainly from small and medium sized enterprises. Two striking examples

Table 2.2 Ownership composition of industrial output (%)

Enterprise	1978	1980	1990	1995	1998
State-owned/controlled	77.6	76.0	54.6	32.6	27.0
Collectives	22.4	23.5	35.6	35.6	36.3
Private	0.0	0.5	9.7	31.8	36.8

are the spectacular growth in TVEs (town and village enterprises) and the industrial growth in the export processing zones in coastal areas. Most of TVE growth was due to the privatization of collective enterprises. Noted Chinese economists like Qian and Wu (2003) believe that private enterprises will play a spectacular role in accelerating the growth rate in the Chinese economy in the next decade, provided there is further reform and liberalization to eliminate the various restrictions and discriminations against private enterprise.

The development of private small and medium-sized enterprises will likely become the new growth engine and the brightest spot of the Chinese economy in coming years. Our optimism is supported by recent evidence from Zhejiang province, which has the fastest development of private enterprises and in which we see the likely pattern of future development for the rest of the country.... Zhejiang represents China's future. In historical perspective Zhejiang had led the country in ownership changes. In 1984 the share of nonstate industrial output (collective and private) in Zhejiang was already more than 50 percent at a time when the national average was 35 percent. Eight years later in 1992 the national average of nonstate industrial output rose to over 50 percent. In 1998 the share of private industry surpassed 50 percent in Zhejiang while the national average stood at 37 percent. Recently many provinces have sent out study groups to visit Zhejiang to find out why it grew faster than other provinces. To us the lesson is clear: faster development of private enterprises. With other provinces learning from Zhejiang's experience we would not be surprised to see the share of private industrial output at the national level surpass 50 percent within the next decade. (Quin and Wu 2003: 56–7)

The most important impact of the Chinese economic reform has been in rural economic reforms since 1978. By dividing the rural economy into two sectors: the agricultural and the RSE (rural small scale enterprises) sector (also called townships and village enterprises on TVE) one can estimate the growth pattern over the period 1978–90. As Sengupta and Lin (1993) estimated, in 1976 the RSE sector accounted for 23.3% of total rural output and 5% of the total rural labor force, but in 1987 these shares rose to 47% and 20.9% respectively. In 1990 these exceeded 50 and 30% respectively. Sengupta and Lin (1993) divided the Chinese rural economy into three regions: the high income, the middle income and the low income regions. The high income region consists of eight provinces: Shanghai, Beijing, Tianjing, Liaoning, Guandong, Jiansu, Zhejiang and Shangdong. The middle income region consists of 13 provinces: Hebei, Shanxi, Neimomgu, Hilin, Heilongjiang, Anhui, Fujian, Jiangxi, Henan, Hubei, Hunan, Sichuan and Xinjiang. The low income region consists of the remaining seven provinces. The high income region had the greatest success in generating rural nonagricultural employment opportunities and income growth. The middle income region contains more than 50% of the total rural surplus labor force and a very low level of per capita income. In the low income region like Gansu and Guizhou provinces nonagricultural employment in 1980 constituted less than 3% of the total rural employment. The empirical estimates of productivity through log linear production functions over 1978–90 show the following results. First of all, the marginal labor productivity of the RSE sector is found to be 3.6 times higher than that of the agricultural sector and the RSE sector is found to have a strong positive externality effect on agricultural production mainly due to improved technology and incentives and more efficient management. Secondly, the high and middle income regions show strong evidence of increasing returns to scale exceeding 1.05 and the capital elasticity uniformly higher than the labor elasticity of production. This trend has continued in the recent period, which lends support to the hypothesis that market-based incentives and openness in global trade have accelerated the rapid income growth in the coastal provinces of the RSE in the high income region.

Two other distinct features of Chinese growth experience provide lessons for India today and tomorrow. One is the Chinese policy on joint ventures (JV) between Chinese and foreign firms. The other is the internationalization of the education sector, initiated by Deng Xiaoping in 1977 and accelerated by Jiang Zemin's call in 1996 for policy reforms to expand China's education through foreign cooperation.

Joint ventures provided significant growth synergy by globalizing rural China. Local governments thus competed for FDI and became eager to establish JVs as quickly as possible. This put pressure on the Chinese government to decentralize the decision making authority over JVs. As a result most open rural counties were allowed to approve FDI projects of under $5 million. Nationwide the number of JV contracts increased fourfold between 1991 and 1993. The FDI in rural China ballooned from $446 million in 1992 to $3.1 billion in 1993. The rural provinces became a focal point of linkage through which foreigners accessed China's domestic market on more favorable terms than the central state preferred. In return for this access the rural provinces received foreign capital equipment or access to international markets that otherwise would have been closed to their exports. Also they enjoyed special tax concessions, e.g., three years tax free, two years half taxes and also inputs at special rates.

Modernizing education policy since Deng's 1992 southern trip was the second most important step in Chinese globalization. Ironically, a country long seen as totalitarian has allowed more than 450,000 of its brightest students and scholars to leave the country in 2000, although about half remained abroad. The tempo continues in the international-ization of Chinese higher education in technical, engineering and management fields. International economic forces pulled people out of China and undermined the state's control. Since 1992 US universities were granted the right to organize Chinese educational exchange programs. US fellowships and grants attracted China's best and brightest and once this started the brain drain process began when the returnees were granted preferential treatments in establishing new enterprises and expanding international exchanges. The new policy adopted in March 1992 declared a strategy to improve services for returnee students from abroad through job introduction centers, greater support for scientific research and preferential policies and subsidies for returnee students and their families. Rather than lamenting over "brain drain", the Chinese government emphasized the "brain gain" from returnee students. It also fostered educational exchanges in a deliberate attempt to internationalize the technical and managerial education system in China. Thus between 1985 to 1991 the percentage of returnee students out of total graduate students was 6.1%, but it rose to 14.1% during 1992–99 and a peak of 18.0% in 1995. One important step in policy followed since 1992 is the provision of incen-tives by which returnees could negotiate their own deals with entrepre-neurial cities such as Shenzhen or Shanghai that offered them preferential policies. The internationalization of the curriculum in tech-nical, vocational and business schools and the strong support for setting up exchanges with US institutions helped the process of an enormous level of deregulation. Even for basic education services China provides a contrast to India. As Dreze and Sen (2002) have stressed, adult literacy rates in India were as low as 34% for women and 62% for men in 1990–91, compared with 68% for Chinese women and 87% for Chinese men. For the two Indian states of Kerala and West Bengal they cited high literacy rates: for Kerala the female and male literacy rates were 92 and 95% in 1981–82 but increased to 98 and 98% in 1990–91. But the record of industrial growth in these two states was depressing.

The communist-led governments in these states were opposed to any liberalization or economic reform in the industrial sector and in West Bengal the education policy over the period 1980–2000 systematically reduced the role of English language up to the secondary level. The contrast to China is very significant. As Zweig (2002) has noted:

> Under internationalization the knowledge of foreign languages, particularly Japanese and English became a valuable commodity with demand five to ten times greater than supply. Organizations fought furiously for these people, helping those with good skills to gain access to the transnational sector and better lives for all. (187)

It is not surprising that the intellectual elites in West Bengal and Kerala have a double standard: they seem to adopt communistic political controls as in China but refuse to follow the Chinese model of education reforms and market-based industrial growth. While sympathetic to the Chinese political ideology, Dreze and Sen tend to follow this double standard by not blaming the leftist states of Kerala and West Bengal for their miserable failure in their records of industrial growth and market reforms.

> China's liberalization program has certain pragmatic features that distinguish it from some other attempts at surging towards a market economy. The market mechanism has been used in China to create additional channels of social and economic opportunities, without attempting to rely on the market itself as a surrogate social system on its own. (Dreze and Sen 2002: 140)

One economic puzzle remains: Why did China globalize and set up economic reforms to improve overall efficiency? By contrast the leftist states of Kerala and West Bengal did not, although they purported to follow the Chinese style of philosophy in their political ideology. There are two plausible answers: one answer lies in the network capital model, advanced by Zweig (2002) which emphasizes horizontal linkages by smaller ethnic Chinese firms that carry out successful transnational exchanges with a modicum of central state interference. This model stresses the role of overseas Chinese business networks such as Taiwan and East Asia, who invested heavily in seeking export markets and cheap offshore centers for export processing in the coastal provinces and TVE in China through small and medium sized firms. By contrast the experience of NRIs in returning to India and building a network of export-oriented firms has yielded mixed results. Except in Bangalore and Hyderabad where the IT sector flourished, the results have been rather disappointing. States like West Bengal and Kerala in spite of their high literacy rates performed very poorly. Even those NRIs who returned to these states to start new enterprises with their own investment found great stumbling blocks if not outright rejection. The double standard of the intellectual elite in these states played their games very well.

The second reason is the rent-seeking propensity of the political leaders and bureaucrats, who wanted to oppose any serious economic reform. This rent-seeking model argues that globalization through economic decentralization empowered the local state vis-à-vis the center by creating a core of developmental communities, which fostered world exchanges with network capital and FDI outside the purview of Beijing's control. This never happened in India. Individual states with higher than average literacy rates or better educational records never developed a successful global linkage. The political leaders found it to their rent-seeking advantage not to introduce any deregulation or any serious reform towards outward orientation. Opportunities for corruption and rents, created by the regulation and political graft system led bureaucrats and politicians to prefer partial reform and partial deregulation. The intellectual game of double standards continues to perpetuate the zero-sum society in India. In states like West Bengal and Kerala the game turned more intense: political largesse generates a cadre of communist party henchmen, which earns enormous rents in opposing any serious economic reforms. Competence and efficiency are sacrificed for rents and grafts. The political leaders turn a blind eye to the spectacular growth experience of China. In China today the people increasingly demand increased access to global markets, better and cheaper products, added comparative advantage for Chinese goods and services and an increased share of the IT processes and services. These new opportunities in the world today create pressure for continued deregulation. China's accession to the WTO would enhance this deregulatory process with increased transparency and more economic efficiency in China's policy setup. India has a lot to learn. West Bengal and Kerala have a long way to go. Beyond the slogans and above the hill!

2.2   NICs in Asia

The high performing Asian economies (HPAEs) showed a remarkable record of high and sustained economic growth in per capita GDP exceeding 6% per year over the period 1965–90 and thereafter. These economies include South Korea, Singapore, Taiwan and Hong Kong (China), known as the "Four Tigers." A recent estimate by a Global Research Project (McMahon and Squire 2003) compared the average per capita GDP growth rate of 83 developing countries over a 31-year period 1968–98. Selected results are reported in Table 2.3.

Here the high-growth category of countries consists of those countries whose average growth rate is at least equal to the mean of the OECD countries. Clearly India has a high growth potential, although it is far below countries such as China, Thailand or Indonesia. Three major forces have been identified behind high growth performance by the empirical growth economists. The first is the investment in physical and human capital per worker. The World Bank study by Page (1994) found for the 11 HPAEs over the period 1965–90 that their investment levels in physical and human capital substantially exceed those for other countries at similar levels of development, thus yielding a more rapid growth of per capital income. A more recent estimate by McMahon and Squire (2003) based on 83 developing countries over a 32-year period 1968–98 identified the investment share of GDP (INV/Y) as the major explanatory variable for high or low growth performance. They found that the threshold value of investment that separates high and low growth performance is 22%. By using a dummy variable D taking the value one if the ratio INV/GDP exceeds 22% they found the following regression estimate

$$\text{Growth} = -3.3 + 0.16(\text{INV/GDP}) + 1.99D$$
$$(2.5) \qquad\qquad (2.2)$$

Table 2.3   Growth experience by per capita GDP growth performance (1968–98)

High-growth		Medium-growth		Low-growth	
China	6.9	Colombia	2.0	Argentina	0.2
Taiwan	6.7	Brazil	2.0	South Africa	−0.3
Korea Republic	6.6	Bangladesh	1.6	Nigeria	−0.3
Singapore	6.0	Mexico	1.3	Peru	−0.5
Hong Kong	5.5	Kenya	0.9	Ghana	−0.8
Thailand	5.3	Sudan	0.4	Haiti	−1.0
Indonesia	4.9				
Malaysia	4.2				
Sri Lanka	3.1				
Chile	2.8				
India	2.6				

with t-values in parentheses. This estimate strongly supports the view that productivity of investment is significantly higher in countries where the rate of investment exceeds the threshold level. On average the growth rate is 1.99 points higher for these countries for which INV/GDP exceeds 22%. Next to investment rate the other most important factor is the inflation rate. They found a threshold value of 18.5% for the inflation rate, above which growth is hindered. The low inflation rate could be interpreted as a proxy for good monetary and fiscal management. The World Bank Report (1993) observed that the high growth rate in the NICs in Asia is largely due to the superior accumulation of physical and human capital and the residual factor which is often termed TFP or productivity growth. Table 2.4 summarizes the World Bank estimates.

The critical importance of productivity growth and the role technical innovations played here offer useful lessons for other countries like India. The econometric estimates by Nadiri and Son (1999) of the output growth decomposition are more revealing, as shown in Table 2.5. Their estimates for 1969–90 also report the average cost elasticity of physical capital (K), human capital (H) and foreign capital (F) and the overall scale of returns as follows:

Cost elasticity	Korea	Taiwan	Singapore	Japan	Malaysia
K	0.39	0.38	0.19	0.57	0.42
H	–0.24	–0.23	–0.11	–0.35	–0.25
F	–0.008	–0.009	–0.002	–0.003	–0.003
Scale	1.13	1.12	1.02	1.25	1.15

Table 2.4   Sources of per capita GDP growth in the Asia–Pacific region (1960–85)

Country	Growth (%)	% real per capita GDP growth accounted for by	
		Factor accumulation	*Productivity growth*
Hong Kong	6.09	44	56
Korea	5.89	63	37
Singapore	6.03	65	13
Taiwan	6.38	58	42
Japan	5.69	82	18
Indonesia	3.72	60	40
Malaysia	4.00	87	13
Thailand	3.82	66	34

Table 2.5   Average yearly output growth over 1969–1990 and its decomposition in NICs in Asia

Output growth	Korea	Taiwan	Singapore	Japan	Malaysia
	9.70	9.71	9.60	5.07	7.62
			Sources of output growth		
Labor	7.09	6.86	7.19	7.19	5.76
Physical capital	33.57	24.30	9.47	50.65	20.77
Human capital	7.66	4.95	3.40	5.45	7.97
Foreign capital	0.69	0.94	0.34	0.24	0.26
Technical progress	18.44	21.52	5.00	39.93	7.90

It is clear that besides physical capital investment two other important factors played a crucial role in the high growth episodes of the NICs in Asia. These are productivity growth through scale economies and cost efficiency and the role of human capital or knowledge. Note the high and negative cost elasticity with respect to human capital H. For Taiwan and Korea it is –0.23 and –0.24 and for Japan –0.35. Also the scale of increasing returns is 1.13, 1.12 and 1.25 for Korea, Taiwan and Japan respectively.

For a comparative perspective on India's growth experience we may refer to the careful econometric estimate by Athukorala and Sen (2002) which incorporated the nonstationarity of the time series data over the period 1955–96 and used GDP growth and nonresidential business sector growth (NRB) as dependent variables. Their regression results for some of their important explanatory variables are as follows.

	X_1	X_2	X_3	X_4	X_5	R^2
GDP growth	0.223	—	–0.011	0.901	—	0.420
	(t = 2.73)		(–2.050)	(1.62)		
Growth of NRB output	—	0.856	—	—	–0.037	0.414
		(5.65)			(–2.49)	

Here X_1 is the national rate of gross domestic capital formation, X_2 is the same for the the nonresidential business sector, X_3 is the cross product of X_1 and the average rate of inflation, X_4 is the cross product of X_1 and an openness index proxied by the ratio to GDP of the total of imports and exports and finally X_5 is the cross product of X_2 and the rate of inflation. These economic results yield several important inferences about India's economic growth. First, the role of investment in the nonresidential business sector combined with openness have a strong positive influence on economic growth. This result is more significant for the period since economic reforms. Secondly, the openness index when combined with nonresidential business investment has a strong positive influence on growth. Finally, their separate estimates for the two components of investment, i.e., investment in equipment and machinery and investment in construction show that the former has a larger growth effect.

The rapid growth episode of NICs in Asia would be incomplete without special reference to Taiwan, which like China exhibited rapid growth in income and exports mainly through the medium and small scale but economically efficient industries. This was noted by Kuznets as growth with equity. It had two important impacts on the economy. One is that high GDP growth per capita did not increase income inequality at all, since growth was so widely distributed. According to the World Bank estimate for the period 1965–89 Taiwan had a GDP growth rate per capita of 6.8%, whereas income inequality measured by the ratio of income shares of the richest 20% and the poorest 20% of the population stood at 5%. Comparable figures for Korea were 7.2% and 7.1% and for India 1.7% and 7.0% respectively. Thus the HPAEs are unique; Taiwan in particular combining rapid and sustained growth with highly equal income distributions. The small and middle sized firms spearheaded the growth process by developing marketing in specialized lines of product development, e.g., software and electronics, and formed a spawning ground for large firms. For example, Acer in Taiwan developed in such a fashion and turned out to be a respectable computer parts supplier. Acer of Taiwan has its own PC sets thus offering new products at the same time as the major US and Japanese companies. The most important thing is that this tempo is continuing in Taiwan in electronics and related fields by the skill and agility of the numerous entrepreneurs belonging to small and medium sized firms. Secondly, the development of export processing zones in Taiwan helped the backward linkages and nurtured other supporting industries outside the zones. Thus application-specific industries got a boost and the indigenous firms in these application-oriented industries such as micro-chips, etc. started developing joint ventures with the multinational companies, as their suppliers but also sometimes as their competitors.

Thus one may conclude that Taiwan's rapid growth experience was largely conditioned on the core competence and efficiency of the small and medium sized enterprises. At a later stage overall growth had its diffusion to other sectors through collaboration and joint ventures with multinational enterprises. This growth was a two-way process. Skill intensity, hard work and choosing the right marketing niche activated the growth process by the small and medium sized enterprises. Government provided active help and support. People shared in the growth dividend and this trend is till continuing in the technology-intensive industries of today.

2.3   Japan's experience

Japan's growth experience is important for India for several reasons. First, it competed successfully with the US and other developed countries well before the NICs in Asia. In modern manufacturing and high-tech products it still leads the world market. Secondly, unlike China it has practiced western-style democracy and invested heavily abroad. According to Maddison (1995) the labor productivity in manufacturing changed dramatically over the period 1950–89. With the US level taken as 100 it changed for Japan from 18 in 1950 to 56 in 1973 and 80 in 1989. In 1995 it exceeded 90. By comparison India had 5 (in 1950), 11 (in 1973) and 20 (in 1989) and Korea 5 (in 1950), 11 (in 1973), 20 (in 1989) and 25 (in 1995). Income inequality did not rise as fast with high growth rate in Japan. World Bank estimates over the period 1965–89 were 5% GDP per capita with growth of 5% inequality. This implied a high participation rate of the middle class and the rural population. Thirdly, Japanese companies like Sony, Panasonic and Hitachi play a very dynamic role in the computer and telecommunication markets in the world today and for this reason alone India has to interact with Japan in trade and foreign investment.

The gross national income per capita (GNI) in 2001 adjusted for purchasing power parity is reported by the World Bank as follows.

	GNI	*Adult illiteracy rate (%)*
Japan	$27,430	3
India	2,450	43
US	34,870	—
UK	24,460	—
China	4,260	16
Korea	18,110	2

It is clear that Japan has reached very close to the US level of per capita national income, exceeding that of the UK and many other European countries. Its adult illiteracy rate has fallen down to less than 2% in 2004 and the average life expectancy at birth in 2000 is 81, exceeding that of the US (77), China (50), Korea (73) and India (63).

What are the major economic reasons for Japan's spectacular growth performance? Many of Japan's experiences were the same as the high growth economies and NICs in Southeast Asia, e.g., high export growth, openness and liberalization, high rate of technological diffusion across different sectors and high rates of productivity and its growth.

It is important to emphasize some of the distinctive features of the Japanese growth experience. First, the major thrust of Japan's industrial policy since the 1950s has been to accelerate industrial growth by decreasing marginal cost through increasing returns to scale by various economic reforms. As Norsworthy and Jang (1992) have estimated, the intensity of productivity growth and technological change for the US and Japan over 1975–81 in the computer and electronics industry is substantial with Japan exceeding the US in several sub-periods. Secondly, Japan has most successfully capitalized on the R&D spillover effects from R&D investment in US companies. In a recent study of bilateral trade between the US and Japan Bernstein and Mohnen (1994) have evaluated the productivity impact of international R&D spillovers between the R&D intensive sectors of the two countries such as telecommunications, microcomputers, scientific instruments, etc. The industries for each country are aggregated by the Fisher index for a single composite sector. The estimated results of spillover effects over the period 1962–88 are shown in Table 2.6.

While the short run elasticities are derived from the short run demand for capital, the long run elasticities are derived from long run capital input demands. Table 2.6 exhibits several important features. First of all, the short run elasticity shows that a 1% increase in the US R&D investment reduces Japanese average variable cost by 0.63%. The long run reduction is much more (i.e., 1.057%). Secondly, the effect of R&D spillover from the US to Japan on Japanese labor productivity is

Table 2.6   Short run and long run spillover effects

	Short run		Long run	
	US	*Japan*	*US*	*Japan*
Average variable cost	0.241	–0.426	0.136	–0.430
Labor/output	–0.014	–3.546	–0.762	–2.058
R&D capital/output	0.026	0.053	0.242	–0.261

more spectacular. Thus in the short run the R&D investment reduces the labor output ratio in the US by 0.014 and in Japan by 3.546 and in the long run by 0.762 in the US and 2.058 in Japan. Bernstein and Mohnen have noted another surprising result: as new R&D-based knowledge is transmitted from the US to Japan, the latter reduces its own R&D investment rate. Note that the US has not reduced its R&D intensity, for example the short and long run R&D intensity increases by 0.026% and 0.242% respectively with the spillover from Japan. This process of internalizing R&D spillover from Japan is the unique feature of Japanese growth. Not only has it borrowed technology from abroad, it has utilized it, improved it and is still on the frontier of efficient technology. This is quite different from the Chinese and or NCI experiences in Asia. Japan never adopted the Chinese policy of almost ignoring the property rights of knowledge capital associated with R&D investment in the US. It also had to circumvent its lack of communication in the English language.

Here the Japanese government played a very active and dynamic role. It relied less on the invisible hand of the competitive market but more on the will of the Japanese government and the industrialists to optimize Japan's gains from international trade through selective interventions in the external and internal sectors of the economy. Internally the state supported developing an industrial structure composed of only a few firms whose market shares are stable over time and they compete continually in reducing average costs through innovations and utilization of R&D capital from abroad. This policy put a strong emphasis on promoting labor productivity through quality improvement and innovations. The innovations were interpreted in Schumpeterian terms very broadly, e.g., the development of new products, products going up on the quality ladder, the adoption of new production technology and the opening up of new markets and lines of investment. As Gao (1997) has emphasized, three basic principles were at the heart of the Japanese productivity movement, (1) the ultimate purpose of promoting productivity was to increase employment, (2) management must consult with labor on how to promote productivity, and (3) the benefits of improved productivity must be distributed between management and labor. Thus through sharing the benefits of innovations industries transformed the competing coalitions within a company to a cooperative production coalition. This helped Japan's comparative advantage in international trade growth and increased export intensity.

An incident during the tour of Japan by the noted management consultant Peter Drucker is worth pointing out here. He was interested in visiting an automobile plant in order to understand why this industry is so efficient in Japan. This was the 1980s. He was told by his host that this plant was currently on strike by the labor union and he could not visit. But that evening, while he was returning from visiting another industry he found the auto plant running. On query he found that the plant was open for reaching the export target agreed to by management and labor before the strike, and that strikes do not affect work to achieve the export target. Such is the cooperative production coalition in Japan! The government in Japan must not only help private industries with easy credit and flexible government loans for aggressive investments in equipment and technology transfers, but also initiate positive institutional reforms at the company level, so that the managerial environment becomes actively supportive of the innovation and R&D effort.

Clearly India has a lot to learn in this age of the new economy, when it has to compete in the world market for the various IT products and new technology-based goods and services.

2.4   India and the US

Recent US growth experience is of critical importance for India for two reasons. The most important reason is the phenomenal growth in the IT sector and in software exports from India over the last decade. This trend is likely to grow in future as the new government of Manmohan Singh is trying very hard like the earlier BJP-led government to provide supports and incentives for this sector. Secondly, India has immense possibilities for forming joint ventures with modern US companies in computers, electronics, pharmaceuticals and bio-tech fields so as to capture the spectacular R&D spillover effects.

Two distinctive features of recent US growth have to be noted. One is the upsurge in productivity growth and technological progress in the modern technology-intensive industries such as computers, telecommunications, electronics and related industries. Thus the careful econometric estimates by Norsworthy and Jang (1992) show that over the period 1959–81 the long run average rate of technical change in the US computer industry was of the order of 3.69% per year. The degree of returns to scale was 2.88 implying a substantial increasing returns to scale. Total factor productivity (TFP) growth which can be thought of as the growth in the productive efficiency of all factors combined is another measure of productivity growth. The average annual TFP growth in the computer industry is about 26%. More recently the empirical study by

Jorgenson and Stiroh (2000) noted two significant impacts of the growth of productivity in the US computer industry on the rest of the economy. First, as the production of computers improves and becomes more efficient, more computing power is being produced from the same input, e.g., learning by doing. This increases the TFP growth for the computer industry and the rest of the economy as a whole. Labor and R&D productivity also grow at both the industry and the aggregate levels, the latter through spillover of frontier knowledge capital. Thus in the four years 2000–04 the US economy exhibited labor productivity growth exceeding 3% on average, thus creating the so-called "jobless growth." Secondly, the computer-using industries are using skilled labor working with better computer equipment and this investment is increasing labor productivity growth. TFP growth 1958–96 was highest in two high-tech industries: (a) industrial machinery and equipment including computers, and (b) electronic equipment including communications equipment at 1.5 and 2.0% per year respectively. As a result average computer prices declined by 18% per year over the period 1960–95 and by 27.6% per year over 1995–98.

The second important feature of US economic growth is the spillover effect of R&D knowledge capital from the US to the rest of the world. Japan and the NICs in Asia have achieved great success in utilizing this knowledge transfer through innovations in computer and telecommunications industries. The development of skills and computer training has also occurred at a rapid pace in NICs in Asia and India. As a result many US companies in the services sector have started large scale outsourcing of jobs in order to reduce costs of production and distribution. This is nothing but the application of the comparative cost theory in international trade under competition. India, along with China and the NICs in Asia and Japan have two niches in this market: to supply skilled technicians at a lower cost and to capture R&D knowledge spillovers. So far India has not paid any attention to the second and most important aspect: sharing the knowledge spillover to improve labor productivity in the long run.

Research in productivity studies has changed in recent times. The earlier studies assumed that economic growth in the short run was largely driven by physical capital investment, while long run growth was due to exogenous technological change or progress. More recent studies by endogenous growth theorists emphasized intangible investment such as R&D that influences technological change directly and spreads the spillover effect to other firms and industries. The international cross-section data of more than 60 countries analyzed by Sengupta (1999) show that countries with higher R&D per worker have higher levels of TP growth and that surges in productivity growth over time may be largely due to increases in R&D investment per worker.

The implications of developing a strong R&D base and its impact on national growth and employment can be analyzed from the following empirical data in Table 2.7 reported by Corley, Michie and Oughton (2002) for the manufacturing sector over the period 1990–98 at 1995 prices.

Here the average employment share is measured by the share of hours worked in low tech and high tech industries. Two results stand out. One is the high productivity in the manufacturing sector in the US which has enabled it to maintain competitive advantage. The performance of the high tech industries in productivity growth has overcompensated the negative growth in employment (not shown in this table) in the low tech industries. Secondly, the R&D investment per hour is highest in the US. Even a small country like Italy has R&D per hour of 1.24. In India even a most optimistic estimate would not exceed 0.04 for the high tech category. Clearly India needs to develop its R&D base in the computer and IT-based industries and has all the potential. Joint ventures and active collaboration with US companies who are on the cutting edge of the latest technology should be deliberately pursued by Indian firms. As a result of improving the FDI environment and liberalization of economic reforms the US FDI to India is sure to increase over the next decade. It is true that China's accession to the WTO and her pro-market liberal policies have increased the attractiveness of China as

Table 2.7 Average levels of output, investment and R&D per hour and the average employment share for US and some OECD countries

Country		Output per hour	Investment per hour	R&D per hour	Average employment share
US	low tech	27.6	2.91	0.31	0.36
	high tech	35.5	4.68	4.21	0.64
UK	low tech	23.1	2.82	0.15	0.38
	high tech	26.2	3.48	2.24	0.62
Denmark	low tech	25.1	4.24	0.20	0.49
	high tech	27.4	4.75	2.12	0.51
Italy	low tech	29.4	5.39	0.05	0.41
	high tech	29.5	5.69	1.24	0.59
Canada	low tech	21.0	2.80	0.15	0.51
	high tech	24.9	3.45	1.69	0.49

a host for US direct investment. Since China opened up telecommunications and other technology-based industries to foreign firms, India now needs to compete with China and other NICs to attract FDI from the US. India's exports from the IT sector has crossed $10 billion in 2003 and has all the potential to grow further. Compared to China it is less than 10%. Both China and Japan have had a huge trade surplus with the US for over a decade and a large share of this surplus is in the form of manufactured and electronic goods and services. In order to achieve this type of success India needs to develop a high quality affordable infrastructure in the IT sector. Only then it can attract major US investment.

2.5 Lessons for India

The growth experiences of NICs in Asia and in countries like China and Japan provide important clues for achieving high growth and successfully competing in world markets today. Indirectly they offer an empirical test of the modern theories of economic growth. In this section we discuss very briefly the important lessons India may consider and adopt. India has much to learn from these growth experiences, especially occasional pitfalls of failure and crisis.

The most important lesson is the need for India to open up in a steady but cautious fashion. This opening up has three features: export promotion (EP), encouraging foreign direct investment (FDI) and liberalizing economic reforms so as to foster economic efficiency all around.

Bhagwati (1999) has emphatically stressed the need for EP strategy. He compared India's growth with Asian NIC growth over the last four decades and concluded that until 1956 India's planning stepped up investment in heavy industries in the public sector with an emphasis on infrastructure. This was exactly the path followed by Korea, Japan and even China. But by the end of the 1950s the policies of the two regimes in India and the NICs in Asia diverged dramatically. India turned to import substitution (IS) strategy, while East Asia to the EP strategy.

The result was that the inducement to invest in the economy was constrained by the growth of demand from the agricultural sector, reflecting in turn the growth of that sector. But agriculture has grown almost nowhere by more than 4 percent per annum over a sustained period of over a decade, so that increment at the margin of India's private investment rate was badly constrained by the fact that it was cut off from the elastic world markets and forced to depend on inevitably sluggish domestic agricultural expansion.... By contrast the East Asian private investment rate began its takeoff to phenomenal levels because East Asia turned to the EP strategy. The elimination of the "bias against exports" and indeed a net (if mild) excess of the effective rate for exports over the effective exchange rate for imports (signifying the relative profitability of the foreign over the home market), ensured that the world markets were profitable to aim for, assuring in turn that the inducement to invest was no longer constrained by the growth in domestic market as in the IS strategy. Private domestic savings were either raised to match the increased private investment by policy deliberately encouraging them or by the sheer prospect of higher returns. (Bhagwati 1999: 30)

How does EP strategy and outward orientation in trade help in stepping up the overall growth rate? Three reasons can be given. One stressed by Bhagwati (1999) is the combined process of forward and backward linkage, i.e., the generation and expectation of substantial export earnings induced the trend of growing investment in importing equipment and R&D knowledge embodying new technical change. Thus Asian NICs, for example, paid only five times as much for high-tech equipment and PCs that were 20 times more productive than domestic equipment. Consider the contrast in car manufacturing in India untill the 1980s. Fiat, Standard and Hindusthan Motors were using obsolete technology under their IS strategy. The same story holds for Russia. The loss to the Indian economy from this IS strategy was phenomenal while the gain to the Asian NICs was striking. The staggering costs of pursuing IS strategy have not yet been assessed by economists for India, but taking the Asian NIC experience it may safely be said to be more than 15% of the total industrial output.

There is a second aspect to the EP strategy, emphasized so appropriately by Bhagwati (1999). This is the role of literacy and education at all levels. Thus the productivity of imported equipment would be greater with a labor force that has a high literacy rate, or more significantly high levels of secondary and/or technical education. According to the UN *Human Development Report* 2003 the adult literacy rate and mean years of schooling for India and selected NICs areas was as follows for the year 1992:

		India		Korea		Malaysia		Thailand	
		Male	*Female*	*Male*	*Female*	*Male*	*Female*	*Male*	*Female*
1	Adult literacy rate as % of age 15+	64	35	99	95	89	72	96	92
2	Mean years of schooling from ages 25 and over	3.5	1.2	11.6	7.1	5.9	5.2	4.4	3.4

The figures for total adult literacy rate for 2000 were:

China	*India*	*Korea*	*Malaysia*	*Thailand*	*Japan*
84	57	98	87	95	99.4

It is clear that India needs a more aggressive policy for raising the level of education and the adult literacy rate. India spent about 4.1% of GNP on public education in 1998, compared to 4.9 in Malaysia, 4.8 in Thailand and 2.3 in China. Its effect on TFP growth has not been great since the proportion of science and technical education has been rather low. Estimates of tertiary students in science as a percentage of all tertiary students are reported as follows over the period 1995–1997: India 14, China 53, Korea 34 and Thailand 21.

The second reason why the EP strategy worked so well for Asian NICs in speeding up their growth rates is based on the networking model. China opened up its industry to heavy investment from Taiwan, and Korea's investment was contributed to in large part by Japan. Other successful NICs invited joint ventures with high-tech companies from abroad through networking and R&D investment. They were able to capitalize on the R&D spillover effects. India's efforts in this direction have been mainly cosmetic. Like the old managing agency system, Indian industries performed as sales and distribution agents of software developed by US companies. The NICs in Asia, Japan and even China developed the manufacturing base and utilized the R&D spillover effects but India has lagged far behind. According to the estimate by the Third Perspective Plan 2001–10 of Malaysia the knowledge-based development index for the year 2000 was as shown in Table 2.8.

Table 2.8   Knowledge-based development index and its components for Asian countries

Country	Knowledge index (rank)	Computer infostructure (rank)	Education and training (rank)	R&D and technology (rank)
US	1	1	8	3
Japan	2	8	10	1
UK	11	9	11	14
Korea	15	16	16	13
Singapore	16	14	19	6
Thailand	18	19	14	19
China	19	18	18	20
Indonesia	21	21	21	21
India	22	20	22	22

Here the computer infostructure is measured through the share of worldwide computer use; education and training rank is based on total government expenditure on education rate, literacy rate and higher education enrollment. The R&D and technology rank is based on high-technology exports as a proportion of manufacturing exports, the number of scientists and engineers in R&D as a percentage of GDP and the average annual number of patents.

It is clear from Table 2.8 that India has to raise its human resources capabilities by appropriate investment in human capital through education and professional training that will enhance their ability to generate and manage new technologies, and like Japan improve this technology for ensuring more efficiency.

A third reason for stepping up the EP strategy for India is to increase the core competence in both manufacturing and IT-related industries. Foreign direct investment and entrepreneurs in Silicon Valley of Indian origin provide some key sources of joint ventures in this direction. We may note that China has followed this line vigorously, first by investment from Taiwan and joint ventures with US companies in the high-tech fields and second by providing incentives through education policies for technical Chinese graduates trained in the US to return to the mainland, invest and start new ventures. By this and other policy reforms China has enjoyed a trade surplus of over $100 billion with the US as of 2003. Since joining the WTO China has adopted greater transparency in economic policy and more competition and market reform. By 1993 China had started to privatize small-scale state-owned enterprises (SOEs), to lay off excess state employees and to establish a social safety net. Many SOEs were neither viable or were saddled with excess workers and for them reallocation of labor was the main concern. About 10 million workers from SOEs and urban collectives were laid off each year between 1996 and 1998. Thus the share of SOEs in total industrial output decreased from 77% in 1978 to 27.0% in 1998 and to lower than 20% in 2003, whereas the share of private enterprises rose from zero in 1978 to 36.8% in 1998 and to higher than 44% in 2003. One important way of reforming the SOEs in China was through diversification of ownership and allowing the workers shares in profits. For example the state telecommunications monopoly was broken up in 1999 into four companies and each of them was asked to seek listings abroad and invite FDI and foreign collaboration. Another important example is the Legend Group started in 1984 which is the largest manufacturer of personal computers (PCs) in China. The company was fully state owned till 1999. In early 2000 the privatization process started as the company distributed 35% of its shares to its managers, engineers and other workers. This set up a precedent for other high-tech state companies to distribute shares to their employees and managers. It is an important lesson for India in its drive to reform the public sector enterprises. As Srinivasan has observed:

> It is still the case that the employees of the public sector and organized manufacture are a labor aristocracy which is a small proportion of the labor force. The aristocracy enjoys relatively high wages, security of employment, pension and health benefits, housing allowance, paid vacation and leave travel concessions and other perquisites none of which is available to the overwhelming majority of the labor force. It is nothing short of scandalous that our political leaders from the left to the right cave in to the demands of this aristocracy by being more generous than the Fifth Pay Commission in setting their salaries while completely ignoring the other recommendations of the bureaucracy. Mahalanobis (1961) was surely right in suggesting that it would seem better to try to attain the highest possible efficiency of labor and increasing productivity and use the additional value obtained in this way to create more employment rather than lower the industrial efficiency by slack or restrictive practices through overstaffing. (Srinivasan 2000: 14)

The East Asian economies with growth miracles seen in the last two decades promote an efficient allocation of labor across sectors through a variety of free market oriented policies. Thus their engine of growth in manufacturing and the IT sector has been the private sector. The outward orientation through EP strategy has exposed these private firms to the rigors of international competition, which helped improve cost and price efficiency. India stands at the other extreme. As Bajpai and Sachs (1996) have noted, workers in large firms in the industrial sector have a virtual guarantee of employment according to the Industrial Disputes Act. For firms employing 100 or more workers, layoffs require the permission of local state governments, which is almost never granted. This type of unproductive policy cutting at the roots of all economic efficiency applies not just to corporate industries but also to nonprofit activities such as universities, hospitals and municipal workers. The situation in some of the state run hospitals in the leftist run state governments in West Bengal, which has a relatively large corporate sector, are so deplorable that the class IV-level workers rule the hospitals and the doctors have to work under their consent. The word "efficiency" is unheard of in this culture! Deng in China must shiver in his grave at this culture. Yet the leftists and intellectuals carry on gleefully in their rent-seeking behavior supporting the leftist government in its colossal loss-causing endeavor.

FDI is another source of outward orientation. The major thrust of East Asian development has been the rapid growth of manufacturing. This rapid development has involved four major instruments: (1) convertibility of the currency for current account transactions, (2) zero or low tariffs and the absence of licensing for capital goods, (3) implicit or explicit subsidization of exports, and (4) export processing zones. This openness in manufacturing exports has given a tremendous boost to improving efficiency through a number of steps, for example (1) more efficient allocation of resources through specialization, comparative advantage and dynamic learning by doing, (2) increased FDI and increased share of R&D external benefits, which in turn helped increase exports, and (3) importing the latest technology and utilizing it for transmission of growth benefits to other sectors of the domestic economy. The last step was vigorously followed by China and Taiwan who energized their medium and small scale enterprises and helped the masses benefit from high growth through increased employment and income. Sachs, Varshney and Bajpai (1999) have correlated an openness index with the FDI to compare India's position in 1994 with some NICs in Asia. This is reported in Table 2.9. Here the openness index is measured by the share of GDP contributed by the total of exports and imports. The comparative evidence is self revealing. The potential loss from not sharing modern technology and R&D spillover from abroad may be analyzed more clearly by analyzing the pattern of US investment in India. Since

Table 2.9   Openness in trade in India and other NICs in Asia (1994)

Country	Openness index	Average tariff rate	FDI (US $mill)	FDI (% of GDP)
Indonesia	55	6	2004	1.4
Korea	55	4	516	0.2
Malaysia	171	9	5206	8.0
Thailand	80	9.3	1715	1.4
India	25	33	574	0.3

the US is the leader in high-tech fields like computers, electronics and pharmaceuticals and is likely to remain so in the near future, it is important to analyze the impact of US investment abroad in Asian countries and India.

Since 1995 the attractiveness of East Asian NICs as US FDI hosts has increased considerably due to their rapid economic growth and stellar economic performance. Thus taking total US FDI investment as 100, its percentage share increased from 0.4% in 1994 to 0.6% in 1998 for China, 0.2% (1994) to 0.2% (1998) for India, 0.7% (1994) to 0.8% (1998) for Korea and 1.8% (1994) to 2.0% (1998) for Singapore. But the income generated as a share to total income changed as follows:

China		India		Korea		Singapore	
1994	*1998*	*1994*	*1998*	*1994*	*1998*	*1994*	*1998*
0.1	0.2	0.2	0.0	0.7	0.8	3.1	2.7

Note that India's share is negligible or zero in 1998.

The sectoral decomposition of US FDI shown in Table 2.10 shows that it is more concentrated in petroleum, electronic and wholesale trade in East Asian developing countries. It is clear from Table 2.10 that the electronics industry attracted a large share of US FDI in East Asian countries, mainly because the capital productivity in this sector was very high and helped boost exports. Most of the successful NICs in East Asia attempted to set up export-processing zones for software and IT-related products by providing various fiscal and other incentives. Many US firms and also Japan used their subsidiaries in developing East Asia for the assembly of final electronic products, which requires labor-intensive production. Sections 806 and 807 of the US Tariff Schedule provide incentives to US firms for carrying out such operations.

Two distinguishing features of US FDI in Asian NICs and India are to be noted. One is that most US firms like Microsoft, Oracle, Motorola

Table 2.10 Sectoral decomposition of US FDI (1998) in %

	All industries		Petroleum (%)	Manufacturing		Wholesale trade (%)	Finance & services (%)
	$mill	*Index*		*Total (%)*	*Electronic (%)*		
All countries	860,723	100	10.0	33.5	3.9	8.0	37.3
Europe	20,934	100	7.1	33.9	3.2	8.2	40.8
Asia	35, 569	100	13.2	40.2	6.5	15.8	4.4
China	5,013	100	18.6	34.1	16.0	13.0	15.0
India	1,684	100	10.4	22.6	2.8	2.6	15.0
Korea	6,528	100	NA	41.0	8.7	11.0	4.5
Singapore	17,514	100	19.0	44.8	25.8	10.7	21.0
Taiwan	4,944	100	0.8	64.6	20.7	10.6	9.9
Thailand	3,537	100	26.3	30.8	7.0	16.0	3.6

Source: Aggarwal (2003).

and Hewlett Packard which have their subsidiaries in India and other Asian countries are not much interested in R&D activities. Partly this may be due to the lack of supply of skilled engineers and technicians in these developing countries. This is a niche where India has great potential. Indian entrepreneurs, especially the Silicon Valley enterprises of Indian origin can enter this niche and enjoy comparative advantage from the supply of skilled engineers and technicians from India. The second feature of US investment in Asian NICs and India is that most US firms are using their subsidiaries in developing East Asia as an export base, where parts and components are imported from the US and then assembled as finished products which in turn are exported back to the US and rest of the world. Indian entrepreneurs have considerable scope to manufacture parts and components through joint ventures and active collaboration. Note from Table 2.10 that India's share of electronic products in the total US FDI in India was barely 2.8% in 1998, whereas China had 16.0%, Korea 8.7%, Taiwan 20.7% and even Singapore had 25.8%.

Finally, outward orientation or openness to world competition is most important for stimulating growth because it helps the innovation process. Innovation may take many forms but the common core is creativity and human capital. The old, obsolete and inefficient methods are discarded in favor of new, current and more efficient methods. World competition helps this process by increasing labor productivity and creating scale economies. With infinitely elastic world demand, economies of scale generated by new innovations can be effectively utilized so as to lower costs and prices. This opens up the door of efficiency by which firms can grow successfully via world competition and thereby increase exports. Even a communist country like China realized this long ago when Deng took the first step in opening up China to world competition. A small step by Deng is a giant leap today. As Jefferson and Rawski (1999) have observed, China's state owned enterprises under the post-reform era started facing severe competition and declining profit margins and as a result adopted a strategy to innovate and achieve cost efficiency. They tested the association between competition and state-owned enterprise efficiency by regression over 496 sample enterprises in 1990. Their result was as follows.

$$\ln(Q/L) = -1.25^* + 0.63^*\ln(K/L) + 0.09^*D_1 + 0.65^*D_2 - 0.11D_3; \ R^2 = 0.32$$
$$(t = -3.04) \ (13.94) \qquad (2.55) \qquad (4.72) \qquad (2.54)$$

where ln is natural logarithm, Q/L = output labor ratio as a measure of labor productivity or a proxy for efficiency, K/L = capital labor ratio as a measure of capital intensity of production, D_1 = firm's demand elasticity for its major product, D_2 = firm's assessment of the overall competitive pressure it faces and D_3 = fraction of nonindustrial capital out of total capital stock. The asterisk denotes significant values at 5% level of t-test. Two points emerge very clearly. One is that the competitive pressure enhances labor productivity significantly. The second is that nonindustrial investment discourages labor productivity. Thus economic reforms erode inefficiency by lowering barriers to new technology and innovations.

The second major lesson for India is that growth of the IT sector and associated R&D exports have to be decentralized. Reforms of the regulated and segmented market structure through competition and openness in trade help a bit, but this process may be slow and at times very weak. Two examples are in the forefront: China's emphasis on town and village enterprises (TVEs) and Taiwan's policy of using small and medium sized enterprises in its export drive for electronic and manufacturing products. India can develop a higher rate of diffusion of growth in the IT sector to other sectors in three different ways One is through forward linkage by using information technology in sectors like manufacturing, trade and services. The use of cell phones, cheaper PC and improved communication devices may develop the accountability of government servants in various public services in agriculture. A beginning has been made by Chief Minister Chandrababu Naidu of one state in computerizing all land registration and recording services and ensuring transparency in government policy. The second way is to promote institutional learning and leadership through networking. A prime example of networking is the association of local, national and international NGOs promoting the spread of learning in the information structure, and also the empowerment of communities in rural areas. The eighth five-year plan (1992–1997) in India proposed an action plan to bring about active collaboration between the NGOs (nongovernmental organizations) and various government investments in rural areas. To facilitate this network three schemes were worked out by the Planning Commission in India, (1) consultancy development services, (2) the establishment of a national grid of NGOs, and (3) emphasis on introducing professional competence and managerial expertise including transparency and accountability. But as Sooryamoorthy and Gangrade (2001) have observed in their cross-sectional study of NGOs in India, NGOs have not been an integral part of rural integrated development. And they have not played a catalytic role in spreading information about new communication tools between the public and the government. The collaborative enterprises have not played any dynamic role.

A third method of knowledge diffusion is through the spread of education. The UNDP estimates in the *Human Development Report* (2004) provide the following statistics of government spending in the recent period. Clearly India's spending on public education compares favorably with China. It spends more of its GDP than China, yet the performance of rural small and medium size enterprises in India has been insignificant. Surely this calls for a drastic overhaul of the educational policy of the government in India.

	Public exp. on education % of GDP		Public exp. on education by level (as % of all levels)		
	1990	*1998–2000*	*Primary*	*Secondary*	*Tertiary*
India	3.9	4.1	39.4	40.5	20.1
Thailand	3.5	5.4	36.0	27.1	24.1
Korea	3.5	3.8	44.9	35.1	8.2
Singapore	—	3.7	27.1	28.1	25.0
Malaysia	5.2	6.2	31.8	32.9	14.4
China	2.3	2.1	37.4	32.2	15.6

The third major lesson for India is to follow an effective policy on monetary and fiscal management. Promoting high savings, maintaining low inflation rates and seeking outward orientation in internal and external competition are the three key areas. The largest difference between India and the rapidly growing NICs in Asia lies in government saving rates. The East Asian economies all have sizeable government saving as a percentage of GDP, while India's government saving has been close to zero. The state-run enterprises and public undertakings in India have been most ineffective in promoting efficiency; as a result their losses have contributed greatly to this state of affairs. A low inflation policy is vital to keeping a high growth tempo, since high inflation has a significant negative impact on growth and also private savings. Industrial policy also needs to maintain a high degree of market competition in the internal economy. Most of the East Asian NICs grew so fast because the private sector provided the engine of growth. China also provides the exemplary record in this direction. Its accession to WTO membership is the surest sign that it intends to follow the competitive path and free competition even in its town and village enterprises. Outside the state-owned enterprises sector, the Chinese economy has closely followed the competitive market model, much like the successful NICs in Asia. In China the non-state sector is relatively unconstrained by government regulation while in India the reverse situation holds. Although some steps have been taken since 2001 and the government of Manmohan Singh has declared a policy of liberalization and market reform in India, the pace is very slow so far and bureaucratic control is still very dominant.

India needs the political will and determination of Deng and Jiang Zemin!

The fourth lesson is how to step up the development of infrastructure in its two components: the information infrastructure and the basic physical infrastructure involving transport, communications, and power and water supply. The latter are generally called social infrastructure services (SIS) or public goods. To the extent that SIS are not like private goods subject to market competition, two types of economic inefficiency have thrived. One is cost inefficiency due to inadequate utilization of capacity and overstaffing. Sometimes this takes the form of dead weight loss. For example, in the states of West Bengal the state run bus transport system in Calcutta has been running at a loss for decades, maintenance policies of new buses are deplorable and their services have much to be desired. Side by side the privately owned buses in some routes allowed by the state run at a profit, their buses are well maintained and there is nearly full capacity utilization. The second inefficiency is the loss due to nonoptimal capacity expansion in the face of rapid growth in demand, which also fails to capture the dynamic economies of scale. Several types of efficient policy measures are needed here, e.g., public ownership with operation contracted to the private sector, privatizing some or all of the operations or following the Chinese style of decentralization discussed before. The critical point here is to enforce economic viability through transparency and accountability of government infrastructure.

From 2005 onward India needs to place more emphasis on the information infrastructure (II), which is so critical to export growth and the overall growth of the new economy. Some facts and figures may tell their own story. The *Human Development Report* (2004) by UNDP reports the following trend in India's exports (Table 2.11). Clearly India's export growth performance is very low compared to China and the NICs in Asia. Its high-technology exports also fare very low. Low R&D expenditures tell part of the story. The other part is told by the inadequate supply of scientists and engineers in R&D. The UNDP report records the number of scientists and engineers in R&D per million people over the period 1996–2000 as follows:

China	*Korea*	*Singapore*	*India*	*Malaysia*	*East Asia*
545	2,319	4,140	157	160	619

Most of the R&D activities in India (75% or more) are in the public sector, while in the Asian NICs they are concentrated in the private sector. The growth potential of R&D investment in the development of IT is phenomenal. Some recent developments are worth pointing out.

Table 2.11   Pattern of India's exports in a comparative framework

	Exports of goods & services (as % of GDP)		*Primary exports*		*Manuf. exports*		*High-tech exports*		*R&D expenditures (as % of GDP) 1996–2000*
			(as % of merchandise exports)						
	1990	*2001*	*1990*	*2001*	*1990*	*2001*	*1990*	*2001*	
China	18	26	27	11	72	89	0	20	1.0
Korea	29	43	6	9	94	91	18	29	2.7
Singapore	184	174	27	11	72	85	39	69	1.9
India	7	14	28	21	71	77	4	6	1.2
Malaysia	75	116	46	19	54	80	36	57	0.4
East Asia/ the Pacific	40	54	—	—	75	86	14	32	—

First of all, one recent estimate projects India's exports of manufactured products to the US to reach $300 billion by 2015 at an annual growth rate of 17% as against the historic rate of 11%. With promotional support for the II, the annual growth rate can exceed 20%. Second, the Indian Planning Commission set up in November 2004 an Investment Commission to attract domestic and foreign investors to set up large projects in the IT sector. This commission should include both medium and small size enterprises as in China and Taiwan. One should note how China followed a policy of heavy reliance on exemptions of customs and other duties for all goods and services used in the production of exports, which clearly encouraged development of export processing industries that rely heavily on imported equipment and intermediate inputs. Thirdly, India has a great potential for tapping the Silicon Valley entrepreneurs of India origin for both technical and managerial collaboration. Finally, many established high-tech and software companies have already started or are planning to start their R&D operations in India. For example Siemens, the German industrial giant has set up a new R&D center in Bangalore for medical and information technology and related products. Indian entrepreneurs should start their own ventures either through collaboration or through venture capitalists. Already the process has begun. Indian companies like Infosys, Satyam Computers, Reliance and Tata Motors are listed on the New York Stock Exchange. In 2004 the leading IT companies in India: i-flex Software and Satyam Computers made their way to Forbes Global's list of 100 best "under a billion dollar" companies. India needs to decentralize this talent pool in the IT sector as happened in China, Taiwan and Singapore. All this depends on speedy growth of the information infrastructure. There exists substantial talent in India to spearhead this growth. We need the leadership and the prudent risk takers.

Finally, one must refer briefly to the economic policy towards agriculture and the development of rural sector enterprises. One has to note that China's boom in growth was first initiated by reforms in agriculture. Thus the agricultural boom in output started as soon as the commune system was replaced by private peasant farming. Next, rural industry was greatly liberalized after 1978 with township and village enterprises (TVEs). They took the lead in economic and technological development zones in coastal open cities and encouraged manufacturing exports. The Chinese government followed a policy of negligible taxation; many of the TVEs oriented to exports were exempt from taxation as the result of special tax privileges. The major source of strength in China's export performance is the dynamic decentralization among the Chinese provinces and rural areas. It is remarkable that these provinces compete directly for attracting direct FDI and for improving the infrastructure of rural development.

The agricultural sector in India has undergone far less reform than other sectors. Private investment in agriculture has grown at less than the national average rate but this is partly a substitute for lower public investment and deteriorating quality of public services. The World Bank country study (2000) pointed out that power capacity in the agricultural sector remains underutilized by more than 15% because of poor maintenance and distribution. This study concluded that allowing greater private trade in products would help reduce price fluctuations and more general reforms would improve the productivity of labor and land use and thereby stimulate agricultural exports. Table 2.12 reports the World Bank estimates of labor productivity and the contribution of the agricultural sector of India in a comparative framework.

It is clear that India's agricultural productivity is far lower compared to the NICs in Asia. It is certainly comparable to China, although the share of agriculture in GDP is less than in India, suggesting significant labor reallocation from agriculture to industry and services. Huang, Lin and Rozelle (2003) have noted three significant developments in agricultural growth in the post reform era (mid 1980s). First, in the post reform period the annual farm labor productivity in value added terms rose from 6.3% in 1979–84 to 18.7% in 1993–97. Much of this increase is due to strong emphasis on research and technological innovations and the introduction of the Household Responsibility System. As they noted, farmers used two measures: a "yield envelope" and an "adopted

Table 2.12 Agricultural productivity and contribution to GDP in selected countries

	GDP ave. annual % growth	Agricultural productivity (value added per agric. worker, 1995 dollars)		Value added as % of GDP		
	1990–2001	1988–90	1998–2000	Agriculture 2001	Industry 2001	Services 2001
China	10.0	227	321	15	52	33
Korea	5.7	7,159	12,374	21	19	60
India	5.9	343	397	24	27	48
Malaysia	6.5	5,680	6,519	8	50	42
Singapore	7.8	27,176	49,905	0	34	66
Japan	1.3	25,293	30,086	1	32	66

yield potential" variable for each crop certified by an agricultural experimental station as highest yielding. This adoption of new technology yielded a steady stream of yield increases for rice, maize and other crops. In addition to producing generic material itself, China has drawn heavily on the international research system, e.g., the international rise research institute. Second, China's agricultural development combined agricultural production with rural enterprises for explaining nonagricultural activities both to generate employment for rural labor and to raise agricultural labor productivity. Thus the share of rural enterprises (RE) in GDP rose from 2 to 4% in the 1970s to 28% in 1997 and dominated the export sector by the mid 1990s, for example, the RE's share of total exports rose from 15% in 1990 to 46% in 1997. The share of nonfarm income in farmers' income rose very sharply from 17% in 1980 to 39% in 1997. The long-term perspective plan of China for 2010 concludes that China will rely more and more on new technology in crop and livestock productivity to raise future agricultural productivity. As Huang, Lin and Rozelle observed: "Technology is at the center of the advancement of agriculture. The exhortation of Jiang Zemin, then President of China, is widely quoted: 'We are counting on breakthroughs in four agricultural research systems. We need to begin reinventing China's agricultural sciences and technology revolution.' The government has begun an ambitious program promoting biotechnology and has pushed a number of high-profile technology projects such as hybrid rice. It has set ambitious funding growth targets."

Taiwan provides another useful example for India, having attained higher agricultural productivity than Malaysia about 20 times during the period 1998–2000. Taiwan has also attained a high degree of decentralization through rural industries maintaining a high degree of economic efficiency. For India the productivity improvement and income growth should be a constant motto in agricultural policy. As T.W. Schultz (1964) noted long ago:

> Studies by Griliches and Gisser show that schooling of farm people is an important explanatory variable of agricultural production and in terms of costs and returns a very profitable investment. Thus, in sum and substance, the man who is bound by traditional agriculture cannot produce much food no matter how rich the land. Thrift and work are not enough to overcome the niggardliness of this type of agriculture. To produce an abundance of farm products requires that the farmer has access to and has the skill and knowledge to use what science knows about soils, plants, animals and machines. (205)

The key importance of knowledge capital in accentuating economic growth has been strongly emphasized in current endogenous growth theory. New knowledge, innovations and learning provide specific organizational competence, which is the source of dynamic increasing returns and creativity.

References

Aggarwal, V.K. (2003) *Winning in Asia, US Style: Market and Nonmarket Strategies for Success*. New York: Palgrave Macmillan.

Athukorala, P. and Sen, K. (2002) *Saving, Investment and Growth in India*. New Delhi: Oxford University Press.

Bajpai, N. and Sachs, J.D. (1996) *India's Economic Reforms*. Working Paper No. 532a, Harvard Institute for International Development. Cambridge: Harvard University.

Bernstein, J. and Mohnen, P. (1994) International R&D spillovers between US and Japanese R&D intensive sectors. *NBER Working Paper No. 4682*. Cambridge, MA: NBER.

Bhagwati, J. (1999) The miracle that did happen: understanding East Asia in comparative perspective. In: E. Thorbecke, and H. Wan, *Taiwan's Development Experience: Lessons on Roles of Government and Market*. Dordrecht: Kluwer Academic Publishers.

Callen, T., Reynolds, P. and Towe, C. (eds) (2001) *India at the Crossroads*. Washington, DC: International Monetary Fund.

Castley, R. (1997) *Korea's Economic Miracle*. Basingstoke: Macmillan – now Palgrave Macmillan.

Corley, M., Michie, J. and Oughton, C. (2002) Technology, growth and employment. *International Review of Applied Economics* 16, 265–76.

Dreze, J. and Sen, Amartya (2002) *India: Development and Participation*. Oxford: Oxford University Press.

Gao, B. (1997) *Economic Idealogy and Japanese Industrial Policy*. New York: Cambridge University Press.

Hope, N., Yang, T. and Li, M. (2003) *How Far Across the River? Chinese Policy Reform at the Millennium*. Stanford: Stanford University Press.

Huang, J., Lin, J. and Rozelle, S. (2003) What will make Chinese agriculture more productive? In: N. Hope, D. Yang and M. Li (eds) *How Far Across the River? Policy Reform at the Millennium*. Stanford: Stanford University Press.

Jefferson, G. and Rawski, T. (1999) China's industrial innovation ladder: a model of endogenous reform. In: G. Jefferson and I. Singh (eds) *Enterprise Reform in China*. New York: Oxford University Press.

Jorgenson, D.W. and Stiroh, K.L. (2000) Raising the speed limit: US economic growth in the information age. In: K.W. Brainard and G. Perry (eds) *Brookings Papers on Economic Activity*. Washington, DC: Brookings Institution.

Krueger, A.O. (2002) *Economic Policy Reforms and the Indian Economy*. Chicago: University of Chicago Press.

Lall, S. (1999) India's manufactured exports: comparative structure and prospect. *World Development* 27, 1769–86.

Maddison, A. (1995) *Explaining the Economic Performance of Nations*. Cheltenham: Edward Elgar.

Mahalanobis, P.C. (1961) *Talks on Planning*. Calcutta: Statistical Publishing Society.

McMahon, G. and Squire, L. (eds) (2003) *Exploring Growth: a Global Research Project*. New York: Palgrave Macmillan.

Nadiri, M. and Son, W. (1999) Sources of growth in East Asian economies. In: T. Fu, C. Huang and C. Lovell, *Economic Efficiency and Productivity Growth in the Asia–Pacific Region*. Cheltenham: Edward Elgar.

Norsworthy, J.R. and Jang, S.L. (1992) *Empirical Measurement and Analysis of Productivity and Technological Change*. Amsterdam: North Holland.

Page, J. (1994) The East Asian miracle: four lessons for development policy. In: NBER: *Macroeconomics Annual*. Cambridge: MIT Press.

Perkins, D.H. (1997) History, politics and the sources of economic growth: China and the East Asian way of growth. In: F. Itoh (ed.) *China in the Twenty-first Century: Politics, Economy and Society*. Tokyo: United Nations University Press.

Qian, Y. and Wu, J. (2003) China's transition to a market economy. In: C.C. Hope, D.T. Yang and M.Y. Li, *How Far Across the River? Chinese Policy Reform at the Millennium*. Stanford: Stanford University Press.

Sachs, J., Varshney, A. and Bajpai, N. (1999) (eds) *India in the Era of Economic Reforms*. New York: Oxford University Press.

Schultz, T.W. (1969) *Transforming Traditional Agriculture*. New Haven: Yale University Press.

Sengupta, J.K. and Lin, B. (1993) Recent rural growth in China: the performance of the rural small scale enterprises 1980–86. *International Review of Applied Economics* 7, 177–96.

Sengupta, J.K. (1999) *New Growth Theory: an Applied Perspective*. Cheltenham: Edward Elgar.

Sengupta, J.K. (2004) *Competition and Growth: Innovation and Selection in Industry Evolution*. New York: Palgrave Macmillan.

Sooryamoorthy, R. and Gangrade, K.D. (2001) *NGOs in India: a Cross-sectional Study*. London: Greenwood Press.

Srinivasan, T.N. (2000) *Eight Lectures on India's Economic Reforms*. New Delhi: Oxford University Press.

UNDP (2003) *Human Development Report*. New York: Oxford University Press.

World Bank (1993) *World Development Report*. New York: Oxford University Press.

World Bank (1996) *The Chinese Economy*. Washington, DC: World Bank.

World Bank (2000) *India: Reducing Poverty, Accelerating Development*. New Delhi: Oxford University Press.

Zweig, D. (2002) *Internationalizing China: Domestic Interests and Global Linkages*. Ithaca: Cornell University Press.

3
Learning from Growth Theory

Economic growth theory provides two types of lessons: one by identifying the key determinants of growth and the other by empirical verification of theory. The first shows which sources and determinants are important and why. The second shows various pitfalls in some of the theories. Here we attempt a historical overview of growth theory and its broad social and economic implications. We discuss only those contributions which have relevance to modern economic growth characterized by market based systems undergoing technological change and worldwide competition. In our view these contributions in growth theory are most important for countries like India which is entering the phase of a "new economy." This new economy is driven by high growth in the information technology (IT) sector and new economic reforms, which favor rapid growth in foreign direct investment and joint ventures in R&D networks.

For growth in the new economy two dynamic forces are most important. One is market efficiency and the other the diffusion of knowledge and information technology. Adam Smith emphasized market efficiency, where growth in productivity is due to the division of labor and specialization of tasks, which in turn depend on the extent of the market. To Alfred Marshall goes the credit of emphasizing the role of increasing returns to scale in an industry's growth. Innovations and technology were emphasized by Schumpeter and Solow as the key factors of growth in industrial economies, while knowledge as human capital and its sectoral diffusion were identified by Lucas and Romer as the essential forces driving the engine of growth. Recently economists have compared economic growth with biological evolution, where adaptivity, learning and interactions between species and the environment are the key factors in evolution.

To Ronald Fisher and Maynard Smith goes the credit of analyzing growth as an evolutionary process.

We discuss here the essential features of the above contributions and show their relevance to growth in India's new economy.

3.1   Market efficiency: Adam Smith

There are four essential components of Adam Smith's market efficiency model. First, there is the so-called "invisible hand" of the competitive market with incentives for maximization of self-interest or profits.

> The taylor does not attempt to make his own shoes but buys them of the shoemaker. The shoemaker does not attempt to make his own clothes but employs a taylor. The farmer attempts to make neither the one or the other, but employs those different artificers. All of them find it for their interest to employ their whole industry in a way in which they have some advantage over their neighbors. (Smith [1776] 1996: 456)

The efficiency of the competitive general equilibrium process is thus highlighted by Adam Smith's model of interdependence of industries, each guided freely by its own maximization objective.

Second, Adam Smith had a theory of economic growth underlying the causes of wealth of nations. To him economic growth did not depend entirely on the division of labor or the market. It was limited primarily by the accumulation of capital, without which the division of labor could not proceed. Also the accumulation of capital in turn depends on individual savings. Thus he believed that overall economic growth depended on capital accumulation and capital accumulation is favored by proper institutions and a compatible culture. Third, Adam Smith's production theory emphasized an evolutionary and growth perspective. Thus several researchers on Smith's economic contributions have argued that his concept of dividing the production process into increasingly simpler processes and thereby improving labor productivity leads ultimately to a continuous discovery process. It also implies "quality ladders" in modern growth theory and also diffusion of knowledge through learning by doing. Inter-firm specialization and inter-organizational collaboration also yield improved capability and competence of the firm. This improves dynamic economic efficiency over time.

Finally, the size of the market and its growth over time are very critical to growth in international trade. Thus a country which can export a product that has a large and elastic world market gains the opportunity to pursue greater division of labor and higher productivity. If the domestic market is small or restrictive, this type of productivity gains is impossible. Thus one of the most important reasons for scale economies at the industry level is the existence of a larger or expanding market. Take Adam Smith's example of the pin factory: if each worker produces entire pins from scratch, productivity is much less than if pins are produced in assembly-line fashion, with each worker specialized to an individual task or step in the process. The key requirement is that the market for pins be large enough so that enough workers can be employed to specialize in different steps of the production process.

Note however that scale economies resulting from the division of labor need not imply geographical *concentration of production*. Consider Smith's pin example again. If each worker concentrates on a distinct part of pin making, there must be enough work for each worker producing that part but the workers themselves need not be concentrated in the same factory, city or nation provided that it is not too difficult to ship different pin parts from worker to worker or from one city or nation to another. Likewise all the parts that go into a PC (personal computer) need not be produced in Silicon Valley in order to profit from the division of labor. These scale economies are thus international: they depend on the size of the world market rather than upon the amount of geographical concentration of production.

This has an important lesson for growth. China utilized this method in its decentralization of production for exports in the town and village enterprises, Taiwan used the small and medium size firms in electronics and IT services and Singapore specialized in software development. India has ample scope for following this policy in the IT sector.

Adam Smith's emphasis on competition and the efficiency it generates has three distinctive features, which characterize rapid episodes of economic growth as observed in the NICs in Asia. First, he points out that the division of labor in the context of an expanding market leads to the establishment of new trades. New trades generate more employment. Secondly, technological change and innovations facilitated by division of labor are viewed as partly endogenous, since they may lead to improvements in technique through "learning by doing," a concept developed by Arrow much later. Taiwan and Japan have exhibited these endogenous innovations in their drive to improve productivity and efficiency in the technology-intensive industries such as microelectronics and software development. Thirdly, as Richardson (1975) points out, Adam Smith was aware that large and growing markets would lead to specialization and interdependence rather than to straightforward concentration. This is because he thought of competition in terms of activity rather than structure and as evolutionary rather than stationary. As Richardson (1975) points out:

> Chamberlin's theory of monopolistic competition does presume an interfirm division of labor the extent of which is limited by the size of the market; to that extent it corresponds much more closely to Smith's vision than does the perfectly competitive model. Nevertheless, it retains a static character foreign to Smith, preferences and production possibilities are given and the equilibrium appropriate to them represents a configuration of production that will remain the same so long as they do not change. We can come closer to Smith's thinking and closer also to economic reality by departing more radically from the framework of assumption underlying our standard competitive models. (355)

Finally, our discussion of Adam Smith's contribution to growth theory would be incomplete if we did not mention the gains from international trade so strongly emphasized by him. It is much more relevant today for the export promotion strategy followed so strongly by the NICs in Asia exhibiting growth miracles. What are the significant economic benefits or gains from free international trade? Several types of gains are discussed by Smith. First, there are the allocative efficiency gains due to international specialization based on absolute differences in costs. This is because international trade enables a country to buy goods from abroad at a lower cost. Secondly, there arises the subjective consumer's surplus as mutual benefits from trade. Foreign trade may in many cases create a demand for the output of resources that would otherwise remain unexploited. Thirdly, foreign trade also transmits technology and knowledge, thereby promoting growth. Thus Smith argued that if China permitted increased foreign trade, it would greatly increase its manufacturing industry, because it would naturally learn to use modern technology and improve efficiency. Looking at China's trade with the US over the last two decades, when it enjoys so large a trade surplus, one notes how true has been Adam Smith's predictions. Even a small rural town in the US today has its tourist shops filled with souvenirs and gift items imported from China!

Thus foreign trade and the EP (export promotion) strategy according to Smith widens the market thereby widening economies of scale, stimulating industrial growth, raising the level of economic incentives and transmitting new technology and innovations. He emphasized in particular the dynamic aspects of evolving gains over time.

3.2   Scale economies: Alfred Marshall

Although scale economies from the division of labor were discussed by Adam Smith, it was Alfred Marshall (1920) who integrated the concept with the theory of evolution of an industry. According to Stigler (1990) the doctrine of external and internal economies was a major Marshallian contribution, which provided a significant analytical reconciliation of competition and increasing returns to scale. There are three aspects of this reconciliation. One is in the theory of firm equilibrium under competition, when externalities are the major source of increasing returns to a firm. Since external increasing returns are not under the control of a firm, its total output may still be subject to diminishing returns. Thus profit maximization and free competition are still compatible along with the existence of decentralized markets with many price taking firms. Secondly, there may be significant costs for a firm of internalizing the externalities due to costs of search and information processing. Hence the returns at the level of a firm may not increase, thus implying a competitive market equilibrium with decentralization. Finally, Marshall suggested that trade knowledge that cannot be kept secret is an important source of productive externality. Thus knowledge diffusion in a broader sense manifesting itself at the level of the industry or the whole economy in terms of increasing returns may be viewed in an evolutionary framework. This framework makes it very close to the evolutionary paradigm of contemporary economics as discussed by Nelson (1995) and others. Recently Raffaelli (2003) has discussed Marshallian contributions on the cumulative aspect of the growth process generated by increasing returns at the level of industry. Thus mechanical standardization spread from one process to another in the same industry and from one industry to another.

The Marshallian tradition of increasing returns was followed up by Allyn Young (1928) who argued that the introduction of a new good was the critical driving force in economic growth and this process has a positive external effect as stressed by Marshall. When new knowledge as in the contemporary information technology sector is viewed as a new good and the increasing returns from this knowledge process, e.g., PC technology can be partly appropriated by a firm in a continuous cumulative fashion, the price taking behavior may be difficult to uphold. One way to salvage the situation is to relax the assumption of one specified good for each firm out of a specified list and to introduce product differentiation as in the Chamberlin model. In this situation an equilibrium can be reached, where each producer operates under increasing returns with marginal cost below average cost but is nevertheless subject to rival competitors offering goods similar but not identical.

The second most important contribution of Marshall is his theory of industry evolution. Marshall used the term "contrivance" to denote innovations and creativity, which he considered to be essential to industry evolution. He discussed the relevance of the Darwinian mix of selection and variation for industry evolution and this was based on the principle of "survival of the fittest" which states that those organisms tend to survive which are best fit to utilize the environment for their growth. But he warned that this principle ignores the fact that those organisms which utilize the environment most may sometimes produce harmful effects. This is especially true because of external diseconomies, when natural organisms are replaced by firms. Three types of harmful effects are discussed by him in the context of industry evolution. One is "economic parasitism" which like its biological counterpart may thrive as a rent-seeking class under this selection process. Second, the short run beneficial effect of the fitness principle may ignore other cooperative principles, less successful in the short run but beneficial to evolutionary success in the long run. Thus he argued in favor of limited protection of appropriate infant industries in the short run in order to alleviate the detrimental effects of selective mechanism of competition, e.g., the sacrifice of the individual to the rigid organization of production as in the Soviet-style commune system. Finally, he warned that the intensive drive to achieve competitive success in industry evolution may sometimes generate externalities that are detrimental to sustainable growth. The experience of China promoting a very high rate of industrial growth at the expense of environment and quality of life is a stark reminder of Marshall's prognosis. Recent emphasis on infrastructure development and the human development index by the World Bank point to the same direction.

A third contribution of Marshall is to extend Adam Smith's division of labor paradigm to include the growth of knowledge. He notes:

> Capital consists in a great part of knowledge and organization; and of this some part is private property and other part is not. Knowledge is our most powerful engine of production; it enables us to subdue Nature and force her to satisfy our wants. Organization aids knowledge; it has many forms, e.g., that of a single business, that of various

businesses in the same trade, that of various trades relatively to one another, and that of the State providing security for all and help for many. (Marshall 1920: 138–9)

Young (1928) extended this view later by showing how increasing returns stimulate economic progress.

Marshall stressed the point that knowledge depends on educating and training and he thought that the British educational system in his time was seriously deficient. He specifically noted that "the absence of a careful general education for the children of the working classes has been hardly less detrimental to industrial progress than the narrow range of the old grammar-school education of the middle classes. The industrial leadership of Germany and of the United States were both enhanced by their superior systems of education" (1920: 208, 211).

Finally, we must point out that Marshall's view of increasing returns to scale as a key factor in industry's growth was quite different from the traditional notion. Thus improved organization is viewed as the central basis of productivity gains. Although greater economic efficiency is a consequence of increased scale, its direct cause is viewed to be improved organization. This is very close to the basic approach of modern endogenous theory of growth.

As an important contribution to the theory of industry evolution one has to mention the ingenious concept of *"a representative firm"* which he developed as a prototype of industry. The representative firm is an average of the individual firms in an industry, average in size, in age, in shares of external and internal economies and in the skill of management. By the analogy of trees which grow, reach their peak and then decay, he emphasized the necessity of studying the distribution of firms in an industry and the various phases of the life cycle. In modern literature on industrial organization these life cycle studies of new products offer important insights into the success and failure of modern industries facing intensive competition due to technology and software development.

For stepping up growth in a developing country two important aspects of the theory of "a representative firm" deserve emphasis by the policy-maker. One is to set up standard or examples of a representative firm in different groups of industries, e.g., high, medium and low growth industries. The frequency of firms coming up close to or exceeding the performance of a group-specific representative firm may then be viewed as a measure of success in the implementation of economic policy aimed at promoting industrial growth. Secondly, as China followed the method of promoting productivity in agricultural farms through standard or target farms and providing various incentives for coming up to the standard, the representative firm may be used as a target for improving productivity and efficiency at the level of an industry. One has to note that most of Marshall's *Industry and Trade* (1919) was devoted to an appraisal of various forms of cooperation requiring more detailed interactions in the organization which are helpful in total factor productivity growth. Thus competition needs to be combined with cooperation.

3.3   Innovation efficiency: Schumpeter

Schumpeter's notion of economic growth and development was highly disaggregative. Three major components of his theory of economic development were: innovations, the entrepreneur and finance. They are closely interrelated. Innovation constitutes the major catalytic force. It includes the introduction of a new product or a new method of production, the opening of a new market, the acquisition of a new source of supply and the reorganization of an existing industry. Innovation destroys old processes and channels and creates new ones. That is why it leads to "creative destruction." The individual entrepreneur is the principal agent of innovation. He is not a business manager or the custodian of a managing system but an innovator who carries out new and creative projects and faces the future market evolving over time. An innovating entrepreneur requires foresight and originality, resolution and determination and above all a vision of the future. He is thus ideally suited for the high-tech world of today dominated by computers, software networks and new communications technology. If the innovator succeeds in this dynamic environment, he earns significant entrepreneurial profits. He invests this profit and the growth cycle continues.

Bank finance and credit provide the means by which the entrepreneur carries out the innovation. According to Schumpeter all innovative investment is financed by credit creation by banks or other finance capitalists who may be now called "venture capitalists." Savings are only the residuals, the results of successful development. The dynamic element is financing. Many creative ways of financing build the opportunity for an entrepreneur to innovate and effect a change from the routine and the status quo. The neoclassical model of equilibrium under free competitive conditions works very well in a static world, but it fails in a dynamic world where innovations introduce new goods, new markets and new technologies. As Schumpeter observed in his 1942 classic *Capitalism, Socialism and Democracy*:

> But in capitalist reality as distinguished from its textbook picture, it is not that kind of competition (i.e. perfect) which counts but the competition from the new commodity, the new technology, the new source of supply, the new type of organization (the largest scale unit of control for instance) – competition which commands a decisive cost or quality advantage and which strikes not at the margin of profits and the outputs of existing firms but at their foundations and their very lives. (124)

We have to discuss in more detail the role of innovations in economic growth and Schumpeter's classic contributions which are so relevant today. He emphasized three dynamic aspects of innovations, which help spur the engine of growth. First, long term growth is basically *evolutionary*. It involves among others new methods of production and technology and the process of "creative destruction." The latter involves replacing the old by the new and thereby increasing efficiency. Second, it involves expansion in market opportunities, e.g., globalization of markets, which provides the incentive to expand capacity and utilize economies of scale. Third, innovation involves R&D investments for improving the production frontier. Several dynamic features of R&D investment by firms are important for industry evolution. Recently Sengupta (2004) has discussed in detail the role of R&D investments and Schumpeterian innovations in the context of dynamic competition and economic evolution of industries. He discussed in particular three important features of R&D investment as it affects growth. First, this investment not only generates knowledge about new technical processes and products, but also enhances the firm's ability to assimilate, export and improve existing "knowledge capital". This has a cumulative impact on industry growth. For example Cohen and Levinthal (1989) have shown with empirical data that R&D investment in semiconductor and other electronic industries provides an in-house technical capability that would keep these firms on the leading edge of the latest technology developed elsewhere. A second aspect of R&D investment within a firm is its spillover effect. Thus R&D investment yields externalities in the form of knowledge transmission which generates new applications both locally and globally. The Asian NICs and China have utilized these externalities and their outward orientation have helped in this process very significantly. Countries like India, Indonesia and Malaysia have great scope in this direction. Finally, R&D expenditures provide the possibility of implicit or explicit collaboration in R&D networking as joint ventures which increases the firms' incentives to invest.

Schumpeter's concept of innovation efficiency has important implications for the creation of new strategic assets by innovating firms. The Schumpeterian view of competition has two facets: static and dynamic. The former takes technology as given, so firms compete only on costs and prices. Thus greater competition reduces prices and/or raises costs thus reducing profits and dwindling assets. At the limit some firms may have to exit. The dynamic aspect of Schumpeterian competition however changes technology at various points on the value chain. Thus successful firms compete in new and innovating ways, bringing them new streams of increased cash flows and profits. In the dynamic context the successful innovator may enjoy "first mover" advantages and monopoly profits due to patents and other barriers. Thus Schumpeterian dynamics is most appropriate for what is sometimes called "the new economy" which emphasizes the dynamic force of competition, rather than the static. This new economy presents through globalization a new world of expanding markets, e.g., e-trade, e-commerce and the Internet economy. This market presents significant economies of scale on the demand side and demand creates its own supply through supply side economies of scale. The NICs in Asia, China and other countries have effectively utilized these opportunities and Japan has successfully challenged the world market in high-tech products. Thus Schumpeter in a basic sense extended Adam Smith's market efficiency model based on division of labor and Alfred Marshall's scale economies model based on internal and external increasing returns in two directions: replacing the old (static) equilibrium by the new and continuing innovation efficiency in the new economy.

In conclusion we must mention that Schumpeter (1934) had stressed the role of democracy to provide leadership in fostering appropriate infrastructure and the institutions for development. To him democracy in the political system and markets in the economic system are functional parallels in that both are competitive systems for selecting leadership in government and in industry. Schumpeter's theory of democracy intended to separate the traditional ties between socialism and democracy. He argued that they may be combined or remain separate. From the economic point of view he favored socialism because it would be a sequel to the economic performance of capitalism at the highest stage. However with regard to its noneconomic functions he favored democracy over the idol of socialism.

Thus the Chinese model of autocratic socialism need not be the only model for faster growth. The Asian NICs could provide a viable alternative. India could mix and match, provided the efficiency goal is kept high.

3.4 Technical progress: Solow

In his classic 1956 paper Solow (1956) proposed an aggregate model of growth with three distinctive features. First, he assumed a neoclassical production function with decreasing returns to capital. The rates of saving and population growth determine the *steady state level* of real income per capita. Thus Solow's model predicts as follows: the higher the rate of saving, the richer the country; also the higher the rate of population growth, the poorer the country. Secondly, growth of total output results from two sources: the accumulation of factor inputs (e.g., physical capital and labor) and the efficiency of factor use (e.g., total factor productivity (TFP)). Since each factor accumulation exhibits diminishing returns according to the neoclassical model, a country cannot rely solely on the accumulation of factor inputs like capital but must have growth in TFP in order to achieve higher long run growth. Solow (1957) applied his model empirically for the US economy and found the surprising result that the output growth of the US economy in the first half of the twentieth century could be mostly attributed to TFP growth. For example the annual TFP growth was estimated to be 2.25% during 1930–49 and 1.5% during 1909–49. This line of research stimulated the upsurge of many growth accounting exercises such as Denison (1967), Jorgenson, Gollop and Fraumeni (1987) and Mankiew, Romer and Weil (1992). These studies extended Solow's methodology to include other factors such as education, economies of scale, resource allocation and advance of knowledge and R&D investments. As Mankiew et al. observed in their international cross-section study, differences in saving (physical capital), education (human capital) and population growth explain most of the international variations in income per capita. Also this model predicts that countries with *similar* technologies and rates of accumulation of physical capital and population growth should converge in income per capita. But multiple or different steady states may emerge with dissimilar technology growth and adoption.

Thirdly, Solow makes a very important distinction between the two effects: the *level effect* and the *growth effect* associated with the long run or steady state income per capita. Thus the two variables: savings rate and population affect the level of long run income per capita but not its growth. Technology measured by TFP has a growth effect over time, since it induces growth in long run income per capita. This growth effect on output may come in different forms, e.g., learning by doing from human capital, and constant returns to knowledge capital with overall increasing returns and productivity improvement per worker through cumulative experience. The effects of technical progress are essentially captured in extended Solow models by the time trend, which reflects the influence of omitted variables other than physical capital and labor such as R&D capital, the natural endowments and infrastructure of institutions such as markets and software development. In underdeveloped countries R&D development and technological improvement may constitute a very small part of GDP but the developed countries invest a more significant percentage of their GDP in R&D and even greater amounts in innovations and other productivity-improving processes. Hence technical progress in the Solow sense is likely to be much larger in the developed and industries countries like the OECD, the US and Japan.

Three important lessons emerge from Solow's contribution to growth, which are useful for emerging countries like India, which has embarked on the growth of its new economy. First, the emphasis on the neoclassical model by Solow showed that competitive markets and their incentive system have made TFP growth possible for the US and other industrial countries. Market flexibility and profit incentives have played a dynamic role in industry growth. Resource reallocation and the complementary augmentation of physical and human capital simultaneously during technical progress have been most helpful. Secondly, technical progress need not comprise technological innovations only. It includes many small and discrete improvements in organization and business policy that help improve labor productivity and efficiency. Recently Solow (1997) has observed that the level of technology is important for log run growth for two reasons as follows:

> The first has to do with policy. A society that would like to accelerate (or decelerate) the pace of technological progress will need some understanding of the micro level process in order to design effective incentives or even to make centralized decisions. That is enough reason to get on with the study of research and development, empirically and theoretically. There is, as I have said, an exciting literature along these lines.
>
> The second reason is the one that moves me. It is a thought that has emerged from the many recent studies of the fate of manufacturing industry in the US, including the inevitable comparison with Japan.

There appear to be two processes at work, not just one. The more obvious one is the occurrence of discrete innovations, some major, some minor, whose development changes the nature of the product or the nature of the production process in existing industries, or may even lead to the creation of recognizably new industries. These innovations are the product, perhaps unintended or unexpected, of an activity that one would clearly describe as research. The less obvious process is usually described as "continuous improvement" of products and processes. It consists of an ongoing series of main improvements in the design and manufacture of standard products. It leads to advances in customer satisfaction in quality, durability and reliability, and to continuing reductions in the cost of production. (20)

Finally, the Solow model provides a strong support to a deliberate policy for education and skill development, especially for the information technology sectors. We may note the illuminating case of state intervention in Korea to promote economic development. Promotion of targeted infant industries with promise of export growth has been a basic part of the state strategy on selective interventions in Korea. More recently electronic and information technologies are being promoted. Table 3.1 from Kim (1997) shows the trend in R&D indicators in Korea. It is clear from Table 3.1 that between 1965 and 1990 R&D expenditure increased more than 500 times. The major take-off has been since the mid-1980s. Note also the reversal of the roles of the public and the private sectors. In 1965 the private sector provided only 10% of total R&D expenditure,

Table 3.1   Major R&D indicators in Korea

	1965	*1975*	*1980*	*1985*	*1990*
R&D expenditure ($mill)	8	88	32.1	1298	4481
gov't	7.2	59	186	247	717
private	0.8	29	135	1051	3764
R&D/manufacturing sales	NA	9.35	0.65	1.51	2.07
R&D/GNP	0.29	0.42	0.58	1.48	1.91
Research institutions	NA	5308	4598	7154	10,434
Universities	NA	2312	8695	14,935	21,332
Companies	NA	2655	5141	18,996	38,737
R&D researchers per 10,000 people	1.0	2.9	4.8	10.1	16.4
Patents (no.)	12,759 (1986)	25,820 (1990)	28,132 (1999)	average growth rate (1986–91) 17.1	

while in 1990 it provided 84%. The growth in research institutes is also very significant. The lesson for emerging countries like India is very clear. A strong education policy and strategies for research and skill development must be imperative for stimulating growth.

3.5   Spillover technology: Lucas

The concept of technical progress in the Solow model was made endogenous by Lucas (1990, 1993) and Paul Romer (1990, 1994). Endogeneity is from intentional investment decisions made by entrepreneurs seeking to maximize profits and earn quasi-monopoly rents due to "first mover" advantages. Thus new technology in the form of human capital accumulation is not a public good but a nonrival input complementary to all other inputs. This nonrival input is only partially excludable since in the form of R&D it yields spillover or external benefits. Due to nonconvexity introduced by this nonrival input the aggregate production function exhibits increasing returns to scale and hence the competitive equilibrium cannot be supported here. Instead one has to seek an equilibrium in the framework of monopolistic competition. Lucas (1993) introduced several new dimensions of endogenous technology. While emphasizing the point that Asian growth miracles cannot in general be explained only by physical capital accumulation alone, he discussed the role of human capital accumulation at school and on the job. The rate of expansion in knowledge in both forms transforms a *level effect* into a *growth effect*. This notion of knowledge capital is important for its "learning by doing" effect. Learning has two types of impact. One is that it increases the total stock of design knowledge by increasing its efficiency. The second is that the human capital employed in research or job training leads to an expansion of the stock of design knowledge. As Arrow (1962) pointed out, information or knowledge capital is not only the product of inventive activity, it is also a nonrival unit with strong complementarity with others' inputs. The productivity of human capital in research is an increasing function of the accumulated knowledge capital. As a result the costs of producing new designs decline over time. This is an important source of the externality or spillover effect in research.

The second dimension of endogenous technology is its spillover effect which is manifest in learning by doing. Lucas has termed this learning spillover technology, which is the source of rapid productivity growth and trade or openness. To the question why does not capital flow from rich to poor countries on a large scale, the answer provided by this theory is that the spillover effect is very small in the poor countries. As Lucas observed:

> Consider two small economies facing the same world prices and similarly endowed like Korea and the Philippines in 1960. Suppose that Korea somehow shifts its workforce onto the production of goods not formerly produced there and continues to do so, while the Philippines continues to produce its traditional goods. Then according to the learning spillover theory, Korean production will grow more rapidly. But in 1960 Korean and Philippine incomes were about the same, so the mix of goods their consumers demanded was about the same. (But now Korean incomes are about three times incomes in the Philippines and about one third of US.) For this scenario to be possible, Korea needed to open up a large difference between the mix of goods produced and the mix consumed, a difference that could widen over time. Thus a large volume of trade is essential to a learning-based growth episode. (1993: 269)

A third dimension of learning spillover technology is that for such learning to continue on a long run sustained basis the workers, managers and entrepreneurs must work continually to improve the technology through what Grossman and Helpman (1991) called "the quality ladder."

Finally, spillover technology is closely associated with Schumpeterian innovation in its many forms, e.g., R&D, new processes and new products and services. The market power is the key source of this innovation process – that generates nonrival outputs through knowledge capital. The incentive of monopoly rents compensates for the cost of generating the nonrival inputs and output. For example R&D as knowledge capital has two facets: nonrival input and nonrival output. The former yields productivity growth of other inputs, e.g., the use of computers at the workplace. The latter generates research output and its spillover may develop new products in other sectors, e.g., the joint venture and research collaboration. Thus the introduction of nonrival goods and services is central to growth. When the fruits of research are allowed to be exploited more openly and broadly by free trade and world competition, then such globalization of trade would have a scale effect thus speeding up growth of the trading countries. In many ways spillover technology allows dynamic externalities to generate dynamic gains from trade. Thus declining computer prices and improved inputs have helped NICs in Asia and China to reap the benefits of spillover technology.

Two important lessons emerge from the analysis of learning spillover technology. One is the importance of R&D at the enterprise level and also technical education oriented to the new information age. Since this type of knowledge capital is a nonrival input, it helps stimulate growth all around. Second, the crucial feature of the knowledge capital using spillover technology is its increasing marginal productivity, which in effect yields unbounded growth. Schmidt (2003) has recently discussed these implications for the Romer and Lucas models.

As an empirical test we consider the time series data on total factor productivity in Korean manufacturing from Kwon (1986) updated till 1994. The production function estimates in log linear form come out as follows :

$$\ln Y = 4.92^{**} - 0.47 \ln R_1 + 0.16 \ln R_2 - 0.57 \ln R_3 + 1.51^{**} \ln N \ (R^2 = 0.99)$$

Here Y is output, R_1 through R_3 are measures of three rival inputs (capital, energy and materials) and N is a proxy for nonrival input measured by labor employed in the export sector. The two asterisks denote significant coefficients at the 1% level of t-test. Clearly the nonrival input (N) has significant increasing returns, implying that a 10% increase in N generates a 15% increase in output. Another indirect way to estimate the impact of dynamic externality is through the efficiency of the export-intensive branches of the manufacturing sector. This efficiency may be measured by the proportion of firms oriented to export-intensive branches which are on the efficiency frontier. Separate empirical studies for the NICs in Asia by Sengupta (1993) have shown that measured by this yardstick most of the outward oriented industries in the export sector have been very efficient. Thus Chen and Tang (1987) found for the electronic industry in Taiwan that the export-oriented firms were 6 to 11% closer to the efficient production frontier than other firms. Kwon (1986) estimated an index of capacity utilization for the Korean manufacturing sector and it is found to rise from 0.46 during 1961–64 to 0.75 in 1970–74 and to nearly full capacity (0.98) in 1985–90.

The experience of Taiwan is more striking. Table 3.2 reports some growth statistics in Taiwan over the period 1995–2000, when the economy underwent transition from the traditional to the modern technology system. Taiwan's export promotion strategy was systematically pursued by the Taiwan government through the export financing and export processing zone with various incentives. From the beginning (the late 1960s) Taiwan made special efforts to promote high-technology exports through publicly funded research laboratories, industrial parts and favorable educational policy. New reforms initiated in 1990 put extra

Table 3.2   Economic growth indicators in Taiwan

	1995	*1998*	*2000*
Export/GDP(%)	42.03	41.32	47.66
Gross investment/GDP(%)	24.93	24.72	22.57
Export growth rate (%)	20.0	−9.42	21.98
Import growth rate (%)	21.33	−8.53	26.49
Literacy rate (%)	94.00	94.9	95.6
Secondary school enrollment rate (%)	95.93	97.21	99.61
Higher education enrollment rate (%)	45.32	51.06	60.85
Output of electronics & information technology			
Total (US $ bill)	15.4	—	69.8
	(1990)		(2005)
Information products	6.9	—	35
	(1990)		(2005)
Consumer electronics	2.3		7.0
	(1990)		(2005)

Source: Khan (2004); the figures for 2005 are forecasts reported by Hobday (1995).

emphasis on technology and skill-intensive activities, e.g., information technology, electronics and machinery, telecommunications equipment and computers. As Table 3.2 shows very clearly, IT products and tele-communications equipment grew at an average annual rate of around 15.1 and 14.0% respectively. As Hobday (1995) points out, the Taiwanese Council for Economic Planning and Development prepared a ten-year plan (1980–89) which provided targets for R&D expenditures and human capital supply. Under an overall imitative technology policy Taiwan followed the world leaders already established in the electronics and information technology. The central objective of both government and private entrepreneurs was to compete by cutting costs through produc-tive efficiency. The state fostered advanced research in state-supported research institutes and their results were transferred to the private sector. In terms of complementary human capital accumulation a deliberate policy of sending trainees abroad and inviting foreign collaborators was pursued. All these show the importance of learning spillover techno-logy which was utilized by Taiwan to the fullest extent.

3.6   Growth as evolution: Ronald Fisher

The contributions of Ronald Fisher (1930) discussed here are in genetic evolution theory, not in economic growth. As a distinguished statistician he made many classic contributions in statistics including genetic evolution. In genetic evolution theory he developed a fundamental theorem of natural selection and its implications are relevant for the theory of economic growth applicable to new emerging economies like India.

Three reasons can be given for the relevance of Fisher's theory of genetic evolution of species for the analysis of economic growth and development. First, it is based on the fitness principle which is closely related to the Darwinian model of survival of the fittest in natural selection. In market competition the most efficient firms tend to acquire a dominant share of the market. Modern management scientists have applied the concept of *core competence* to explain this trend of dominant market share. It is very closely related to the fitness principle of natural selection in genetic evolution theory. Secondly, the economic models of entry and exit by firms in industry evolution are comparable to the genetic process of competition. Thus in genetic models of species evolution "entry" is comparable to invasion of one species by another. Game-theoretic models have been applied here to explain why some species' populations are successful in preventing invasion. The evolutionary strategies they follow help to maintain a stable population through gains in fitness. Fitness is comparable to economic efficiency in the economic theory of the firm. Thus the fitness frontier in Fisherian dynamics is comparable to the economic efficiency frontier, which in a dynamic context separates the two groups of firms: one on the frontier and the other below. Models of two-person games with Cournot–Nash equilibrium solutions are most appropriate here. Such models in dynamic forms generalize the Fisherian replicator dynamics by introducing the strategy interactions of the two groups of players in a fluctuating environment. Thirdly, the Fisherian model of fitness dynamics is very similar to the evolutionary model of a firm in its capacity to learn how to change its internal decision rules when the environment changes and its profit maximization goals go unfulfilled. Nelson and Winter (1982) constructed an evolutionary model of economic change in this context. The concept of evolutionary competition has been applied by Metcalfe (1985) and others to model the dynamic evolution of technologies. The key point in their approach is as follows: not only the average representative firm or representative technology matters but also their distribution in the whole population. They obtain the interesting result that the rate of change of average unit costs is proportional to the weighted variance in unit costs in the industry. This result is very similar to Fisher's result. If one assumes that the variance of unit costs is higher in the initial phase of evolution of a new technology and falls as technology (or the associated product) matures, then this would generate a pattern of firm growth, where mature technologies would show a slower rate of productivity growth than the new technologies. But as competition proceeds and some competing firms are eliminated by new designs, the surviving firms are likely to have not only a higher average productivity but a lower productivity variance. But this may lead to a switch to a new technology paradigm, as new streams of innovations follow. Clearly this provides a dynamic characterization of industry growth, which captures the essence of the Schumpeterian concept of "creative destruction." Winter (1984) has discussed this dimension of Schumpeterian competition in alternative technological regimes.

Three aspects of Fisherian dynamics are most relevant for the economic models of growth of technology and the industry. First, the concept of fitness which is defined by the relative growth rate of the population of a certain species defines a trajectory over time, where the fitness of a mixed population is the arithmetic mean of the fitness of its components. Individual fitness depends on the population size and the environment. Second, the average fitness of the population never decreases over time in the course of natural selection. This generalizes the Darwinian survival of the fittest principle for the diploid case, which is probably the reason why Fisher's theorem is said to be fundamental. Thus Fisher's theorem says that the logarithm of population size under natural selection always has a nonnegative acceleration. Finally, the adaptations and mutations may change the rates of fitness of a population. Thus the rate of change in the growth rate of a population is viewed as a function of the environment, the rate of change in the environment and the natural growth rate. In a fixed environment any population should eventually be able to reach its equilibrium growth rate depending on the environment. But in a fluctuating environment or density-dependent fitness multiple equilibria are possible and departures from such equilibria may be more frequent.

The above concepts of Fisherian dynamics are directly applicable to the Schumpeterian framework of dynamic innovations. Sengupta (2004) has recently applied this framework in terms of a model of hypercompetition. Competition has been most intense in recent times in high technology industries. Declining prices and costs, accelerating global demand and increasing innovation have intensified the competitive pressure. Following Schumpeter's dynamic innovation approach D'Aveni (1994) has termed this state as hypercompetition. He argues that this hypercompetitive world resembles the Darwinian world of survival of the fittest, where the rival competitors get crushed, if they are not on the leading edge of the innovation efficiency frontier. Competition today has two facets: static and dynamic. The former takes technology as given, so firms compete only on prices and costs. Thus greater competition reduces prices and/or raises costs, which squeeze profits. At the limit some firms or technologies may have to exit. The dynamic competition however changes technology at various points of the value chain, thus challenging firms to compete in new innovating ways. Thus the successful firms in an industry transform their technologies so as to create new strategic assets. Thus competition can bring new profits or increased losses to a firm depending on whether it is following a static or dynamic strategy.

Three areas of efficiency are central to hypercompetition. They are comparable to the superior fitness and/or adaptability in Fisherian dynamics. These are: innovation efficiency, access efficiency and resource efficiency. Racing up the escalator ladder in the arena of R&D, new processes and software constitutes innovation efficiency. Access efficiency is racing up the escalation ladder in the stronghold arena. By building barriers around a stronghold, the successful firm or company reaps monopoly profits that can be used to fund aggressive price and advertisement strategies. Finally, the dynamic resourcefulness of firms involving the creation of new strategic assets at various points of the value chain generates resource efficiency. Companies seek to find the best use for their resources or assets even going over to a global setting. Hypercompetitive firms must use their assets to build their next temporary advantage before their competition. For example IBM bet the company on the 360 series computers and the bet paid off in the 1960s. But it could not sustain the position because it failed to keep up a strong position in the next temporary advantage, e.g., the personal computer market. Instead tiny companies such as Apple and Microsoft became giants by seizing the next advantage.

Two important lessons emerge. The new economy in emerging countries like India and the NICs in Asia is facing hypercompetition in world markets today. The dynamic side of competition is more important than the static side in this market, where more emphasis on knowledge capital and innovation efficiency is required. New economic policies by the state and flexible strategies by entrepreneurs are absolute necessities for success. Secondly, the core competence of an organizational efficiency, which comprises dynamic fitness in Fisher's theorem must be adopted as the key strategy for growth in today's fluctuating and evolving world markets. The examples of Asian NICs are ample proofs that they have understood this message.

References

Arrow, K.J. (1962) The economic implications of learning by doing. *Review of Economic Studies* 29, 155–74.

Chen, T. and Tang, D. (1987) Comparing technical efficiencies in a developing economy. *Journal of Development Economies* 26, 25–31.

Cohen, W.M. and Levinthal, D.A. (1989) Innovation and learning; the two facets of R&D. *Economic Journal* 99, 569–96.

D'Aveni, R.A. (1994) *Hypercompetition: Managing the Dynamics of Strategic Maneuvering*. New York: Free Press.

Denison, E.F. (1967) *Why Growth Rates Differ?* Washington, DC: Brookings Institution.

Fisher, R.A. (1930) *The Genetical Theory of Natural Selection*. Oxford: Clarendon Press.

Grossman, G.M. and Helpman, E. (1991) Quality ladders and product cycles. *Quarterly Journal of Economics* 106, 557–86.

Hobday, M. (1995) *Innovation in East Asia: the Challenge to Japan*. Aldershot: Edward Elgar.

Jorgenson, D.W., Gollop. F.M. and Fraumeni, B.M. (1987) *Productivity and US Economic Growth*. Cambridge: Harvard University Press.

Khan, H.A. (2004) *Interpreting East Asian Growth and Innovation*. New York: Palgrave Macmillan.

Kim, L. (1997) Imitation to innovation: the dynamics of Korea's technological learning. In L. Kim and R. Nelson (eds) *Technology, Learning and Innovation: Experiences of Newly Industrializing Economies*. New York: Cambridge University Press.

Kwon, J.K. (1986) Capacity utilization, economies of scale and technical change in the growth of total factor productivity: an explanation of South Korean manufacturing growth. *Journal of Development Economics* 24, 75–89.

Loasby, B.J. (1990) Firms, markets and the principle of continuity. In: J.K. Whitaker (ed.) *Centenary Essays on Alfred Marshall*. Cambridge: Cambridge University Press.

Lucas, R.E. (1990) Why does not capital flow from rich to poor countries? *American Economic Review* 80, 92–96.

Lucas, R.E. (1993) Making a miracle. *Econometrica* 61, 251–72.

Mankiw, N. Romer, D. and Weil, D. (1992) A contribution to the empirics of growth. *Quarterly Journal of Economics* 107, 407–37.

Marshall, Alfred (1919) *Industry and Trade*. London: Macmillan.

Marshall, A. (1920) *Principles of Economics* (8th edn) London: Macmillan.

Metcalfe, J.S. (1985) On the diffusion of innovation and the evolution of technology. In: G., Williams, J. Bryan and G. Brown, (eds) *Knowns and Unknowns in Technical Change*. London: Technical Change Center.

Nelson, R. and Winter, S. (1982) *An Evolutionary Theory of Economic Change*. Cambridge: Harvard University Press.

Nelson R.R. (1995) Recent evolutionary theorizing about economic change. *Journal of Economic Literature* 33, 48–90.

Raffaelli, T. (2003) *Marshall's Evolutionary Economics*. London: Routledge.

Richardson G.B. (1975) Adam Smith on competition and increasing returns. In: A. Skinner and T. Wilson, *Essays on Adam Smith*. Oxford: Clarendon Press.

Romer, P.M. (1990) Endogenous technological change. *Journal of Political Economy*, 98: 71–102.

Romer, P.M. (1994) The origins of endogenous growth. *Journal of Economic Perspectives* 8, 3–22.

Schmidt, G.W. (2003) *Dynamics of Endogenous Economic Growth*. Amsterdam: Elsevier.

Schumpeter, J. (1934) *The Theory of Economic Development*. Cambridge: Harvard University Press.

Schumpeter, J. (1942) *Capitalism, Socialism and Democracy*. New York: Harper Brothers.

Sengupta, J.K. (1993) Growth in NICs in Asia: some tests of new growth theory. *Journal of Development Studies* 29, 342–57.

Sengupta, J.K. (1998) *New Growth Theory: an Applied Perspective*. Cheltenham: Edward Elgar.

Sengupta, J.K. (2002) Model of hypercompetition. *International Journal of Systems Science* 33, 669–75.

Sengupta, J.K. (2004) *Competition and Growth: Innovations and Selection in Industry Evolution*. New York: Palgrave Macmillan.

Shionoya, Y. (1997) *Schumpeter and the Idea of Social Science*. New York: Cambridge University Press.

Smith, Adam [1776] (1996) *An Inquiry into the Nature and Causes of the Wealth of Nations*. Oxford: Oxford University Press.

Solow, R.M. (1956) A contribution to the theory of economic growth. *Quarterly Journal of Economics* 70, 65–94.

Solow, R.M. (1957) Technical change and the aggregate production function. *Review of Economics and Statistics* 39, 312–20.

Solow, R.M. (1997) *Learning from Learning by Doing: Lessons for Economic Growth*. Stanford: Stanford University Press.

Stigler, G.J. (1990) The place of Marshall's Principles in the development of economics. In: J.K. Whitaker, (ed.) *Centenary Essays on Alfred Marshall*. Cambridge: Cambridge University Press.

Winter, S. (1984) Schumpeterian competition in alternative technological regimes. *Journal of Economic Behavior and Organization* 5, 287–320.

Young, A. (1928) Increasing returns and economic progress. *Economic Journal* 38, 527–42.

4
Growth of the IT Industry: India and the World

The information technology (IT) sector in an economy has many dimensions, each of which influences the growth process significantly. First, it brings in a new era of industrial revolution through its impact both locally and globally. This impact is generated through innovations in software technology and data processing capabilities. Managerial skills and work performance in plants get a tremendous boost. Second, the key component of the IT system is knowledge capital and organizational knowhow, which are always complementary to other inputs. This complementarity generates spillover effects in other industries using IT services. Third, the IT input is not subject to diminishing returns, so that its growth contributions need not decline over time, i.e., it has a steady state growth effect rather than a level effect. Finally, the investment in IT input through R&D and related expenditures helps improve the efficiency of the IT sector itself and this efficiency spreads to other manufacturing, processing, distribution and service sectors through learning by doing, externalities and forward linkages to other sectors.

Our object here is threefold. First, we attempt to analyze the growth and efficiency of the computer industry in the US and discuss the role of the IT sector in India. Secondly, we discuss some implications of the IT policy pursued in India, and the need for taking a new direction. Finally, we analyze the role of the IT inputs in improving economic efficiency in the other industrial, agricultural and service sectors in India.

4.1   Fitness principle and core competence

The fitness principle underlying Fisher's fundamental theorem of natural selection in unlimited environments has dominated the thinking of population biologists for a long time. Fisher's theorem states that the average fitness of the population of species never decreases in the course of natural selection in unlimited environments. This generalizes the Darwinian principle of the survival of the fittest for the diploid case, which is probably the reason why the theorem is said to be fundamental. Recently, adaptivity in the selection process has been introduced in population dynamics in two related ways. One is to postulate that the rate of change in the growth rate of a species is a function of the environment, the rate of change in the environment and the growth rate. The second is to apply the evolutionary stable strategies proposed by John Maynard Smith, which fits the world of predator–prey dynamics.

The fitness principle with adaptivity in the environment has been applied to the market dynamics of competition in an economic framework in several ways. One is the theory of dynamic evolution of firms based on models of industry growth emphasizing the concept of evolutionary efficiency. This approach, discussed by Nelson and Winter (1982), Dosi (1984) and Metcalfe (1994) considers two basic economic aspects of dynamic competition, when the overall demand is growing at a positive rate. One is that the price declines over time at a rate equal to the rate of decline in average practice unit costs. Secondly, the rate of decline in average practice unit costs over time reflecting the average fitness critically depends on the innovation flow in the industry. Thus firms with more efficient innovations may lead the industry's growth and evolution. On the reverse side the firms decline under dynamic competition, if they do not keep up on the leading edge of the efficiency frontier.

In order to understand the growth of the information industry (IT) involving computers, telecommunications and microelectronics one has to realize that competition dynamics has been most intense in recent times in the new technology-based industries such as microcomputers, telecommunications and bio-engineering firms. Declining prices and costs, accelerating global demand and increasing innovation and cost efficiency have intensified the competitive pressure resulting in increasing inter-firm variance in sales. Following Schumpeter's dynamic innovation approach D'Aveni (1994) has characterized this state as hypercompetition. He argues that this type of hypercompetitive world resembles in many ways the Darwinian world of survival of the fittest, where rival competitors get crushed if they are not on the leading edge of the innovation and cost efficiency frontier.

This hypercompetition has generated several other dynamic economic forces that are most important in determining the industry evolution over time. The first is the creation of intra- and inter-industry externalities by the introduction of new "knowledge capital" in the IT sector. Learning by doing and technological diffusion to other industries have accelerated the overall tempo of growth. In the theory of hypercompetition discussed by Sengupta (2002) this type of knowledge diffusion and transmission is called "access efficiency" or networking efficiency or externalities. The second dynamic force is the demand side economies of scale which generated a strong positive feedback in today's information economy. Shapiro and Varian (1999) have strongly emphasized this aspect. They argued for example that Microsoft's dominance today is based primarily on the demand side economies of scale. The customers of Microsoft value its operating systems because they are widely used in the industry. The expanding global demand helps in exploiting the benefits of cost economies through expansion of scale. The third dynamic force is the creation of new strategic assets by successful firms in the industry. This is sometimes called "dynamic resourcefulness" in management science literature. This view holds that competition has two facets: static and dynamic. The former takes technology as given, so firms compete only on reducing costs and prices. The dynamic or Schumpeterian competition however changes technology at various points on the value chain. Thus the successful firms in an industry transform their technologies so as to create new strategic assets.

These three areas of efficiency central to hypercompetition constitute the most important forces of dynamic efficiency, which is different from the production and allocative efficiency underlying static competition. These sources of dynamic efficiency may be better understood if we view efficiency as an escalation ladder, where the firms grow in dynamic efficiency by racing up the ladder. Survival of the fittest remains the dominating principle of success in dynamic competition. Thus racing up the escalation ladder in the arena of R&D, developing new processes and software and new knowledge capital constitutes innovation efficiency. This efficiency or core competence is the foundation of the growth of the new economy.

4.2   Growth of the IT industry in the US

The computer industry is one of the fastest growing sectors in the US economy. During 1981–90 the annual rate of sales grew by about 13% and some companies grew much faster, e.g., Compaq by 64.3%, Conner Peripherals 128.3%, Dell 45.6% and Silicon Graphics by 59.1%. More recently the average sales growth has been sustained. Three important aspects of this growth phenomenon are to be noted. First, the information flow between business has been the primary differentiation for business and trade in this digital age, e.g., e-Bay, e-commerce and the Internet market have expanded by leaps and bounds. Economists have been very slow in understanding the behavior of the rapidly expanding corporations in the IT sector, which has sometimes been called hyper-growth, for example the phenomenal growth of Cray Research Corporation. But this growth has not always been one of equilibrium and balance. Companies have two basic options when they seek to build new-growth businesses. They can try to take an existing market from an incumbent competitor with *sustaining* R&D and innovations, or they can try to take on a competitor with *disruptive* innovations by capturing the incumbent's worst customers or by creating a new market. This highlights the need for following new strategies in the hypercompetitive age, e.g., instead of designing products and services that dictate consumers' behavior, consumers' needs should continually generate information so as to improve the design of the IT product. Secondly, competition and technological change has been most rapid in the computer industry today and its impact on cost efficiency and productivity growth has been most significant for the US economy over the last two decades. Thus Norsworthy and Jang (1992) have empirically found for the US computer industry a productivity growth rate of 2% per year for the period 1958–89, while for the recent period 1992–98 the growth rate estimated by others exceeded 2.5% per year on the average. Increased R&D investment and expanding "knowledge capital" have contributed significantly to this productivity growth. They helped reduce marginal costs and prices, which led to increases in overall demand. Thus according to the recent estimate by Jorgenson and Stiroh (2000) the price decline for personal computers has accelerated in recent years reaching nearly 28% per year from 1995 to 1998. Significant economies of scale and learning curve effects have often been the key to this rapid price decline.

Productivity growth and efficiency changes in the US computer industry have been the main focus of research in many recent studies of high-tech industries like microelectronics, computers, semiconductors and telecommunications. Norsworthy and Jang (1992) are probably the first to provide a detailed empirical study of the US computer industry comprising mainframe, mini and microcomputers (PCs) over three sub-periods 1959–67, 1967–75 and 1975–81 and the whole period 1959–81. They estimated a translog total cost function by nonlinear maximum likelihood and measured scale economies and technological progress. In a modified and simplified version (with fixed factor prices) their translog cost function appeared as follows:

$$\ln TC = b_0 + b_1 \ln y(t) + b_2 T$$

Here T is a time trend variable used as a dummy for the state of technology. Cumulative output or cumulative R&D investment have also been suggested as a proxy for technological change. The inverse of the parameter b_1 can be interpreted as the degree of returns to scale. Hence $1/b_1$ must equal one if there is CRS (constant returns to scale). The Hicks-neutral technical change is defined by a pure shift of the cost function that leaves the factor shares unchanged. The average annual shift in the cost function is therefore b_2. On differentiating (11) one obtains

$$\Delta TC/TC = b_1 (\Delta y/y(t)) + b_2$$

According to Norsworthy and Jang (1992) the estimate for b_2 turns out to be (−0.0369) for the whole period 1959–81, whereas $\hat{b}_1 = 0.3477$ and both are significant at 10% level. This suggests that the long run average rate of technical change (or progress) is 3.69% per year in the US computer industry over the 23 years 1959–81 and the degree of returns to scale (S) is $1/\hat{b}_1 = 2.876$. Both are substantial. The technical change for the three sub-periods 1959–67, 1967–75 and 1975–81 were −0.037, −0.051 and −0.041 suggesting no definite trend, although when production workers (b_{2L}) and nonproduction workers (b_{2N}) are used as explanatory variables, the degree of production-worker saving decreases through time from $\hat{b}_{2L} = -0.011$ in 1959–67 to $\hat{b}_{2L} = -0.004$ in 1975–81. Our DEA models use more up-to-date firm-wise data to estimate technological progress (see Table 4.2).

Technological developments in the US computer industry since 1981 have followed two distinct patterns in the new information age. One is the important role of R&D investment in both human capital and shared investment network. The theory predicts that technical uncertainties in R&D investment outcomes can be hedged considerably by pursuing multiple conceptual approaches in parallel. This has precisely what has happened in the computer industry through networking in R&D; see, e.g., Shapiro and Varian (1999).

The second important trend in the US computer industry is the pattern of product cycle and its changes over time in recent years. Thore et al. (1996) have argued that in the computer industry the rapid growth of a firm depends on its success in bringing a continuous stream of new products. Each product goes through a typical life cycle of R&D, market introduction, maturation and eventual obsolescence. Two trends are important in this evolution: the market initially expands (this is sometimes called economies of scale in demand, see e.g., Shapiro and Varian (1999)) and competition becomes more intense (this is sometimes called hypercompetition, see e.g., Sengupta (2002)). To supply the expanding market, scale economies and learning curve effects are exploited along with technical progress and this is accompanied by falling prices. Thus many early niche markets in the computer industry such as the markets for laptops or palm PCs have now grown into mass markets. As the manufacturers scramble to shorten the time to market, the R&D and commercialization phase of each cycle becomes shorter. As the products gradually penetrate an ever-expanding market, the upswing and maturation phases become longer and longer thus generating accelerated growth.

Investment in R&D inputs and innovations in product designs and marketing affect future productivity growth to a significant degree. This has been well established by the empirical studies of Norsworthy and Jang and others. Also these inputs have significant spillover effects on other firms in the industry. Viewing research output as designs, the human capital aspect of R&D expenditures emphasizes the knowledge of how to work blueprints. A single firm's research may be assisted by the cumulative number of designs invested by all the firms in the industry, e.g., software development by Microsoft.

Finally, in the computer industry today no company stays with a single life cycle, due to rapidly changing technology patterns. The managerial challenge is to bring an optional stream of new "vintages" of its products and as each company does so, the process of technological evolution continues forward in the industry. Hence the cost and efficiency analysis of firms in this industry have to be analyzed in three phases over the whole period.

Phase 1   Rising or maintaining efficiency over time on the average. This may be due to learning by doing, scale economies or changing product-mix, where some component products are still climbing their life cycles.

Phase 2   Falling or not maintaining efficiency over time on the average. This may be due to diseconomies of scale, technological regress or product components in their declining life cycles.

Phase 3   Time paths exhibiting mixtures of rising and falling or, falling and rising efficiency. This may be due to firms' inability to maintain an efficiency uptrend due to intense competition and aging product components and/or problems in supply chain management.

The computer industry in the US is at the top of the fastest growing sectors in the US economy over the 16 year period 1985–2000. The average sales growth of all the companies in the SIC codes 3570 and 3571 is about 12.8% per year on the average for the period 1985–94, and it is slightly higher (13.1%) for 1995–2000. Some companies like Dell and Silicon Graphics grew much faster over the whole period 1985–2000, e.g., an average of 22.4% per year.

Demand growth involved intense market competition followed by increasing technological diversity with greater utilization of economies of scope and learning by doing. All these resulted in increasing cost efficiency and falling prices.

It is useful to separate the demand growth and rapid technological evolution for analytical purposes. Although demand growth has played a key role in technological evolution, the latter has advanced on its own due to R&D investment in both hardware and software. The dynamic role of R&D investment in the companies on the leading edge of competition had dramatically improved the performance of computers, e.g., microprocessor development by Intel and IBM and their diverse range of applications in almost all the manufacturing industries. Technology in new hardware improved due to the development of new software and the latter developed at a rapid rate due to demand from domestic and international users.

Three aspects of the evolution of demand are important in the growth of the computer sector. One is the increase in volume of demand due to globalization of trade. The expansion of international trade in both hardware and software markets has been spearheaded by the rapid advance of software development by the subsidiaries of leading US companies in Asian countries like Taiwan, Korea, Singapore and India. The second aspect of demand growth is due to the significant economies of scale in demand rather than supply. The elasticity of demand with respect to total industrial output has exceeded 2.91 over the whole period 1985–2000, whereas the income elasticity of demand has been about 1.92. Since the value of a network goes up as the square of the number of users, demand growth has generated further investment in expanding the networks through interlocking and other linkages in the network economy. The third aspect of demand growth is due to interlinked demand, i.e., transmission of demand from one arena to other arenas.

The demand pattern may be modeled as a first order Markov process. Net sales data are used as a proxy for demand. These data are obtained from Standard and Poor's Compustat files for the period 1985–2000. Denoting y_t as net sales in years t the model is of the form

$$y_t = \alpha + \beta \, y_{t-1} + \varepsilon_t$$

Since the β coefficient indicates the growth parameter its estimates for some selected firms are as shown in Table 4.1. Here the last column is a measure of productive efficiency by the nonparametric method known as data envelopment analysis with 1.0 indicating highest efficiency on the average based on three typical years 1987, 1991 and 1998.

Sengupta (2002) applied this efficiency method to analyze a set of 22 companies in the US computer industry over a 16-year period 1985–2000. The selected companies are from a larger set of 40 companies, some of which did not survive. Standard and Poor's Compustat Database (SIC Code 3570 and 3571) provides the main source of input and output data. As outputs we used net sales revenue realized including incomes from various computer services. Nine inputs are selected from the Compustat Database representing both financially related input variables such as manufacturing costs and market costs and also "net capital employed" at the end of the reporting period. Of all the nine input variables three are most important from an economic viewpoint, e.g., R&D expense, net plant expenditure and the total cost of goods sold. Note that R&D expenditure here includes not only software

Table 4.1   Estimates of demand growth and efficiency

	$\hat{\beta}$	$t_{\hat{\beta}}$	R^2	*Efficiency index*
Dell	1.495	41.181	0.994	1.00
Compaq	1.276	28.728	0.988	1.00
HP	1.116	26.664	0.986	1.00
Sun	1.107	31.810	0.990	0.96
Toshiba	1.043	9.480	0.899	0.98
Silicon Graphics	0.994	9.470	0.899	0.64
Sequent	0.990	9.407	0.897	0.66
Hitachi	0.718	4.607	0.669	0.64
Apple	0.699	4.427	0.650	0.70
Data General	0.721	10.212	0.681	0.59
Average (22 firms)	**1.102**	**6.172**	**0.901**	**0.89**

development but also all marketing costs which include advertising, research and development, networking and any other selling expenses in general. Data restricts us from using only the research component of this variable.

For measuring technical change over time we use the nonparametric efficiency method known as DEA (data envelopment analysis) to estimate Solow-type technical progress based on observed data on growth of inputs and outputs for 22 companies in the Compustat data available from Standard and Poor's Databank: R&D expense, net plant and expenditure and cost of goods sold. The cost of goods sold includes marketing and administrative costs along with manufacturing costs. The estimates do not impose the restriction of CRS as in the Solow model, hence this is called scale unadjusted models.

The average annual technical progress for the whole period 1985–2000 is about 12.1% for 22 companies and 10.8% for the ten companies in Table 4.2. This is much lower than the estimate of 26% for the period 1959–81 obtained by Norsworthy and Jang (1992). Also it is clear from Table 4.2 that the ten companies selected here exhibit much higher technical progress in the recent period 1995–2000 compared to the earlier period 1985–89. When CRS technology is imposed, we use the nonparametric model (2) with the additional condition (3) and the estimate for scale adjusted technical change is much higher, i.e., about 21.1% for the whole period 1985–2000 for all 22 companies. This is only slightly lower than the estimate of Norsworthy and Jang. The

Table 4.2   Annual average technical change based on scale unadjusted models

	Technical progress			*Average 1985–2000*
	1985–89	*1990–94*	*1995–2000*	
Dell	0.042	0.642	0.320	0.335
Compaq	0.024	0.361	0.164	0.183
HP	0.064	0.050	0.107	0.074
Sun	0.050	0.055	0.049	0.051
Toshiba	0.038	0.024	0.105	0.056
Silicon Graphics	0.062	0.066	0.057	0.062
Sequent	0.022	0.060	0.036	0.039
Hitachi	0.044	0.024	0.107	0.058
Apple	0.030	0.112	0.315	0.152
Data General	0.049	0.110	0.061	0.073

Note: These estimates assume variable returns to scale.

scale efficiency measurement exhibited in Table 4.3 shows an average of 1.403 for the whole period for ten companies and 1.341 for all 22 companies. These estimates of RTS (returns to scale) are much lower than the estimates of Norsworthy and Jang (1992) for an earlier period 1959–81.

Finally, we have in Table 4.4 the estimates of nonradial efficiency measures which allow the overall efficiency measures to be decomposed

Table 4.3   Annual average scale coefficients of the scale unadjusted models

	1985–89	*1990–94*	*1995–2000*	*Average*
				1985–2000
Dell	1.618	1.007	1.065	1.230
Compaq	1.607	1.165	0.963	1.578
HP	1.170	1.269	2.011	1.150
Sun	1.161	1.280	0.956	1.466
Toshiba	1.530	1.066	1.989	1.526
Silicon Graphics	1.016	1.035	1.749	1.267
Sequent	1.653	1.292	1.451	1.465
Hitachi	1.513	1.020	1.991	1.508
Apple	1.587	1.546	0.469	1.534
Data General	1.260	1.278	1.387	1.308

Table 4.4   Nonradial average efficiency measures θ_i^* (t)

	1985–89			*1990–94*			*1995–2000*		
	θ_1^* (t)	θ_2^* (t)	θ_3^* (t)	θ_1^* (t)	θ_2^* (t)	θ_3^* (t)	θ_1^* (t)	θ_2^* (t)	θ_3^* (t)
Dell	0.61	0.44	0.47	1.0	1.0	1.0	1.0	1.0	1.0
Compaq	0.40	0.54	0.50	1.0	1.0	1.0	0.33	0.60	0.75
HP	0.49	1.0	0.47	0.55	0.80	1.0	1.0	1.0	1.0
Sun	1.0	1.0	1.0	1.0	1.0	1.0	0.42	0.24	0.67
Toshiba	0.49	0.62	0.72	1.0	1.0	1.0	1.0	1.0	1.0
Silicon Graphics	1.0	1.0	1.0	1.0	1.0	1.0	0.25	0.25	0.38
Sequent	1.0	1.0	1.0	1.0	1.0	1.0	0.50	0.54	0.48
Hitachi	0.40	0.68	0.65	1.0	1.0	1.0	0.94	0.84	1.0
Apple	0.52	0.69	0.64	0.51	0.44	0.76	1.0	1.0	1.0
Data General	1.0	1.0	1.0	1.0	1.0	1.0	0.48	0.54	0.77

Note: Here the three inputs are: R&D expenditures, net plant and equipment and cost of goods sold and theta is the respective non-radial efficiency measure.

into three components, e.g., R&D (θ_1^*), net plant expenditure (θ_2^*) and cost of goods sold (θ_3^*). The importance of R&D input is clearly revealed. Companies which have experienced substantial growth in sales have also exhibited strong efficiency in the R&D input utilization – e.g., Dell, Sequent, Sun and Data General.

The leaders in phase 1 (rising phase) of the growth frontier may be identified by the number of years the company remained efficient on the average. Based on the estimates of nonradial efficiency Dell, Toshiba, Silicon Graphics, Sun and Data General are leaders (six out of nine times they retained growth efficiency with an average market share of 25%) but in terms of R&D efficiency only Sun, Silicon Graphics, Sequent and Data General maintained their leadership (four out of nine times with an average market share of 12%). Most of the other companies belonged to phase 3, e.g., Apple did not do well for the period 1985–1994, but in the recent period (1995–2000) it picked up growth efficiency. The experiences of Silicon Graphics and Toshiba are similar. For the set of ten companies analyzed here, none stayed in phase 2 (declining) continuously, although from the overall set of 42 companies many did not survive at all, hence we had to include only 22 companies in our comparison data set.

Tables 4.5 and 4.6 show the contributions of R&D in the growth efficiency framework. Note that the R&D expenses as defined here include not only software development and research but also all types of marketing expenses. Data limitations prevent us from considering

Table 4.5 Impact of R&D inputs on growth of sales

	1985–89		1990–94		1995–2000	
	θ^*	β_2^*	θ^*	β_2^*	θ^*	β_2^*
Dell	1.00	2.71	1.00	0.15	0.75	0.08
Compaq	0.97	0.03	1.00	0.002	0.95	0.001
HP	1.00	1.89	0.93	0.10	0.88	0.002
Sun	1.00	0.001	1.00	0.13	0.97	1.79
Toshiba	0.93	1.56	1.00	0.12	0.82	0.09
Silicon Graphics	0.99	0.02	0.95	1.41	0.87	0.001
Sequent	0.72	0.80	0.92	0.001	0.84	0.002
Hitachi	0.88	0.07	0.98	0.21	0.55	0.00
Apple	1.00	1.21	0.87	0.92	0.68	0.001
Data General	0.90	0.92	0.62	0.54	0.81	0.65

Note: Here θ^* denotes the efficiency measure and β_2^* is the coefficient measuring the impact of R&D on the sales growth of companies.

only the research-based expenses here. The companies which are leading firms in Table 4.4 show a very high elasticity on the average. Specifically their marketing innovations have contributed to significant declines in costs, which have led to declining prices. This also explains the fact that a company like Dell which does very little in pure software development research excels in growth efficiency. Only more detailed data can decompose the sources of such anomaly.

On an overall basis it is clear that technological progress has been significantly higher for those leading firms which have maintained growth efficiency on the average. Growth efficiency is a relative measure of long run growth, which is distinguished from *level efficiency* by Solow, since the latter does not include growth effect due to technological progress and labor productivity.

	Technical progress (%)		R&D efficiency (%)	
	1985–89	*1995–2000*	*1985–89*	*1995–2000*
A. Leading firms	25	30	28	30
B. Non-leading firms	14	16	15	17

In an economic environment of rapid technical change and intense market competition, growth efficiency reflects more accurately the efficiency ladder. On the average our empirical results showed that the leading growth efficiency companies enjoyed increased market shares in terms of sales growth. Laggards and growth inefficient firms showed poorest sales growth figures. Also the R&D investment expenditure played a very significant role in explaining the efficiency behavior of leading firms. The overall regression of the log linear production function showed a highly significant value of 0.162 (significant at 1% level of t) for the coefficient of ln R&D expenditure, whereas net plant and expenditure in logs contributed only 0.009 which is not significant at even 5% level of t statistics. It is remarkable that the leaders in growth efficiency invariably exhibited R&D efficiency to a significant degree.

Recently Thomas and D'Aveni (2004) have analyzed empirical data of every publicly-listed manufacturing firm in the US economy over the period 1950–2002 and found a monotonic shift towards hypercompetition with increasing structural instability. A prominent feature of hypercompetition is the *pervasive innovation* throughout the extended value chain. As in Schumpeter's concept of "creative destruction" this rapid sequence of innovations erodes established competitive positions and makes possible the creation of new competitive positions. One of the most prominent consequences of hypercompetition is volatility in corporate performance and a shift towards temporary competitive advantage. Another consequence is the decay of existing competitive positions for firms that fail to create new competitive positions faster than their old positions erode. As the turbulence of the hypercompetitive environment increases, the competitively weak firms are likely to fail, exits increase thus yielding market share and profits to the successful hypercompetitive firms. Thus today's market is greatly influenced by the exits of firms in a manufacturing industry which contribute greatly to the increasing degree of churn in an industry's membership.

The revolution of the information age is changing the face of the industrial world today. As Bill Gates (1999) has pointed out, most customer transactions in the US today will become self-service digital transactions and intermediaries will evolve to add value or perish.

> Has your management team familiarized itself with the Internet and taken time to prepare a vision of how it will change your business in the next decade? Are you working with your IT team to implement that vision technically? (Gates 1999: 71)

Two implications of the Internet revolution are worth pointing out. In pre-Internet days the only way consumers could get goods from most manufacturers was through tiers of distributors and retailers. Today any manufacturer can provide the Internet equivalent of a factory outlet. Secondly, most Web merchants, e.g., e-Bay, or Amazon.com offer flexible pricing, i.e., a promise to match the lowest price a consumer can find.

The globalization of demand and trade and the use of IT networks in communications imply that US growth of IT technology will have a diffusion effect on its externalities. One may refer to the work of Laursen (1999) who estimated a technology-gap model of international competitiveness, where changes in trade performance are explained in terms of changes in unit labor costs, investment, catching up, a structural market effect (i.e., the advantage coming from being initially specialized in the classes of products that grew more in terms of exports), a structural technology effect (i.e., the advantage coming from being initially specialized in the product classes that grew more in terms of patents) and a technology adaptation effect (i.e., the ability to move actively into the technological sectors with above-average rates of growth). The statistical results for OECD countries in 1996 gave no support for the structural technology effect to have an impact on market shares, while a significant effect is found for the technology growth adaptation effect and the structural market effect. Thus it is important for national systems of innovation to actively move into sectors offering above-average technological opportunity rather than being fortunately specialized initially.

4.3   The new economy and the Indian IT industry

The new economy is characterized by two key features: information technology (IT) and innovations. India has begun its quest for information technology but the full potential is yet to be realized. Innovations complement the IT process by investing in managerial skills, which have often been called "the core competence" by managerial experts, e.g., Prahalad and Hamel (1990). India has an enormous potential here. The successful growth episodes of Southeast Asian countries provide ample evidence of how the IT sector can speed up the tempo of overall growth by spreading growth to other sectors through forward and backward linkages. Forward linkages occur when other sectors like manufacturing, transportation and trade use the services of the IT sector. By such linkages the productivity of these sectors gets a boost. Backward linkages occur when the IT sector demands skilled personnel and goods and services from other sectors notably trade, commerce, transportation and communication. India has a long history of central planning of more than five decades with the associated policy of heavy government investment in large industries and inward oriented economic strategies. The recent growth of the IT sector in India has provided new challenges which demand substantial economic reforms. One of the major reforms is to reorient government policy so that the IT sector growth can be transmitted to other sectors. Transparency and liberalization in policy are the key factors which may help this process. The examples of China and Taiwan are most striking in this regard. Growth of the IT sector helped the other sectors to grow and this process of growth transmission helped the small and medium scale industries to grow. Hence the need for a new orientation of the planning process in India. How to spread the growth transmission? How to involve the other sectors to participate in the information superhighway so as to improve their productivity and efficiency?

It is instructive to review in this connection the growth experience of Taiwan in its electronics industry. In the early 1950s it produced only transistor radios but now it produces various components of personal computers, advanced workstations, PC monitors and a host of other microelectronic products. Large companies such as Tatung and Acer have flourished from world exports. But what is surprising is that a number of small firms such as Sampo and United Microelectronic have shown tremendous sales growth during 1995–2004. Total exports from the electronics sector grew from $4.1 billion in 1980 to $25.2 bn in 1995. The most important feature of this export growth is the dominance of the small and medium size firms with less than 300 employees. Hobday (1995) has estimated the various components of output of the IT sector based on electronics and information technology in Taiwan for the year 1990 as shown in Table 4.6.

Two types of economic policies were adopted by the government of Taiwan. In May 1979 the government put forth the Science and Technology Development Program identifying the information technology systems as the key area of emphasis for future R&D. The Council for Economic Planning and Development prepared a ten-year plan 1980–89 which provided targets for R&D expenditures and human capital supply in terms of skilled personnel. By all indicators targets were realized and plans succeeded and by the 1990s Taiwanese firms started gaining prominence as innovative designers of PCs and electronic and telecommunication products. Datatech for example, gained enormous success. Also during this time Taiwan exceeded the UK to become the fifth largest producer of semiconductors in the world. Government policy adopted the overall initiative strategy and exhorted domestic firms to compete by cutting costs through productive efficiency. The government took the overall responsibility for acquiring advanced technology from abroad and fostered advanced research by training skilled personnel. Secondly, the mutual interactions and R&D collaboration among the various strategic firms in the IT industry were fostered by deliberate government policies and this helped exploit the externalities

Table 4.6   Output produced and forecast for the various IT industries in Taiwan (US billion $)

	Output 1990	Forecast 2005	Average annual growth
Information products	6.9	35.0	15.1
Automation	2.8	12.1	12.5
Consumer electronics	2.3	5.5	7.0
Telecommunications	1.9	10.2	14.0
Semiconductors	1.5	7.0	14.0
Total	15.4	69.8	14.0

of R&D expenditures for the growth of the IT sector. There was a combined effect from strategic interactions among the following five types of subsection: foreign companies, high-technology startup companies, government sponsored ventures, local manufacturing groups and leadership roles with innovating business leaders. The design and implementation of such plans should be the joint responsibility of both government and business leaders and a continual follow-up of the success or failure in achieving the targets should be mandatory. Plans need to be realized rather than indicative. Secondly, medium and small scale industries have to be involved in the planning process. There exist several avenues for doing this. One is through "outsourcing" by which IT services can be exported to several lines of business, e.g., publishing, networking, R&D research and various trade and communication services. A second avenue is the decentralization of IT services through interaction and joint ventures. Recent developments in the IT sector in India since 2002 are promising in this direction, because of liberalization and economic reforms.

The upsurge of economic activity heightened by the IT-based enterprises in India in recent times has taken several forms. First, the global entrepreneurs in the US and Europe have now discovered the potential of India's future in information technology. Hence they have started a steady stream of subsidiaries and joint ventures. Secondly, the outsourcing trend worldwide has shifted IT sector related services to Bangalore, Hyderabad, Chennai and other cities of India, where the cost of skilled personnel is 80 to 90% heaper. In classical international trade theory one critical assumption is that people cannot move across countries but goods can. But today's PC network has allowed IT services to move across national boundaries. This has facilitated the almost free movement of skilled services, e.g., publishing, trade, distribution and finance. Thirdly, consultancy companies in India like TCS (Tata Consultancy Services) have expanded their sales of IT services in Europe and the US in the design and implementation of information networks for public and private enterprises. Finally, the successful NIE countries like Korea, Singapore, China and Taiwan have discovered new opportunities in exploring R&D collaboration and joint ventures in the manufacture and sale of telecommunications products, e.g., cell phones, microelectronics and optimal products.

It is useful to review these developments in more specific terms. First, Microsoft, Hewlett Packard, Motorola, Oracle and more recently Dell Computers have opened their subsidiaries in Bangalore, Hyderabad, Calcutta and other cities. They have established their training campus in order to tap the skilled personnel available. Bill Gates of Microsoft visits India every year to tap the services of skilled students even at college level. These software companies are now facing competitors from Europe. For example, SAP AG, the German software major in business solutions software has already started negotiations with leading IT vendors in India for global partnership to develop business applications and business products in Net Weaver, its latest technology platform, and announced plans to hire more than 2,000 people. Secondly, countries like Korea and China have started joint ventures in IT products in India. For example, LG CNS Global, a subsidiary of South Korean Chaebol's IT services firm has recently set up its India office of software development in Bangalore to provide specialized services to business enterprises in India and abroad. China's computer maker Lenovo, which has recently acquired IBM's PC business and the Kejian Corporation of China have launched ventures in PC and mobile phone products in India. Similarly, Hyundai Mobile, a unit of South Korea's Hyundai Corporation has started its mobile phone business in India. All these developments have driven down the cost of telephone and software services in India and the trend is almost certain to continue. However the trend in adopting the business software products and applications for Indian business is still very slow. Thirdly, there are many complementary products in the IT sector besides software development where India has ample scope for developing joint ventures with international companies. For example, Inten, the world's largest chipmaker announced plans in 2004 to spend $40 million over the next two years to expand its operations in India. Cisco Systems, a global network major signed a contract with VSNL in India in November 2004 to deploy broadband metro Ethernet solution providing broadband services at less than Rs. 1000 ($25) per month. Finally, India's entrepreneurs in the IT sector have started exploring foreign markets, e.g., TCS has recently tied up with a South Korean firm to tap the IT market in the NIE countries of Southeast Asia. Infosys is doing the same in China and South Korea. Also many private Indian companies, for example Tatas, Infosys, Satyam and Reliance are now registered with the NYSE (New York Stock Exchange) thus making them eligible for participation in the global capital market at competitive interest rates.

Several interesting developments in the Indian IT sector are to be noted. One is the study by ILO published in December 2004 which reported in its World Employment Report 2004–2005 that the service sector including IT services has seen impressive improvements in productive employment. The agricultural sector in recent years has witnessed the smallest improvement in productivity but greater employment growth than the industrial sector, which had the highest improvement in productivity but at the cost of very little improvement in employment. Secondly, India has entered into free trade agreement on economic cooperation with the Gulf Cooperative Council to liberalize trade and investment relations. India's PC sales were expected to grow throughout 2005 to 4 million and more and its foreign exchange reserves hit $130.62 billion in the week ending 17 December 2004 thus exceeding Singapore's records. The tempo of foreign direct investment in India especially in the IT sector has started increasing at a rapid rate. Three phases are observed here. In the first phase IT services, marketing and distribution have been the primary focus through "outsourcing." The second phase is marked by the sale and development of software programs and business applications, where international giants like Microsoft, Oracle, Silicon Graphics (software Quark) and SAP AG (Germany) have opened their subsidiaries in Bangalore, Hyderabad and Chennai. Some cities in India like Calcutta are making serious attempts through the creation of special industrial and export zones to attract foreign direct investment in the software technology sector. The third and most recent phase is the trend where R&D leaders in the international field in the IT sector have selected India as the innovation hub. Two important sectors are healthcare and the environment, where there exist big opportunities to drive growth in the global IT industry. This opens up a big window of growth opportunity for the Indian IT industry for inviting foreign direct investment (FDI). India's trade with China has recently crossed $10 billion with an impressive growth of 82.5% in the first ten months of 2004. An equal opportunity exists for expanding trade with the other high growth NICs in Southeast Asia. As Nrayana Murthy, the Infosys chairman has noted: India will need about $480 billion in FDI over 2005–2015 to become a developed nation. An important component of this FDI should be in reply to R&D and the development of knowledge capital in the whole economy. It is useful in this connection to refer to the four components of the knowledge-based development index in the year 2000 constructed by the Third Perspective Plan in Malaysia:

(a) Computer knowledge infostructure measured through the share of worldwide computer use, i.e., computers per 1,000, connection to Internet and computer usage per capita.
(b) Information structure based on investment in telecommunications, TV sets, newspaper circulation.

Table 4.7   Knowledge-based development index for selected countries in 2000

	Index A	Index B	Index C	Index D	Index E
US	1	10	8	3	1
Japan	8	3	10	1	2
Canada	3	12	5	15	9
UK	9	8	11	14	11
Korea (South)	16	11	16	13	15
Singapore	14	16	19	6	16
Malaysia	17	17	17	16	17
Thailand	19	21	14	19	18
China	18	199	18	20	19
Indonesia	21	20	21	21	21
India	20	22	22	22	22

(c) Education and training based on total expenditure on education per capita, literacy rate, student–teacher ratio in primary and secondary education and higher education enrollment.

(d) R&D and technology which includes high-technology exports as a proportion of manufacturing exports, number of scientists and engineers in R&D, total expenditure on R&D as percent of GDP and the average annual number of patents.

The country-wise position of these components of the knowledge-based development index in 2000 with E denoting the overall knowledge index is reported in Table 4.7 in terms of ranks with one indicating the highest. This table indicates in a very rough way the gap in knowledge-based economic structure for countries in Asia compared to advanced industrial countries. Since human resource competitiveness relies most heavily on these knowledge-based development indicators, national economic policy in India for the coming decade should heavily emphasize the target of raising these indices A to D. Building successful joint ventures with international leading companies through FDI may be the key to enhance the core competence of Indian IT companies.

4.4   Growth transmission: from old to new

Growth transmission refers to the diffusion of the growth process at three levels. One is through international trade, the second through domestic trade from one region to another and another thorough knowledge and the transfer from one sector or industry to another. In all these diffusion processes three factors play a major role. The first is the *knowledge effect*. It depends on the size of capital stock and learning by doing which can be measured by a country's or industry's past level of cumulative output. The second has been termed *competition effect* by Helpman (2004). It may have both positive and negative effects on growth. Thus foreign competition may lower profits of the domestic producers and retard their growth. But it may also raise incentive to innovate in R&D, thereby inducing business leaders to push in new directions. The third force is the *externality effect* whereby skills and creativity move from the leading sector to other sectors.

The concept of a *new economy* embodies these three aspects in a dynamic context. The NICs in Southeast Asia have exploited these effects over the last two decades and continue to do it now. India now faces the dawn of the new economy and it has a number of comparative advantages over Asian NICs. First of all, technical skills in IT products and services and language skills in English are readily available. The quality of engineering and technical education though small in proportion to the overall labor force is very high, thanks to the IITs in India. IIT graduates get easy admissions to MIT, Stanford and other top universities in the US. Secondly, India could easily follow the trade pattern of China with Taiwan, which earned for China enormous gains from trade. The NRIs and Indian expatriates in Silicon Valley and the large number of Indian venture capitalists in the IT sector in the US may provide as much knowledge capital to India, as Taiwan provided to China or Japan provided to South Korea. It is significant to note that the prime minister of India declared in January 2005 the appointment of a knowledge commission at a high level. It should actively pursue methods of tapping this huge knowledge capital from successful entrepreneurs in Silicon Valley with Indian origins. Finally, the IIMs like the IITs in India have a significant role to play. The potential managerial talent in India is very significant. An outward-oriented economy fostering international competitiveness may tap this potential. Compared to Taiwan or China India appears to be superior in this respect but the IIMs have yet to play their dynamic role in boosting managerial leadership and innovative entrepreneurship in India. Over the last four decades IIMs have laid utmost emphasis on job creation in the managerial field But they have lacked applied research and an emphasis on building new entrepreneurs and future business leaders. The latter aspect is most important for medium and small scale industries as the experiences of China and Taiwan show. The IIM curricula have closely followed the format of business schools in the US but only in theoretical outline. The applied part in business applications and myriads of industrial case studies, which emphasize the sources of growth in successful companies are conspicuous by their absence. Management education in India failed to emphasize strategies which not only borrow advanced technology but help to transplant it and improve it through a continual process of training, research and new development. Look at the contrast with Taiwan's policy since the 1980s. It decided to follow world leaders in already established technologies by competing through cutting costs through improved productive efficiency. The government not only took the responsibility for acquiring technology from abroad but actively fostered research through research institutes, management schools and private sector laboratories. The crucial thing to note is that all these results are finally transferred to the private sector. The ultimate responsibility thus shifted to private entrepreneurs. By taking advantage of government support and incentives many start-up companies prospered. Private firms including small and medium enterprises found synergies with each other and with R&D institutions forming an integrated network. The remarkable outcome is the stellar success in the information industry. As a result by 1993 Taiwan surpassed the UK as the world's fifth largest producer of semiconductors. By 1995 the total value output of IT products was nearly $20 billion US dollars, making Taiwan one of the top three exporting countries of IT products. PCs made by Acer, Mitac and Ta Tung are now competitive with those made in the US and Japan. Many peripheral products have gained top market shares in the world, such as monitors (57%), computer mice (70%), printed circuit boards (65%) and LCD panels (20%).

A measure of technological progress is the number of US patents awarded to Taiwanese inventors: individuals, institutions and industries. These increased rapidly in the 1990s and outnumbered all other East Asian NIEs including South Korea, Singapore and Hong Kong. Thus the number of US patents granted to Taiwan increased from 30 in 1976 to 900 in 1991, whereas South Korea increased from 20 in 1976 to 300 in 1991. India and China never exceeded 20.

The critical point to note is that high-tech advances have not been limited to electronics and IT products in Taiwan, they also spread very fast to such areas as chemicals, specialty materials and machinery, e.g., high-speed fiber spinning and high-value fiber technologies useful for development of the textile industry. Another important development was the establishment of the China Engine Corporation in 1995 for manufacturing a common automotive power train, the result of an R&D consortium consisting of ITRI, four domestic manufacturers and the British Lotus Engineering Company.

It is important to note two recent developments as of 2005. One is the appointment of a knowledge commission by the Indian government, which is charged with the task of pinpointing critical areas of managerial education in the country for IT and related sectors. A second development is the founding of a center in Mumbai by Harvard University, which intends to develop industrial cooperation with the education and research institutes so as to boost the tempo of growth in the next decade, when India is likely to emerge as a world leader.

It is important now to discuss the various effects of growth transmission, from old to new and from large to medium scale. Taiwan provides the key example of spectacular success here. Consider the knowledge effect which emphasizes the various channels of transfer of knowledge capital from IT to other sectors and from domestic to international arenas by taking advantage of the gains from trade. Consider Taiwan's example. In 1990 the Executive Yuan put forward a six-year national development plan which identified ten emerging industries and eight key high technology processes. These are sectors and enterprises with a demonstrated technology foundation, manufacturing capability and sales experience. Its successful completion yielded sales over $60 billion in US dollars, which is about 25.5% of all manufacturing. The value added was 40% and exports about US $34 billion accounting for 32% of the total export value of manufacturing.

Traditional industries mainly in the manufacturing sector were actively helped by government through the Bureau of Industrial Development and the Medium and Small Enterprises Service. Besides various ITRI (Industrial Technology and Research Institute) laboratories the China Productivity Center helps to improve management quality. Modern industrial technology has four basic phases: design, materials, processing and quality. By improving each of these phases the value of manufacturing products can be significantly improved and the real costs per unit reduced. A notable example is the use of carbon fiber composite materials in bicycles and other sports equipment. In the 1970s the average price of a Taiwan-made bicycle was under US $50. In 1984 Taiwan started developing a carbon fiber resin system for bicycle frames. In 1988 the newly designed carbon fiber bicycles were introduced and rapidly became popular with a 25 fold increase in unit price. Similar composite materials technology has also been used in tennis rackets, golf clubs and other sporting goods and Taiwan has become the largest exporter in the world of these products.

India needs to make a sequential plan of selecting a few key industries and using them to spread new technology. Agriculture and rural industries may provide the starting point. Exports of dried flowers, new research products in herbal medicines, varieties of silk products and handicraft goods and services come readily to mind. China has carved out a market niche in these products in its export trade with the US and India has ample scope in boosting export trade here. Alongside agriculture is the manufacturing sector, where India should adopt, develop and improve products which are highly income elastic in world markets today. Starting from the IT sector the scope here is enormous. Technology diffusion here may take many forms, e.g., direct technology transfer from foreign direct investment, technical consulting, cooperative R&D and strategic alliances and spin-off companies. The primary need for India today is to gradually build up foreign distribution, sales channels and up- and down-stream cooperation. Supply networks need to be developed in electronics, telecommunications and service industries. There is software development by Indian engineers and technicians but the diffusion process both at home and abroad is very weak. What we need now is to foster a user friendly technology diffusion process. Thus when a technology or software is developed by a public or private research organization, the economic environment should be such that it can be readily followed up by manufacturing the product and marketing it worldwide. Thus strategies for opening up new markets and new lines of business have to be actively followed up by the central and state governments in India.

Economists have emphasized the role of learning by doing in the knowledge effect. The learning process has a cumulative impact of knowledge capital. It helps speed up the specialization process. When the stock of knowledge capital crosses a threshold in a particular sector, the favored sector expands at a faster rate which dominates the growth of the overall economy in the long run. Thus the IT sector has to be viewed as a favored sector where the knowledge capital has crossed the threshold and is ready to experience fastest growth, pulling TFP growth in the other sectors. The sheer size of export market growth and the learning by doing effect may help rejuvenate other related sectors.

The "competition effect" utilizes the market mechanism to speed up growth. By opening up to international markets technology spreads faster and specialization moves forward. One has to note that the new economy in the US today is due to the arrival and gradual absorption of a new general-purpose technology (GPT), which will gradually spread to the rest of the world. This GPT may have to be absorbed by other countries if they seek growth in exports and outward-looking growth. One channel of international diffusion of GPT will be foreign direct investment (FDI), especially where the full use of the new technology requires organizational changes. But the speed of diffusion depends on the local circumstances, particularly on the characteristics of local markets, managerial skills and the business environment. If firms and enterprises are protected by import restrictions or regulatory constraints, they are unlikely to feel the pressure to make the efficiency enhancing changes permitted by the new technology. Workplaces must be organized in new ways to achieve optimal use of new technology. The IITs and IIMs need to develop improved methods of training and hands-on education in India for improved skills in the new technology and its requirements.

One has to note that the US has no monopoly on new ideas, new skills or on willingness to translate them into lucrative applications. Silicon Valley in California is only a melting pot, bringing together not only Americans but also British, Chinese, Indians and people of many other nationalities to translate new ideas and new skills into viable business applications and successful business ventures. India has already started boosting its IT and GPT sectors by expanding computational and community capacity. Bangalore is now called the Silicon Valley of India. But it needs to be a central hub like the melting pot of Silicon Valley. In this respect it has two economic weaknesses. The technological diffusion has not spread to smaller cities in India, so that its impact on regional growth has been very insignificant. State governments in India have yet to develop a consensus for attracting IT-related businesses through special incentives as happened in China and Taiwan. The states of West Bengal have set up special zones in Salt Lake for IT and related technology-based firms but the policy so far has been bogged down by indecision and inner conflicts in the CPM government. It is ironic that this leftist government seeks to follow the Chinese model as its party philosophy; yet the Chinese have embraced market reforms all the way and every province and local area have been given authority to propose various local incentives in order to attract FDI and spread it around the rural and township areas. It is heartening to note that India has now started taking baby steps to move in this direction. An example is Kochi's info park in India. Fourteen months after it started it is now home to 24 IT companies like Wipro, TCS and Spanish IT companies like DITRD and ACS. The example of Taiwan needs to be mentioned here. The Hsin-Chu Science based Industrial Park was started by Taiwan in 1983 with about 35 participating companies but it has attracted high-tech companies and skilled scientists and engineers from overseas. By 1993 the number of companies had reached 150, providing employment for

30,000 with a total business revenue of NT $130 billion accounting for 2% of GNP in 1993. Between 1983 and 1994 about 25% of central government's non-defense projects were carried out by ITRI which helped commercialize many high-tech products; thus patents awarded to ITRI both domestic and international increased very rapidly from five in 1980 to more than 400 in 2000.

A second fundamental weakness in technology diffusion patterns in India is the policy of separation of R&D and skill formation between the government, universities and public research institutions and the private business sector. Mutual distrust has fanned a climate of non cooperation in research ventures. Look at the example of Taiwan. In 1993 ITRI transferred 209 technologies to 297 private companies in the Hsin-Chu Park including UMC (1980), TSMC (1987) and the recently founded VSIC (1994) which will manufacture 16 megabyte DRAM and other sub-micron devices. About 50% of the companies in the Park have established technical relationships such as joint R&D, technology transfer and technical services. Many universities and public research institutes have taken active part in various R&D and training projects of ITRI and the Park's companies. High-tech industries have increased in recent years (1995–2000) their R&D spending to over 5% of total sales revenue, which equal more than five times the average R&D expenditure of the whole manufacturing industry.

The "externality effect" emphasizes two key aspects of the transfer of new information technology from the hub to the periphery. One is the joint effect of R&D expenditure, cooperative ventures through subsidiaries and building networks for utilizing comparative gains from inter-regional trade. The second is the spread of knowledge capital through education and in-company training and conferences in applications software. Lin (1998) has provided data exhibiting the technology diffusion initiated by ITRI (see Table 4.8). ITRI has helped upgrade traditional industries in various ways: programmable logic control, precision mould design, electroless plating of plastics, processing of metals and plastics, chemical and biochemical treatment of waste water, risk analysis and management and total quality improvement. In 1991 ITRI started developing technology for making aircraft components with the aim of helping small and medium sized companies enter the aviation and aerospace markets.

Liberalization and economic reforms have been the key innovation driver in India. Liberalization has stimulated the rapid growth of innovation-driven industries such as information technology, communications technology, biotechnology and pharmaceutical industries. The "knowledge

Table 4.8   Technology diffusion of ITRI in Taiwan

		1992	1995
Technology transfers	projects	143	280
	companies	262	418
Joint R&D	cases	411	1,004
Conferences	number	643	880
Patents approved	cases	274	368
Technical training programs	number attending	40,150	59,492
Technology services	cases	37,141	50,944
	companies	21,943	27,061

economy" is now a significant component of the national economy and it has a significant spillover effect. Korgaonker (2004) has recently surveyed the structure and growth of IT and its impact on manufacturing. He noted heavy dependence on technology licensing as a source of technology acquisition with very little equity participation. The collaborations were mainly from the US, the UK and Germany. He comments:

> Unfortunately the Indian firms were unable or unwilling to master the basic knowledge and processes for technical development, so innovation suffered. The Indian model, instead of being "assimilate and innovate" degenerated into "adopt and obsolete". (111)

A recent World Bank study noted that as regards the search for technological services, cooperation or interaction between industrial firms and technology and management institutions is very limited.

Korgaonker (2004) has also discussed the IT industry performance in India in three major areas: software development, venture capital and e-commerce. Software sector development is mainly export driven with over 60% annual growth. It accounts for about 2% of India's GDP and is expected to reach 7.7% by 2008. Of these software exports, 62% go to the US, 24% to Europe and 4% to Japan. A recent major trend is offshore software development. Thus offshore services in 2001–02 contributed 44% of total exports, with onsite services accounting for 56% of export revenues. IT-enabled service applications in India include customer interaction services, business outsourcing and management, medical transcription, legal databases, payroll and human resources services and website services. By outsourcing these services large companies in the US, UK and Europe including Fortune 500 companies gain significantly in terms of cost, quality and time. Leading IT service providers like Ireland and Singapore now "back end" their operations in India because of availability of skilled Indian personnel.

The role of venture capital on innovation and R&D development involves four stages: idea generation, start-up, growth and exit in the form of shifting to newer products or ideas. The venture capital industry, which is so important in the remarkable growth of the IT industry in Silicon Valley is at its infancy in India. According to Indian Venture Capital Association estimates, the domestic and offshore venture capital funds provide about Rs 22 billion, of which about 52% is directed to technology and related R&D. The venture capital industry has a vast potential in India for the various components of the IT sector like software development, biotechnology, telecommunications, media entertainment, medicine and health and agriculture-based industries. The agriculture-based rural industries are especially important for applications of IT technology. Examples of Chinese village and township industries and Taiwanese development of rural electronics industries come readily to mind. Export of processed dried flowers, modernization of handicraft industries through private sector initiative, creating a toy industry with modern designs so as to compete in the world market are some of the new areas worthy of new innovations by venture capitalists in the private sector. Two types of changes in policies are needed here. One concerns the high-level educational institutions including IITs and IIMs who must share the responsibility for encouraging entrepreneurship, R&D joint ventures and incubators. The relation between private industrial firms find the universities cum public research organizations must be one of active cooperation, rather than passive indifference. The US example may be worth following. Private donations and support in the US have built up the top universities, whereas in India this support is negligible or nonexistent. It is no wonder that top business and technical schools like Harvard, MIT, Stanford and Wharton School have produced generations of top business leaders in the US. What India needs is to foster active collaboration in R&D training so as to create technology and innovation incubators for the modern information age. A second type of policy needed for the success of venture capital industry is to create and continue a suitable tax and legal environment which promotes transparency, competitive efficiency and a level playing field between domestic and foreign venture capitalists.

A final point is the maintenance and improvement of quality of the products and services exported by India to world markets. A closely related area is the development of e-commerce and Internet trade. The government of India has taken some good initiatives in this regard. By the Information Technology Act of 2000 the government has introduced a policy of permitting the entry of private ISPs (internet service providers) and allowed them to set up international gateways and Internet access through cable television infrastructure. By looking at the phenomenal growth of Internet trade in the US, it is easy to infer that a similar trend would follow in India in the coming decade and the overall economic policy in India must recognize this fact and plan accordingly.

To conclude this section we may note three important points for fostering India's economic growth in the present decade. First, it has to understand the IT market in the US, where India has to compete. The US is the world market where hypercompetition prevails. To succeed in this market enhancing core competence in export industries is of primary importance. Secondly, the IT sector has reached a stage in India where innovations in several forms are needed. Venture capital, and active collaboration in R&D between the private and public sector in India is urgently called for. The educational institutions have a dynamic and catalytic role to play. Creativity may not be lacking in India. What it lacks is the paradigm of an IT-friendly environment. Finally, there is no lack of business leadership in the private sector in India. It needs to wake up to its responsibilities, and should invest in building better educational institutions and better research institutes. To compete and succeed in world markets today this is most important. India today needs the one-pointedness of goal of a Chinese entrepreneur, the zeal of a Taiwanese businessman, the creativity of a Japanese technician and above all the value systems of an average American who contributes so heavily to the cause of education. Even the University of California at Santa Barbara where I work gets an average of over $30 million a year as outright donations from private households and businesses. The top schools get more than $300 million a year. Herein lies the strength of the US. It is the apex in the building of human capital.

4.5   World competition: today and tomorrow

World competition today is influenced by two basic forces. One is technology spreading over the world by international trade. The second is through learning by doing through the use of personal computers and other IT products. Both are interrelated. Helpmann (2004) has considered the case where learning by doing becomes international in scope in the sense that it spreads equally over domestic and foreign firms. Under these circumstances both countries, the domestic and the foreign, have the same stocks of knowledge and their patterns of specialization are determined by comparative advantage, i.e., by their intrinsic productivity levels, which are determined primarily by their core competence or efficiency. The growth rate of an industry's stock of knowledge is then determined by the intrinsic productivity level of the country that specializes in this industry and by the speed of learning and size. Grossman and Helpman (1995) have shown that this pattern of interdependence of trade with learning by doing can produce a variety of growth patterns. Trade may drive a country to specialize in a sector with low growth potential thus slowing down its long run growth. Or it can drive a country to specialize in a sector with high growth potential, thereby boosting its long run growth.

The high performing countries of Southeast Asia have followed the path of specialization in sectors with high growth potential. Learning by doing in Japan, Taiwan and China has manifested in the form of borrowing and imitating the most efficient technology in the world and then altering the specialization pattern from the old to the new. Old technology has been replaced by new. All the means available to the government at the central and state levels have been deployed. FDI, high incentives for inviting expatriates with modern skills and building a large and integrated R&D network have been some of the major strategies. Japan not only borrowed the latest technology in the world, but improved it and made it user friendly to developing countries like the Middle East, Africa and Latin America. With such improved and cheaper technology around the US cannot compete very easily, because Japan has the comparative advantage in this improved technology. Taiwan, South Korea and China are following a similar trend.

One has to note that these successful NICs in Asia have two major deficiencies when compared with India. They lack proficiency in the English language and have less natural resources and technical knowledge. Hence India can alter its specialization pattern in favor of the high growth potential sector and accelerate its rate of long term growth.

It is useful to examine the scope of learning by doing in the IT sector in India and some recent trends shaping the IT services marketplace in India. One major trend is that India maintains its offshore leadership position in "outsourcing" as a method of delivery of IT services. By moving jobs offshore the companies in the US and Europe are not only saving money and reducing domestic staff, they are creating an opportunity to increase the long term strategic value of IT. The mantra for companies that outsource offshore is to keep strategic tasks in-house and outsource the rest. According to AMR research the number of software and IT service jobs in

India will increase by 1.5 million to 2.0 million by 2008. This increase represents about 40% compound annual growth rate. This prediction is consistent with the business growth of IT companies over the last five years. For example Infosys and Wipro increased their revenues by 40 and 36% in the year 2004 and increased employment by 46 and 35% respectively.

Because of IT labor productivity gains and minimal IT spending increases, AMR research estimates that US jobs in IT services will grow at less than 1.5% or roughly 700,000 workers over the years 2004–08. Since India's capacity in IT services will grow by 1.5 million IT workers, the net result is that not only the demand created by 700,000 new jobs be filled by India, but that 800,000 existing US jobs will also migrate to India. The 30 to 50% cost savings offered by India is too large a benefit to ignore by US companies facing stiff competition.

As one researcher in IT services in India has observed: the growth in India-supplied resources for IT work is a train that cannot be stopped. Despite the overheated political rhetoric, the net impact on most IT organizations in India has been minimal so far. But to sustain comparative advantage in the future, India has to adequately prepare in order to face competition from China, Taiwan, Singapore and other countries like Malaysia and Vietnam. Three steps are essential:

1 intensify packaged software application development;
2 accelerate the process of next-generation consulting;
3 develop R&D organizations through active collaborations with domestic and foreign companies.

India's offshore IT development centers for packaged business application vendors are taking on increasingly complex responsibilities. Offshoring/outsourcing has been used not only for custom application development (AD) but also by packaged application software vendors to good effect. Several competitors exist for packaged AD offshoring such as Eastern Europe, China and Vietnam but India is the most popular and it gets the largest percentage of business from the US and UK. Two examples may be cited. One is Baan, now called SSA which is one of the pioneers in leveraging Indian resources for AD. This company set up its Mumbai development center in 1989 and its Hyderabad development center in 1995. Oracle, SAP and i2 Technologies are the other vendors. People Soft, which was acquired by Oracle in December 2004 leverages Indian resources for development through two contractors. One has to note that India's popularity as a destination is mainly due to its core competence and quality.

Next-stage consulting is an area which has a huge growth potential. It is essentially designed to turn technology-focused IT workers into business-focused IT manpower. This is done through process restructuring that maximizes the value of onsite and offshore employees. The traditional consulting model exemplified by TCS (Tata Consulting Services) offering IT services on-site to US enterprises is now dead. The next-generation consulting model combines global delivery that capitalizes on low-cost resources with high-quality strategic consulting. Knowledge and resources must flow seamlessly between the customer's site and the service provider's global locations. Thus partner-based consulting companies with large numbers of high-priced onsite staff are facing extreme pricing and cost pressures as their clients look for lower cost solutions to their existing problems.

Two recent examples may be noted. One is Infosys Consulting Inc. a wholly-owned US based subsidiary being managed by partners from CGE&Y, Deloitte and EDS. The new firm will use Infosys India's resources onsite and offshore to deliver higher value but lower cost consulting. At the other end of the spectrum, IBM recently bought Daksh, an Indian company that provides offshore call center services. IBM gets access to low-cost agencies, which should help it with its Sprint Call Center outsourcing. It is clear that India has a huge potential for growth in this area and many other companies should pitch in.

Finally, India has a huge potential in R&D development and innovations. The global companies have already realized this potential and flocked to India's door. Microsoft, the global software company in software services and business solutions recently launched its research facility in Bangalore. Other companies include Pervasive Software, Polaris and Nucleus Software Laboratory. The India Semiconductor Association unveiled its ISA Technovation initiative in 2005 in universities and research institutions to institutionalize patent awareness. Clearly India has a huge growth potential here and many other domestic companies should pitch in. As IT researchers have observed, Indian IT companies have not paid much attention to expanding their domestic markets, unlike Japan, Taiwan and South Korea, where the domestic market has expanded the decentralization of IT jobs and services.

The dynamics of India's competitiveness in the global IT services market today are characterized by the following trends:

1   continued growth and demand for outside buyers for resources in India;
2   proven track record through credible vendor and quality maintenance;

3 more multinational companies scaling operations in India like IBM, Oracle, etc.;
4 continued demand by the US and UK for offshore services requiring English speaking capabilities;
5 continued buildup of physical campus to meet the growth of outsourced business in the multiple hub cities, e.g., Bangalore, Delhi, Chennai, Hyderabad, Pune and Calcutta;
6 continued quality of the Indian labor pool.

To achieve rapid growth in its IT sector and thereby overall growth, India has to incorporate these dynamics of global competition and to sustain its comparative advantage through continued learning by doing over time. As the noted management science expert Peter Drucker observed: In today's competitive world you need an organization that is a *change leader*, not just an innovator.

In the new economy India should build organizations in IT and other sectors so that they become change-leaders. That is the future. There is no other way.

References

D'Aveni, R.A. (1994) *Hypercompetition: Managing the Dynamics of Strategic Maneuvering*. New York: Free Press.

Dosi, G. (1984) *Technical Change and Industrial Transformation*. Basingstoke Macmillan – now Palgrave Macmillan.

Gates, B. (1999) *Business at the Speed of Thought*. New York: Werner Books.

Grossman, G.M. and Helpman, E. (1995) Technology and trade. In: K.G.M. Grossman, and K. Rogoff, (eds) *Handbook of International Economics* Vol. 3. Amsterdam: Elsevier.

Helpman, E. (2004) *The Mystery of Economic Growth*. Cambridge: Harvard University Press.

Hobday, M. (1995) *Innovation in East Asia: the Challenge to Japan*. Adershot: Edward Elgar.

Jorgenson, D.W. and Stiroh, K.J. (2000) Raising the speed limit: US economic growth in the information age. In: *Brookings Papers on Economic Activity*. Washington, DC: Brookings Institutions.

Korgaonker, M. (2004) The Indian experience. In: P. Drysdale, (ed.) *The New Economy in East Asia and the Pacific*. London: Routledge Curzon.

Laursen, K. (1999): The impact of technological opportunity on the dynamics of trade performance. *Structural Change and Economic Dynamics* 10, 341–57.

Lin, O.C. (1998) Science and technology policy and its influence on economic development in Taiwan. In: H.S. Rowen (ed.) *Behind East Asian Growth*. London: Routledge.

Metcalfe, J.S. (1994) Competition, evolution and the capital market. *Metroeconomica* 4, 127–54.

Nelson, R. and Winter, S. (1982): *An Evolutionary Theory of Economic Change*. Cambridge, MA: Harvard University Press.

Norsworthy, J.R. and Jang, S.L. (1992) *Empirical Measurement and Analysis of Productivity and Technological Change*. Amsterdam: North Holland.

Prahalad, C.K. and Hamel, G. (1990) The core competence of the corporation. *Harvard Business Review* 66, 79–91.

Prahalad, C.K. and Hamel, G. (1994) *Competing for the Future*. Cambridge, MA: Harvard Business School Press.

Sengupta, J.K. (2002) Model of hypercompetition. *International Journal of Systems Science* 33, 669–75.

Shapiro, C. and Varian, H. (1999) *Information Rules: a Strategic Guide to the Network Economy*. Cambridge, MA: Harvard Business School Press.

Thomas, L.G. and D'Aveni, R. (2004): The rise of hypercompetition in the US manufacturing sector 1950–2002. Mimeo paper, Atlanta, GA: Business School, Emory University.

Thore, S., Phillips, F., Ruefli, T. and Yue, P. (1996) DEA and the management of the product cycle: the US computer industry. *Computers and Operations Research* 23, 341–56.

5
Science and Technology in India's Growth

India has entered the phase of a "new economy" since the late 1990s. This economy is characterized by a number of features, each of which affects growth and development to a significant degree. The major features are as follows:

1 increasing role of the information oriented sector utilizing information and communication technology (ICT);
2 accelerating trends in openness in trade with specialization in technology-intensive exports;
3 building R&D investment and human capital for the ICT based sectors, and;
4 proactive policy of government in market enhancing and competitive strategies of domestic firms in domestic and world trade.

The US has taken the lead in ICT but others like Japan, South Korea and Taiwan are catching up. The NICs in Southeast Asia have taken the lead in openness in world trade over the last two decades. They adopted increased specialization in technology-intensive goods and services and improved their competitiveness, which has boosted their exports and overall growth. Taiwan and Japan have achieved their growth success through building human capital and learning by doing. China has adopted the competitive market model where the government has steadily followed a proactive policy of economic reform facilitating the process of technology transfer from abroad and providing incentives for medium and small firms in ICT industries. South Korea and Taiwan have also steadily followed market enhancing strategies in their government economic policies.

The key to the new economy is openness, competition, transparency and technology diffusion. To foster creativity, knowledge innovation and boost domestic and foreign trade is the goal of the new economy. The NICs in Southeast Asia are attaining such goals and catching up with industrially developed countries. India has all the potential to reach such goals. But it has to take responsibility. Federal and state governments, private entrepreneurs and professional managers and research and educational institutions need to pitch in. How? As Schumpeter observed, the path of successful innovation today is the process of "creative destruction." One has to destroy the old mores that are inefficient, the old rules that lack market enhancment and old rules of business that ignore ICT technology. Two important catalytic forces are the private sector and the education sector. Both creativity in research and competence in trade depend on these two sectors and the government has a complementary role.

Out objective here is to discuss the economic role of these catalytic forces in India's economic growth. We consider an international framework with three interrelated scenarios. One is India's increasing participation in world trade, starting with the IT sector and moving to other manufacturing and trading sectors. The second is spreading the message of knowledge innovation from IT to other sectors, especially medium and small enterprises in rural and township arenas as in China and Taiwan. The third is India's leading role in increasingly absorbing the spillover benefits of US and international information technology and associated R&D. These three scenarios emphasize three important economic effects: the *competitive effect* of world markets, the *linkage effect* in domestic fields and the *externality effect* through research and development.

5.1   Competitiveness and specialization

The competitive effect emphasizes the principle of competitive advantage through which firms grow and industry evolves. Porter (1990) has identified several sources of competitive advantage which are crucial for industry growth. Recently D'Aveni (1994) has emphasized the efficiency aspects of the competitive advantage principle which dominates the technology-intensive market structure of today. This market structure has been called hypercompetitive. Following Schumpeter's dynamic innovations approach he argues that this new type of market resembles the Darwinian world of survival of the fittest, where the rival competitors get crushed if they are not on the leading edge of the innovation efficiency frontier. Besides innovations effi-ciency, three other dynamic forces are important. One is the first mover advantage, which is most important in the software market and its growth in India. Early movers gain advantages by reaping substantial economies of scale through learning curve effects and establishing reliable customer channels through brand loyalty. The second dynamic force is the market enhancing strategy of a competitive market. This has sometimes been called demand-side economies of scale, which generates a strong positive feedback for the information-based economy today. The growth of the Internet economy and e-commerce in the US provide a clear example. The third source of dynamic efficiency can be better understood if we view efficiency as an escalation ladder. Access efficiency is the third force, whereby firms grow by racing up the escalation ladder in the stronghold arena. Thus by building barriers around a stronghold, the firms reap monopoly profits that can be used to fund aggressive price strategies and new investments in R&D. Porter (1990) identified six major barriers to entry that firms normally use to create and sustain a stronghold advantage, e.g., dynamic economies of scale, product differentiation, large capital requirement, large switching costs and specific cost advantages due to favorable locations, low-cost inputs or even government subsidies and incentive programs.

For India's software industries the competitive effect has mainly come from international trade and foreign direct investment. The principle of competitive advantage then gets transformed as the principle of comparative advantage. A country has a comparative advantage in the good that is relatively intensive in the country's abundant factor. Take for example India's software and information technology oriented industry. Over the last decade its growth has been phenomenal and this is mostly due to high growth in exports to the US and Europe. Why? There are three main reasons. One is the comparative cost advantage of IT serves in India. To the US and Europe the comparative cost of Indian IT services is 20 to 40% cheaper. Hence the fast tempo of outsourcing of IT related jobs to India. Second, we see the recent upsurge of foreign companies investing in the IT sector in Bangalore, Hyderabad, Chennai and Kolkata. These investments usually take four forms: technical services through consultancy, data entry and storage, software package develop-ment and R&D services. It is only recently over the last two years that India has emphasized software package development and R&D services in its IT exports. But these are precisely the two sub-sectors where exports are most highly income elastic and India has a superior compar-ative advantage compared to China, Taiwan and Singapore. In 1994

India's export share in software package development and R&D services was of the order of 10 and 1, whereas China had 60 and 3 respectively. Clearly, India needs to catch up. Note that India's software exports from Bangalore alone exceeded 4 billion dollars by the end of 2004, but its record of growth in exports of R&D services was still very negligible. One good sign is that foreign IT giants are moving their R&D divisions to India, since they realize India's superior comparative advantage over the NICs in Southeast Asia. Thus Microsoft Research (India) launched its research facility in Bangalore in January 2005, followed by Pervasive Software, Inc., a global value leader in infrastructure software, ISI (India Semiconductor Institute) with its Technovation initiative to institution-alize patent awareness in India and Nucleus Software Exports based in the US. Recently Hewlett Packard (HP) started a joint venture with the Indian Institutes of Technology for a computing research center. A third reason for rapid export growth from the IT sector in India is the steady rate of restructuring of IT services in India. Three obvious signs are apparent. One is that India is looking for exports to other countries besides the US and UK. The NICs in Asia, the Middle East and Africa are important outlets. Second, the volume of IT services trade with NICs in Asia including China has started to go up significantly. Recently, China has ventured in joint investment with Indian companies. For example in January 2005, South China's Shenzhen city sent some 1,000 software managers to be trained in India in software and communication skills. Likewise there has developed active collaboration with Indian companies in the telecommunication sector. Thirdly, India's economic prospects for the five years (2005–09 remain robust. In January 2005 the Indian government revised the economic growth rate to 8.5% during 2003–04 from 8.2% estimated earlier. According to the international forecasting group Global Insight Inc. all the important economic factors such as strong profit growth of IT companies, their restructuring, higher-than-ever foreign exchange reserves and the strengthening of the Indian rupee against the US dollar point to a steady growth rate of national income by more than 7% on the average. Challenges like stiff competi-tion from China and NICs in Southeast Asia that threaten growth of the IT sector in India have also opened up new opportunities for IT service providers in the IT market, making it among the fastest growing market in the Asia–Pacific region, second only to the Chinese market.

In terms of the linkage effect India's record of performance has been very poor. Although the Indian IT services industry is one of the largest offshore IT services its domestic market has yet to see comparable growth. The examples of China and Taiwan provide striking contrasts to India in this regard. The former countries have been eminently successful in expanding IT services markets in the domestic front through medium, small-scale and rural townships in coastal areas. Even the individual states and/or districts have been permitted to invite FDI in the IT services sector through various incentives. The record of performance of the domestic IT services market in India was evaluated by Gartner Dataquest in October 2003. This international firm conducts intensive face-to-face vendor research in the IT sector covering more than 350 qualitative and quantitative interviews across the Asia–Pacific region. Twenty-five vendors in all areas of IT services were interviewed in some detail in 2004 and these include the following: HCL Technologies, GTL, Hexaware Technologies, ICICI Infotech, iFlex Solutions, Infosys Technologies, ITC Infotech, Kshema Technologies, Patni Computer Systems, Polaris Software Lab, Syntel India, Tata Infotech, Wipro Infotech, Zensar Technologies and NSE.IT. Besides the above companies, revenue data earned by multinational corporations from the domestic market in India such as IBM, HP and Accenture were also used for generating the forecast for IT industry in India up to the year 2008. Some of the key findings are as follows:

1 During 2003 the IT services industry grew 15% over 2002 to $1.66 billion. The market is forecast to grow at a compound annual growth rate (CAGR) of 17.4% through 2008 to $3.7 billion. But this forecast of market size does not include transfer pricing, revenue of captive offshore and on-site facilities. When these are included, the software exports from Banglore alone will reach $6.0 billion US dollars. By 2008 this figure is likely to go up to $7.5 billion.

2 Through 2008, product support services accounting for about 28.1% of the total Indian IT services market are expected to grow faster than the professional services.

3 Development and integration services revenue accounted for the largest share of the total IT services market in India of about 57% growing at a CAGR of 16.4% from 2003 through 2008.

4 Consulting services revenue had a small decline of about $2 million in 2003, primarily due to the stiff competition from China and other NICs in Southeast Asia. But with restructuring this market is expected to grow at a CAGR of 16.2% from 2003 through 2008.

5 The banking, financial and insurance services and the telecom sector, which have been the leaders in deploying IT services in their operation would play a significant market enhancing role with a CAGR not less than 15.0% through 2008.

When market dynamics is viewed in terms of enhancing the domestic market, the externality effect opens up new opportunities for IT service providers in the Indian IT market. Exploiting these opportunities has not only a level effect in the form of increasing employment and income but also a growth effect in the form of long term research in human capital and skills. The international spillover of R&D investment in knowledge capital can be more effectively utilized in India, due to its talent pool in IT skills and collaboration with the Indian managerial pool in Silicon Valley. That India has a significant comparative advantage in this arena is apparent from the multinational giants knocking at India's doors in Bangalore, Hyderabad and Kolkata. It is clear that India has to restructure its IT operations along the lines the market dynamics change so as to tap its comparative advantages. The following strategies of growth and diversification are of critical importance, if the externality effect has to be tapped so that the domestic market expands and domestic jobs are created.

1   The domestic service providers catering to the demands by the multinational corporations (MNCs) in the R&D area must look for opportunities to form complementary alliances and joint ventures.
2   Local service providers in the software package development area must look to modify technology from abroad so as to make it more suitable and cost effective in India and other developing countries in Asia, Africa and the Middle East. Thus Indian service providers must look for subcontracting opportunities in the "mega deals" signed by global IT giants in IT services and products. The policy of Japan to borrow global technology and improve it should be the goal of Indian services providers in software research and development.
3   The consulting services area of the IT market is undergoing a rapid shift due to intense competition from other NICs in Asia. On the one hand, outsourcing of jobs from the US is moving at a fast rate, on the other hand, other NICs in Southeast Asia are now in direct competition with Indian service providers. India has a clear need to restructure its technical competence in order to tap these opportunities. Thus MNC service providers in India must leverage their ability to tap into the knowledge of global best practices from their global operations to differentiate themselves from local competition. Some recent trends may be worth noting. US based Agilent Technologies, a world leader in testing and measurement technology, software solutions for communications, life sciences and chemical industries have recently expanded their investment in India by more than 40%. Convergys Corporation, the world's largest call center operator

has planned to double the number of jobs in India during 2005 from its current level of 10,000.

4 The international R&D spillover effect in informational technology has been much less utilized in India compared to other NICs in Asia. For example Korea, Japan and Taiwan witnessed an average yearly output growth of 9.70, 5.07 and 9.71 over the period 1969–90 and the percentage contributions to output growth due to technical progress were 18.44, 30.93 and 21.52% respectively. This is from the careful econometric estimate by Nadiri and Son (1999). The comparable figures for India would not exceed 1.0 for the contribution of technical progress measured by the time shift of the translog cost function.

5.2   Growth strategy for the new economy

The new economy in India poses challenges for business, government and the labor force. Entrepreneurs and managers not only have to be professional but also develop efficiency to compete in world trade.

Let us begin with the managerial challenge and perspective of the respected management expert Peter Drucker (2000). On 22 August 2000 he was asked two questions about the future shape of a successful business venture in the IT-oriented world.

1 Several years ago you set down the five do's and three don'ts of innovation. If you were to create those rules for innovation today, what would they be?
2 What do you believe is the future of business on the Internet?

His answer to the first question was: Today you need an organization that is a change leader, not just an innovator. Five years ago you had an enormous amount of literature on creativity. Most of creativity is the normal amount of hard and systematic work. Fifteen years ago everyone wanted to be an innovative company, but unless you are *a change leader* you won't have the mindset for innovation. Innovation has to have a systematic approach. And innovation is very unpredictable. Look, you have a zipper on your pants, don't you? The five do's and three don'ts of innovation are:

Do
1 analyze the opportunities
2 go out to look, to ask, to listen

3   keep it simple, keep it focused
4   start small – try to do one specific thing
5   aim at market leadership.

Don't
1   try to be clever
2   diversify, splinter or do too many things at once
3   try to innovate for the future.

The answer to the second question was: I think if e-commerce takes only a relatively small part of the total consumer business (and it may take a fairly large part) it will have a profound impact and will force existing distribution channels to change radically. I think one high probability guess is a system that uses e-commerce to sell and a physical location to deliver. That is already being developed very rapidly in Japan and other NICs in Asia. Ito-Yokado is probably the world's largest retailer today. And they own among other things the Japanese 7-Eleven stores. Japan has 10,000 7-Elevens. Increasingly they have deals with all kinds of suppliers where customers buy online and pick up at the nearest 7-Eleven. At Japanese 7-Elevens the online pickup system already accounts for about 40% of what the store sells. Similarly for the first time selling, making and delivery are separated. The center of power has been shifting to distribution now over the last 50 years. That's accelerated several orders of magnitude. How many manufacturing plants will survive? Not many. But so far the distributor has squandered that power. The distributors already have the brands, but only a very few of the very big manufacturers have brands that have real standing in the consumer market.

In other areas, the design of a product, its manufacture, marketing and servicing will become separate businesses. They will be owned by the same financial control but basically run as separate businesses. Ford is considered a manufacturing company, but they don't manufacture anything. They assemble. This is a radical break with the mass-production concept. So its changes are very profound and very deep and very long lasting. And we are just beginning to understand what it all means.

The new economy in the future requires continual restructuring of services from Indian IT services providers. This calls for two types of growth strategies: one for the domestic market and the other for the world market. Both strategies should look to market enhancing and cost efficiency, so that domestic jobs are created and the middle class get a fair share of the fastest growth of the Indian IT sector.

Consider for example a strategy for creating a country-wide e-commerce business in India. In the US the annual sales exceeded 150 billion in 2004 and are going at a fast rate in Japan and other NICs in Asia. Obviously, India has a huge potential here. But it has to look into the problems of market enhancing and reduce or eliminate the barriers. Some of the biggest barriers to creating a global e-commerce and Internet business are the lack of physical information and payment infrastructures. But infrastructure constraints which are so critical in Indian cities and small townships can be overcome by thinking creatively as you localize a business model. The trick is to shift your thinking from *what is missing* to *what is available* locally. Consider some examples. One is Japan where credit cards are not widely used for e-commerce i.e., less than 10%. But many consumers in Japan regularly used convenience stores e.g., 7-Eleven Japan has a payment acceptance service for products and services purchased from Web merchants. Since 2001 7-Eleven Japan has gone one step further to allow consumers to pick up and pay for merchandise bought on the Web at any of its 10,000 stores in Japan. Consider a second example with business to business (B to B) commerce in India. Many small businesses in India do not have Internet access or even personal computers. So how can a US-based B to B firm or a large provider in Mumbai connect with small Indian suppliers in Bolpur or Kochi? Since India has relatively abundant cheap labor, a B to B e-commerce venture can afford to have real people visiting each small supplier in Indian towns or rural areas manually collecting orders, invoices and payments. This information can be entered into a Net-based information system that can communicate with Mumbai and also US-based buyers. At the Indian end of the network, "human-ware" can substitute for hardware and software.

The Net has made the world smaller and the time is not far off when the marketplace will welcome the creation of a number of truly global e-commerce companies. India has all the cards needed to succeed in this globalization of trade and commerce.

Recent government policy reforms offer some silver lining in this arena. First, it has eased the rules for issue of fresh equity to foreign investors and liberalized foreign loans and preference shares into equity. Secondly, access to the Internet has been made easier by government steps to reduce the costs further. In order to expand the world market for Indian products and services from its IT sector two strategies are most important. One is to borrow, imitate and improve the latest technology and develop R&D infrastructure. Japan and more recently Taiwan and China have been following this strategy with great success.

Taiwan has earmarked special industrial zones and parks with adequate incentives to foster growth in this area. India has great scope here. This is evident from the recent trend adopted by the US-based Technology Museum of Innovations, which sought more nominations for its 2005 awards from India. Borrow and then improve IT technology in its various business applications should be the motto of Indian entrepreneurs. Research activity should be broadly viewed as Schumpeterian innovation and not simply as engineering technology. Two trends are to be noted. One is that process management and general IT management services in India, both onsite and offshore are expected to grow at a compound annual growth rate of 17.4% and 21.9% respectively with a growing focus of core competency. Secondly, the banking, financial, insurance and telecom sectors are increasing their current trend in deploying IT in their operations. While these sectors will continue to remain large spenders, government spending on deploying IT is on the rise and also represents an attractive market. Some of the "mega deals" that have gone to large multinational company service providers in Bangalore indicate two major trends: growing maturity of Indian enterprises in outsourcing and their preference for service providers capable of offering them global best practice technology and services.

The second type of growth strategy is to forecast the areas of comparative advantage in the next five to eight years and plan for switching from low to high comparative advantage areas. This should be the design of a proactive restructuring policy in the provision of IT services onsite and offshore.

As an example of this type of forecasting we may refer to the simple regression study by Harrigan (1995) based on a panel of 20 countries over 15 years and country specific fixed effects from OECD data. The regression study tests the Rybcyzinski theorem which explains the change in the pattern of production to that of endowments and skills. For two industries the results are as follows:

Iron and steel:
output=constant+0.824 capital−2.311 skilled labor
−0.590 unskilled labor
Printing and publishing:
output=constant+0.570 capital+1.089 skilled labor
−0.529 unskilled labor

with t-statistics (in absolute value) between 2 and 3.5 for each estimated coefficient. From these results Harrigan infers that capital is a source of comparative advantage in these industries, while skilled labor is a source of comparative advantage in printing and publishing but not in iron and steel. Unskilled labor is a source of comparative disadvantage in both industries. Most of his results are similarly sensible. Similar results are obtained by Leamer and Levinsohn (1995). Similar regressions performed over IT sector data in India would reveal the optimal choice of restructuring operations. For example the services with highest comparative advantage should be given top priority, then the next highest and so on. This involves sequential planning. India's economic reform policies should incorporate strategies oriented to this type of sequential planning for the IT sector.

Two implications of this sequential planning may be stressed here. One is the need for strategic support as more jobs are outsourced from the US and Europe. The second is the task of training and skill development so as to turn technology-focused IT workers into business-focused IT workers. This calls for replacement strategies that keep local and remote groups staffed with high quality junior workers who can increase their skills and responsibilities. Despite the rumors of IT job losses in the US due to offshore outsourcing, recent US Department of Labor statistics indicate that the number of jobs currently lost is still relatively small. The Department's statistics show that the Computer System Design and Related Services industry sector of the US economy lost only 20,000 or 1.7% during 2004. In the same period the Computer Hardware, Peripheral and Semiconductor industries have reduced the number of workers by 70,000 or 3.4%. However, many of these job losses from within industry sectors are the result of the weak US economy and are not directly attributable to offshore outsourcing. AMR Research Inc. predicts that the number of software and IT services jobs in India will increase by 1.5 million to 2.0 million by 2008. This represents about a 40% compound annual growth rate. As examples we may refer to Infosys and Wipro which increased their staffing by 46 and 35% respectively in 2004 with their revenues increasing by 40 and 36% respectively. The AMR Research Report also concludes that existing IT staff in India do not have adequate skills to manage relationships with the offshore service provider and the IT companies in India companies must adopt sequential planning strategies for optimal restructuring and training for skill development.

5.3   Education and skill development

The need for specialization in world trade in IT services requires a strategy for skill development in India. Three points must be stressed at the outset. The private sector's role in tertiary, technical and management education must be accentuated. So far India's record of performance here is insignificant. Secondly, one has to recognize the fact that skill development and specialization in IT services come in all forms as in the Schumpeterian concept of innovations. Changes in design, improvement of software or developing business applications both onsite and offshore all involve skill development. The transition from basic research to business applications is the urgent need in the restructuring of IT services and their applications in domestic business. Finally, gender bias in technical and managerial education has to be reduced progressively, so that women can play a large role in various IT services like publishing, banking and insurance, transport and online communications.

Recent endogenous models of growth education and skill development play a dynamic role in raising the long run rate of growth of an economy. They raise people's productive capacity just as tangible physical capital and hence are called human capital. However direct measures of human capital investment or their returns are not available for international comparison over a wide range of countries. Hence we have to depend on some proxy measures of human capital through such indicators as (a) improvement in education in primary and secondary levels, (b) the enrollment in tertiary education with emphasis on science and engineering, (c) contribution to growth due to R&D effect and, (d) the quality factor in technological services used in India.

Hayami (2001) has reported (see Table 5.1) on improvements in education (World Development Reports of the World Bank), where improvement is measured as the increase in average gross enrollment ratios at primary and secondary levels. Gross enrollment ratio is defined as the ratio of total enrollment, regardless of age, to the population of the age group.

The average life expectancy measure reported in Table 5.1 is a proxy for health reflecting the level of investment in healthcare. Note that the human development index (HDI) used by UNDP (United Nations Development Program) to measure human development is a weighted average of educational attainment, life expectancy and per capita income. Expressing the index into a scale of zero (minimum) to one (maximum), the HDI provides a proxy measure of a country's relative position in human development. Countries with an HDI below 0.5 are considered to have a low level of human development, those between 0.5 and 0.8 a medium level and those above 0.8 a high level. Over the years 1960–92 the overall HDI for the developing countries as defined by UNDP Report increased from 0.260 to 0.541, whereas in East Asia, the region

Table 5.1   Improvements in education in selected countries

	Average school enrollment ratio (%)			Average life expectancy at birth (years)		
	1965	*1995*	*Increase*	*1960*	*1995*	*Increase*
Africa (sub-Saharan)	23	50	27	43	52	9
Kenya	29	67	38	47	53	6
South Asia	46	69	23	47	61	14
Bangladesh	31	62	31	46	58	12
India	51	72	21	47	62	15
East Asia	63	88	25	44	68	24
China	67	94	27	43	69	26
Thailand	46	71	25	52	69	17
S. Korea	68	98	30	53	72	19
Latin America	60	84	24	54	69	15
Brazil	62	94	16	52	67	15
Argentina	65	98	33	67	73	6
High Income (OECD)	84	100	16	70	78	8
UK	79	100	21	71	77	6
USA	98	100	2	70	77	7
Japan	91	99	8	68	80	12
World	58	82	24	53	67	14

with the largest increase, the HDI value increased from 0.255 to 0.653, i.e., about two and a half times. A selected set of HDI values for the year 1992 and other statistics are given in Table 5.2. The Human Development Reports published by UNDP also list the number of scientists and technicians per 1,000 people over the period 1988–92 as follows:

	Scientists and engineers (per 1,000 people) 1988–92	Education as % total gov. expenditure 1990	Pupil/teacher ratio (1990)	
			Primary	*Secondary*
Hong Kong	—	17.4	27	23
China	1.6	12.4	22	15
Singapore	1.8	—	26	
S. Korea	2.3	22.4	34	25
India	0.3	11.2	47	
Kenya	—	16.7	31	
Malaysia	0.4	18.8	20	19
LDCs in world	—	—	45	—
World	—	—	—	—

Table 5.2 HDI and other indicators of development

	HDI 1992	Real GDP per capita (PP $) 1992	Gross enrollment ratio (%) 1st–3rd grade	Education (% of GNP) 1980	1990	Education as % of total govt. expenditure:	
						Primary & secondary 1990	Higher education 1990
Japan	0.937	20,520	77	—	—	—	—
US	0.937	23,760	95	—	—	—	—
Hong Kong	0.905	20,340	70	—	3.0	71	29
China	0.594	1,950	55	1.8	2.3	67	19
Singapore	0.878	18,330	68	—	—	—	—
S. Korea	0.882	9,250	79	2.0	3.6	79	7
India	0.439	1,230	55	2.3	3.5	71	17
Indonesia	0.637	2,950	60	—	—	23	13
Kenya	0.481	1,400	57	4.6	6.8	77	15
LDCs	0.337	2,591	54	1.5	—	—	—
World	0.759	5,410	58	—	—	—	—

A number of economic trends are observed from these statistics. Hayami (2001) used the data from Table 5.1 to fit a regression line for gross school enrollment ratio (E) on long of national income (Log Y) as follows:

$$E = 4.4 + 10.4 \log Y; \quad R^2 = 0.84$$
$$(t = 5.9)$$

This has a high explanatory value in terms of R^2 and a significant coefficient of 10.4 for the effect of national income on average annual (gross) school enrollment ratios for primary and secondary levels of education. The East Asian economies except Thailand diverge upward from the regression line, suggesting that these economies (e.g., Singapore, South Korea and China) invest in education more heavily than the average. India was far behind the average school enrollment ratio in 1995 compared to China, South Korea, Thailand, Brazil and Argentina. In 1995 the regional average GDP per capita in East Asia was only about one-fourth that of Latin America, but the average school enrollment ratio was about the same in East Asia and Latin America. It is reasonable to hypothesize that the high rate of investment in education was an important factor behind the high economic growth in East Asia relative to other countries and regions.

Secondly, India's share of scientists and engineers is almost one-sixth that of China and almost one-eighth that of South Korea. Hong Kong's share, though not estimated by the UNDP report, would exceed that of South Korea. It is important to note that both South Korea and Taiwan were able to expand their skill base through cooperation with US aid which directly contributed to the rapid expansion of education within South Korea and Taiwan and made oversees training and education possible for many science and technical graduates including some of its future economic policymakers. Transfer of technical skills and management techniques also occurred through FDI from the US. Noland and Pack (2003) have estimated the share of science and engineering students in tertiary education in various years from the UNESCO Statistical Yearbooks as follows

India *(1964)*	*Japan* *(1955)*	*S. Korea* *(1956)*	*Malaysia* *(1967)*	*Philippines* *(1957)*
0.062	0.152	0.206	0.142	0.145

As Noland and Pack (2003) observed: South Korea's endowment of human capital in 1960 was high relative to its income level and it continued to accumulate human capital rapidly after the Second World War just like Japan. Its students were relatively concentrated in science and engineering and in the succeeding three decades the qualitative transformation of education was very rapid, e.g., by the 1990s almost 40% of Korean tertiary students were in these fields, well above the OECD mean. The experience of other successful NICs in Southeast Asia in rapid skill development was very similar. India has to follow this route in order to expedite its growth rate.

Thirdly, the private sector including private business and foreign enterprises operating in India have to play a more dynamic role in technical, tertiary and managerial education. So far only the government or the public sector has been solely responsible for this field of education. But the experiences of US, Japan and other industrial countries have shown that the private sector's contribution has been very significant. In the US the best universities and schools of business are almost 90% private. Corporate contributions, private endowments and national research grants have provided their main source of growth, e.g., Harvard, Stanford, MIT, Chicago and so on. Even high schools and technical colleges run by private support have proved their efficiency and competence. The NICs in East Asia have also

Table 5.3   Components of knowledge-index 2000

	Overall knowledge index	*Computer infrastructure*	*Education and training*	*R&D and technical knowledge*
US	1	1	8	3
Japan	2	8	10	1
S. Korea	15	16	16	13
Singapore	16	14	19	6
Malaysia	17	17	17	16
Thailand	18	19	14	19
China	19	18	18	20
Indonesia	21	21	21	21
India	22	20	22	22

emphasized the role of private sector participation in skill development. This may be seen in Table 5.3 which reproduces the country position by rank by the components of the knowledge-based development index 2000 estimated by the Third Perspective Plan 2001–2010 in Malaysia.

Here the column "computer infrastructure" is measured through the share of worldwide computer use: computers per 1,000, computer per capita and connections to the Internet. The third column "education and training" is based on total expenditure on education per capita both public and private, literacy rate, pupil–teacher ratio in primary and secondary levels and higher education enrollment. Finally, the fourth column "R&D and technical knowledge" is based on the following: high-technology exports as proportion of manufacturing exports, number of scientists and engineers in R&D, total expenditure (private and public) or R&D as percent of GDP and average annual number of patents. Note that India's rank is lower than Thailand, China and Indonesia. India has two distinct strategies to follow. One is to augment the rate of foreign direct investment (FDI) in IT and related sectors and provide incentives for on the job training and skill development. The second is to help domestic business in the private sector raise human resources capabilities by appropriate investment in human capital through higher education and professional training. Tax incentives and fiscal policies are the instruments that can be used as in China by the local and regional authorities in direct competition.

Fourthly, one has to realize that skill development and investment in knowledge capital are as vital as the need to invest in primary and secondary education in India. It is time to eliminate poverty by directing more resources toward primary and secondary education. But as Stiglitz (2003) has observed:

> the flip side of that argument is that it is very hard to close the knowledge gap or the technology gap (which is so critical for the IT sector and its export performance) without having people who are able to transfer technology knowledge from the more developed to the less developed countries. You do need to have a coterie of individuals who are able to absorb knowledge, translate that knowledge and adapt that knowledge to the situation in the country at hand. That is why today there is an increasing emphasis on higher education as part of a development strategy. The countries in East Asia recognized this very early; countries like Korea made that an explicit part of their development strategy. I think that was part of the key to their economic success.

Clearly the private sector has much to contribute to a national strategy for reducing the technology and knowledge gap. As Stiglitz has noted, it is very important to have close links between research and higher education institutions and private industry. This is one of the areas in which the US has been most successful. Around major US universities like MIT or Stanford a whole host of companies have developed cooperative ventures whose job has been to take the ideas produced in the universities and research laboratories and translate them into products and services which then spread all over the world market. Finally, the maturity of India as a country destination for the global delivery of IT services in terms of scale, quantity and quality of resources bodes well for India's ability to maintain its leadership position for the next decade. As the "country to emulate" for offshore IT services, India must continuously raise the standard of country-level business practices and investments to ensure that India outpaces the activities of smaller country locations. For this the national government policy in India must be proactive to the dynamics of India's competitiveness and skill development in the global IT services market. Both private and public investment strategies are needed for the expansion of IT service categories that are beyond the applications-related services.

5.4   NIC models in Asia: Taiwan, China and Korea

The skill development and education policies for the IT sector in NICs in Asia have played a major role in their success stories on rapid growth over the last two decades. Lessons from their experience are most useful for India, since NICs in Asia provide a variety of economic models to choose from. The Chinese leadership follows the model of capitalism and involvement in the world economy on the one hand, and political authoritarianism and commitment to traditional Chinese culture of Confucianism on the other. Taiwan is a fully-fledged democracy in the Western style. The state followed here an all-out strategy to open up the economy, invite FDI on a large scale and fostered the growth of private investment by market enhancing and competence enlarging strategies. Their miracle consisted in the enormous growth rates in private investment to levels that are almost unparalleled in the experience elsewhere now or historically. South Korea, hereafter called Korea, vigorously followed a proactive industrial policy resulting in an export boom amounting to 30 to 40% of GDP and much of it consisted of nontraditional exports (e.g., color television sets, PC monitors). This was preceded by large investment into infrastructure that was so critical for the export drive.

There exist several common points in the education and skill development policies of these three countries: Taiwan, China and Korea, although they differ in their economic policies.

First, FDI and export promotion strategies highlighted the need for rapid skill development in these countries. The exchange of knowledge and information through this network proved most beneficial for growth in exports. Secondly, primary and secondary education was stressed by government policy along with tertiary and higher education with a science and engineering orientation so that the technology gap could be reduced very fast. Thirdly, the tempo of world competition was sustained through increased investment on research and process improvement. Finally, the private sector took up the challenge in intensifying their R&D investment and the government helped transfer the new technology improvements in their state-supported laboratories to the private sector. In particular, application-oriented research was emphasized, so that it could help the competitive strategies of these high export-performance countries of Southeast Asia.

5.4.1   The case of Taiwan

The neoclassical interpretation of Taiwan's success story has been that its rapid growth was primarily due to a low level of trade protection, the availability of inputs to exporters at international prices, limited inflation and competitive factor markets. The basic fiscal incentive program was the Statute for the Encouragement of Investment which was prevalent for the period 1961 to 1990. This statute targeted specific industries for both domestic and foreign firms for augmenting the tempo of exports, from labor-intensive to technology-intensive goods and services, and various tax exemptions and accelerated depreciation allowances were allowed for these specific industries. The statute was replaced in 1990 by a new statute for the upgrading of industry, whereby firms were eligible for tax relief based on their R&D and socially favored expenditure. However the new statute retained some industry-specific incentives in the high-technology sector with its objective set for expanding exports.

But all these developments and industrial liberalization policies needed a spurt in skill development and the building of knowledge capital fit for world competitive markets. Hence another set of state policies were followed, which favored the development of the manufacturing sector through strategies designed to identify, transfer, diffuse and efficiently absorb foreign technologies and then to undertake innovations in various forms. The Industrial Technology Research Institute (ITRI) and the Hsinchu Science Park provided channels for exploiting large economies of scale in R&D investment and also economies of scope. As a result this huge state support for research and its transfer to the private sector at the product/process stage generated a high growth rate of R&D investment by the private sector. Thus the volume of R&D investment by the private sector increased about nine-fold between 1980 and 1990 and this growth tempo has been sustained since.

Two interesting points about R&D development are to be noted. One is that most of the increase in R&D investment and the related industrial development was based on firms with fewer than 100 employees. Hence the technology diffusion helped improve the middle class to a significant degree. Secondly, the government also encouraged the creation of venture capital funds to provide capital for new start-up enterprises which participated in the process of technology transfer. The protection of intellectual property rights for the newly developed R&D processes and products was also tightened after 1990. This provided a favorable climate for R&D investment in the private sector including both domestic and foreign enterprises.

How has the accumulation of human capital and related R&D efforts helped the growth of productivity in the industrial sector in Taiwan? This question is important for two reasons. One is to assess the market enhancing effect of human capital through increasing labor productivity. The other is to evaluate the externality effect in Taiwan's export market. These two effects are very strongly emphasized by the current endogenous theories of growth advanced by Romer, Lucas and others.

Recently Wang and Tsai (2002) have estimated the effect of R&D investment in Taiwan's manufacturing firms on productivity growth and also the rates of return of such Cobb–Douglas production function

$$Q_{it} = A_o e^{\lambda t} L_{it}^{\alpha} K_{it}^{1-\alpha} R_{it}^{\gamma}$$

where Q, L, K and R respectively represent value added, labor, physical capital and R&D capital. The R&D capital is measured by the stock of knowledge of the firm at time t, λ is the rate of disembodied technical change, A_o is a constant and the parameters α and γ are the output elasticity of labor and R&D capital. Constant returns to scale have been assumed for the conventional inputs L and K. A sample of 136 firms over the seven-year period 1994–2000 is obtained from Taiwan Stock Exchange data set. The regression estimates after correcting for first order serial correlation are shown in Table 5.4.

Two results are most striking. One is that the R&D capital elasticity lying between 0.18 and 0.20 is significant at the 1% level, this result showing a significant impact of R&D on productivity growth. Secondly, when the sample is divided into two groups: high-tech and non high-tech, the results are distinctly different. The R&D elasticity for high-tech firms is around 0.30 which is about six times that of the non high-tech firms. Another way of looking at the R&D effect is to analyze its average rate of return by industry-groups and also the average annual rates of TFP (total factor productivity) growth (%). The estimated results are in Tables 5.5 and 5.6. The results in Table 5.5 show that the average rates of return on R&D capital is around 35% for the high-tech firms (electronics) which is about four times the return in other industries with an average of 8 to 10%. Finally, Table 5.6 uses the conventional definition of TFP as the ratio of Q to $(L^{\alpha}K^{1-\alpha})$ and estimates TFP growth (%). Clearly the high-tech firms (e.g., electronics) had the highest TFP growth of about 13% in 2000; also there is a dramatic decline in 1998 due perhaps to the Asian financial crisis for the period 1997 (IV) to 1999 (I).

Table 5.4   Production function estimates

	α	γ	λ	R^2
All firms (N = 136)	0.485**	0.187**	0.037*	0.352
High-tech firms (N = 43)	0.305**	0.297**	0.125**	0.468
Other firms (N = 93)	0.674**	0.055	0.021	0.326

Note: One and two asterisks denote significant t-values at 5 and 1% respectively.

Table 5.5   Average rates of return on R&D investment (%)

Industry	1996	1998	2000
Food	9.79	8.97	8.96
	(2.50)	(1.75)	(0.95)
Chemicals	8.54	7.96	7.84
	(1.36)	(1.93)	(0.89)
Textiles	9.60	8.94	8.75
	(2.37)	(1.11)	(0.95)
Machinery	8.32	8.08	8.03
	(2.12)	(1.16)	(1.14)
Metals	10.73	9.88	9.90
	(2.67)	(2.44)	(2.01)
Electronics	36.84	35.31	35.12
	(4.97)	(4.23)	(3.91)

Note: Figures in parentheses are standard errors.

The information and communications technology (ICT) sector has influenced Taiwan's rapid growth rate to a significant degree. Since 1990 it has become a leading producer of computer hardware in the world. It also plays an important role in the global PC (personal computer) market today. The computer hardware industry contributes to Taiwan's economy through increased production and employment but also through R&D investment, exports and technology innovations. Recently Hu and Chan (2001) analyzed the main trends in the Taiwanese growth pattern in the ICT sector (see Table 5.6).

Table 5.6   Average annual rates of TFP growth (%)

Industry	1996	1998	2000
Food	5.14	−16.01	5.73
	(2.23)	(5.82)	(2.78)
Chemicals	2.31	−19.63	5.46
	(2.72)	(3.76)	(1.72)
Textiles	1.24	−15.28	7.39
	(2.11)	(2.71)	(2.39)
Machinery	4.12	−15.82	8.33
	(2.97)	(5.92)	(2.97)
Metals	2.78	−1.19	−1.49
	(1.98)	(1.45)	(2.51)
Electronics	6.39	−7.26	13.21
	(2.44)	(2.85)	(1.99)

First, in computer hardware production Taiwan has maintained an impressive record of growth as follows:

| | Manufacturing | | | | Total | |
| | Domestic | | Offshore | | | |
	Value ($ mill)	*Growth rate (%)*	*Value ($ mill)*	*Growth rate (%)*	*Value ($ mill)*	*Growth rate (%)*
1995	14,071	21.5	5,472	82.2	19,543	3.40
1998	19,240	1.9	14,536	28.8	33,776	11.9
2000	23,209	10.4	24,867	35.3	48,076	20.5

The growth rates of Taiwan's computer software production are equally impressive. It rose from 18.34% in 1997 to 24.40% in 2000 on an overall basis. But its three component branches grew at different rates.

	1997	*2000*
product market	11.94	16.95
project market	31.39	25.00
service market	14.07	42.00
overall	18.34	24.40

The recent popularity of e-business and e-commerce can explain the rapid growth rates of the project and services markets. In 2000 packaged software accounted for about 86% of total software exports and anti-virus programs made by Trade Inc. for 41% of package software exports.

Secondly, the details of IT sector data show that almost all R&D expenditure is for applied research and technological development e.g., the electrical and electronic machinery industry allocates about 75% of total R&D expenditure to technological development and 25% to applied research. Recently government policies have switched to promoting ICT use to create domestic demand for software and information services. These are important lessons for India to learn.

Finally, the Taiwanese government has actively promoted inward investment and technology transfer, by helping local companies to develop specialized capabilities, seek out export opportunities and exploit them. Overall Taiwan imports more technology than it exports. In 1999 the electrical and electronic industry employed 9.63% of all employees in Taiwan, one of the highest proportions in the world. This suggests that ICT manufacturing has moved from being a labor-intensive to being a technology-intensive industry.

The transition to a technology-intensive economy was facilitated by building human capital and skill formation. The emphasis on learning and education is a deep tradition of the Chinese culture. Taiwan's Constitution Article 164 proclaims that no less than 15% of the national budget shall be allocated to education, culture and science and so shall be 20% of the provincial budget and 25% of the county budget. Article 18 of the Second Amendment in 1993 has further outlined the roles of science and engineering in national development. Lin (1998) has estimated the Table 5.7 from the UNESCO Yearbook. It is clear that Taiwan has more engineering graduates than other industrial countries such as the US and Germany. India's rank is far lower.

Taiwan's technologies were originally borrowed from Japan and the US. By establishing backward linkages with the suppliers both domestic and foreign and forward linkages with customers both foreign and domestic the ICT sector in Taiwan has developed profitable niches of advantage. This strategy helped strengthen Taiwan to develop a strong position in consumer electronics, small machineries and sporting goods.

Technology diffusion across small and medium sized enterprises has also played an important role in additional employment for the middle class. Since the 1970s Taiwan has built up foreign distribution and sales channels through supply and research networks. Table 5.8 summarizes the pattern of technology diffusion through the active participation of ITRI (Industrial Technology Research Institute). It is clear that the

Table 5.7 Engineering graduates per 10,000 population in selected countries (1989)

South Korea	6.70	US	2.70
Japan	6.62	Germany	1.55
Singapore	4.84	China (1992)	1.30
Taiwan	4.00	India	0.34

Table 5.8 Technology diffusion through ITRI

		1992	*1995*
Technology transfers:	Projects	143	280
	Companies	262	418
Contract research & joint R&D	Cases	411	1,004
Patents approved	Cases	274	368
Technology services	Companies	21,943	27,061

process of technology transfer is smoothed by the increasing pool of skilled manpower. As soon as a new technology is developed in a government laboratory, the private business sector can readily follow it up and if possible develop it commercially for the world market.

One may note that in national comparisons conducted by the International Management Development Institute (IMD) Taiwan has been ranked high since the 1990s. Among the Asian NICs, Taiwan and Singapore have alternated in being number one in science and technology in the study.

5.4.2   The Chinese model

China's economic policy is very similar to that of Taiwan. The two countries helped each other in their growth of the ICT sector. During the 1990s China became the largest offshore production base for Taiwan's computer hardware industry and the largest host country for Taiwan's outward investment. Taiwan is China's fourth largest source of China's FDI; this investment accounted for only 7.76% of China's cumulative total FDI. Taiwan's official statistics show that the electronic and electrical appliance industry accounted for about 28% of total indirect mainland investment over 1991–2000. In 2000 this industry was the dominant host industry accounting for about 56.2% of indirect mainland investment.

Accumulation of human capital, learning by doing, and skill development have played a dynamic role in China's rapid development. One way to describe this role is through the concept of a national system of innovation (NSI) discussed by Nelson (1996). The NSI consists of those organizations, institutions and linkages in a country which generate, diffuse and apply scientific and technological knowledge. The stock of knowledge contained in NSI includes R&D investments and the experience of scientific and technical personnel in a country. While the proportion of scientists and engineers in relation to the total working population is relatively low in China, the absolute number is large. Note that a natural comparative advantage in R&D arising from a large human capital can offset the disadvantage due to a lack of accumulated scientific and technical knowledge. Thus even if China does not have any natural comparative advantage in performing R&D, it may overcome an initial lack of research experience due to its size, which may yield increasing returns to scale in production. In spite of its low GDP per capita China has built up a well developed technological infrastructure, partly to serve the advanced military sector and partly to increase exports overseas.

Table 5.9   R&D expenditure patterns in Asian countries

	R&D as % of GDP	% RD by sectors			Share of US patent (1993)	High-tech exports (mil ECU)
		Business	Higher Education	Government		
US (1993)	2.67	69.6	15.8	10.8	50.1	172,066
Japan (1993)	2.92	66.0	20.1	9.3	24.2	180,778
Korea (1991)	2.33	71.5	7.2	4.4	0.9	22,760
Taiwan (1992)	1.82	52.6	14.4	11.6	1.4	—
Singapore (1993)	1.12	62.0	15.8	2.2	—	27,139
Malaysia (1989)	0.37	45.8	9.0	46.0	—	11,095
China (1992)	0.61	22.7	17.7	49.9	0.10	12,064

Source: OECD 1994.

Table 5.9 provides the R&D statistics of China in relation to other countries. Although China's share of R&D in GDP is only 0.61, it devotes a large part (22.7%) to the private business sector. The trend since 1992 has increased the share of the private business sector to 30% and higher. Secondly, the IT industry has grown most rapidly in China, e.g. from 1990 to 1999 it grew by 32.1% per year compared with a total overall industry figure of 14.2% and national economy growth of 9.7%. In 2000 the output of the IT industry exceeded US \$120 billion and exports reached \$55.1 billion, up by 41.2% from 1999. China has the largest mobile phone network in Asia exceeding even that of Japan. At the end of 2000 there were 19 personal computers (PCs) per 1,000 people in China compared with only 4 per 1,000 people in the year 1996. In 2000 China produced more PCs, mobile phones, color TV sets, telephones, audio devices, video disks and magnetic heads than any other country in the world. Table 5.10 reports the growth pattern of the

Table 5.10   Production of major electronic goods in China (1995–2000)

Product	*1995*	*2000*
PCs	449,000 sets	8.6 million sets
Switches	11.23 million lines	62.37 million lines
Software	US \$82.1 million	\$2.72 billion
Color TV	19.12 million sets	37.42 million sets
Mobile phones	13,000 sets	52.1 million sets

Source: China National Statistics Bureau, 2001.

different sub-sectors of the IT sector in China. It is to be noted that in recent years the public expenditure on education and infrastructure were increased with about 10% for social welfare purposes, e.g. a social safety net. This was noted by Qian and Weingast (1997) who observed: "This naturally raises the following question: why did China not follow the examples of Latin America or India in which rent seeking and political pressures have led to more government revenue being used for unproductive social expenditures and politically motivated redistribution?" Their answer was that China followed a process of intense competition, e.g., "In China regional competition to become rich quickly is intense and every region tries to attract more capital, better quality labor and better technology." Competition raises the opportunity costs of using revenue for unproductive expenditures as in India or Latin America. In India the pressure of regional political groups provides local and state governments with incentives for spreading more on welfare redistribution which has a high dose of rent seeking. This means a lack of concentration on productive investment which is growth seeking rather than rent seeking. The growth of TVEs generated an important externality effect: competition with SOEs helped growth in 2000; China sustained the tempo of high growth rates in software and cell phone markets.

One other development needs to be noted, i.e., the recent growth in e-commerce and Internet demand. E-commerce first appeared in China in 1993 but it did not grow until 1997. By the end of 2000 there existed more than 1,500 e-commerce sites involving such businesses as finance, airlines, electrical appliances, IT products, etc. In 2000 the e-commerce transactions had a value of US $9.34 billion of which $9.29 billion was from B to B (business to business). The important point to note is that the development of e-business sites has been paralleled by the development of a national information infrastructure. Thus the implementation of modern digital information projects was carried out in customs, banking, trade and governmental transactions. All these have provided the basic hardware foundation for the development of e-trade in China.

The rapid growth of the IT industry in China can be attributed to the government's emphasis on technology and marketing innovations. Thus since 1995 more large and medium sized electronic enterprises have established their own R&D centers with an impressive record of investment. Thus there are about 2,000 major research achievements in each year, which has brought about breakthroughs in fields as diverse as local area digital switching, large scale computing and software development platforms and thin film transistor industrial manufacturing technologies.

Two important characteristics of Chinese development of the IT industry have to be noted. First, this development involved significant diffusions to rural and township industries with low to medium scale operations. Thus like Taiwan the benefits of rapid development in the IT industry were shared on a large scale. This pattern of decentralization kept up the incentives to innovate and invest by the private sector. Second, China very successfully developed a structure market of preserving federalism with induced incentives for local governments.

The second aspect needs more discussion. Recently Qian and Weingast (1997) have emphasized the point that the success of Chinese economic reform rests in large part on the success of new township and village enterprises (TVEs), which are the enterprise owned by township and village governments. These enterprises show a record of efficiency far greater than the state owned enterprises (SOEs). Note that TVEs are not actually private firms, though they enjoy considerable incentives to perform efficiently. These firms are set up and maintained by local governments. Qian and Weingast have called this system "market-preserving federalism," where widespread decentralization occurs through devolving power from central to local governments. Special incentives are provided to TVEs, e.g., better secured property rights, less social obligations for workers and budget constraints in the form of profit and loss. This devolution of power has allowed considerable flexibility in management of these TVEs. Initially the TVEs started on the south coast but are now spreading out and Chinese local governments have competed to enhance their power by creating firms with profit-maximizing profiles. One noteworthy feature is the pattern of usage of profits of these TVEs by local governments. For the last ten years about 90% of after-tax profits in TVEs were used for reinvestment and various public efficiencies in the SOEs. The World Bank estimates reported by Jefferson and Singh (1999) have reported the following regression analysis:

$$\ln(Q/L) = \underset{(t=3.4)}{-1.25^*} + 0.63\ln(K/L) + \underset{(2.55)}{0.09^*\,COMP} + \underset{(4.72)}{0.65^*\,PCOMP} - \underset{(2.54)}{0.11^*}\frac{NK}{K};$$

$$R^2 = 0.32$$
$$n = 496$$

based on 1990 data of 496 state owned enterprises. Here Q=output, L=labor, K=capital stock, COMP=firm's estimated demand elasticity for its major project, PCOMP=firm's assessment of the overall competitive pressure it faces and NK/K=fraction of nonindustrial capital stock. The asterisk denotes significance of t-statistics at 5% level.

Since Q/L is a measure of labor productivity, the above regression shows a significant impact of competition (COMP and PCOMP) on labor productivity.

Furthermore the overall estimates of expenditure on innovations and research during 1985–89 as a percentage of the total value of industrial output were as follows:

	SOE	Urban cooperatives	TVE
1989	8.2	8.3	11.5

But the number of upper level technicians and scientists as a percentage of the total workforce in 1989 was 4.0, 2.4 and 2.2. This suggests a more dominant role of the state-controlled enterprises in the R&D sector but in more recent years this picture has changed very fast.

5.4.3   The Korean experience

South Korea's export boom amounted to about 35% of GDP during the 1990s and much of it consisted of nontraditional goods such as color television sets and electronic goods. The increased exports provided the foreign exchange necessary to pay for imported raw materials, intermediate inputs and imported machinery. The state adopted a proactive export promotion strategy, e.g., a government subsidized organization, the Korean Trade Promotion Corporation (KOTRA) was established to promote exports and perform market research.

Market research, particularly for the world market and its competition is very important. This research provides estimates of price and income elasticity with respect to world income and helps restructure various IT services according to changes in elasticity. Recent econometric studies based on OECD data (1973–92) reported by Fagerberg (1996) show that the impact of price and nonprice competitiveness is very unequal across various sections of an economy. In general the price variables appear to have an impact on trade especially in low tech industries and the technology variables are significant in most sectors but particularly in chemical and computer industries. Table 5.11 provides the relevant estimates for OECD countries. Here nonprice competition is measured by a composite index of patents and R&D expenditures and econometric studies support the view that nonprice competition affects exports positively and imports negatively.

The record of export performance in IT products and services has been significantly positive for Korea. Table 5.12 shows the share of ICT products and services in total merchandise exports through 1980–89. It

Table 5.11 Price and non-price sources of international competitiveness (from OECD STAN database)

Sector	R&D as % of value added	Sources of R&D intensity		
		Technology	*Price/cost*	*Investment*
Drugs	21	4/5	2/4	1/5
Electronics	18	3/5	3/4	1/5
Computers	16	4/5	2/4	2/5
Transport w/aerospace	14	3/5	2/4	0
Electrical machinery	11	3/5	2/4	0
Industrial chemicals	9	1	3/4	0
Plastics	3	4/5	2/4	2/5

Table 5.12 Share of ICT sector in total merchandise exports

	1980	*1989*	*1998*
Japan	14	28	rose higher
US	8	13	—
Singapore	14	34	rose higher
South Korea	10	22	rose higher
Taiwan	14	25	rose higher
Hong Kong	12	16	rose higher
France	4	7	—

is clear that Japan and NICs in Asia had the highest shares of ICT products (office machinery, telecom equipment and electronics) in total merchandise exports in 1980 and 1989 and its growth has been sustained in the last decade. The success of the export promotion strategy depended on government subsidization and incentive policy. This policy also concentrated on increasing skill development and human capital. The UNESCO Statistics on the share of science and engineering students in the tertiary education sector show the following pattern:

	Share %
India (1964)	0.062
Japan (1955)	0.152
Korea (1956)	0.206
Malaysia (1967)	0.142

During 1995–97 Korea's share increased to 34%. The contribution of this human capital accumulation to total factor productivity (TFP) growth in Korea was significant. Table 5.13 reports the TFP growth for selected countries. One major reason for growth in total factor productivity in Korea was the proactive government policy which continuously monitored the progress of export-oriented firms and enterprises. Subsidies in credit policy and protection in the domestic market were contingent on the export performance of the firms. Thus the Economic Planning Board of the Korean government continuously compared the realized exports with targets set by the Board and here firms were forced to improve productivity in order to lower marginal costs. This led to intensive efforts by firms to import and assimilate improved foreign technology and best practice processes of production.

It is instructive to assess the performance of the IT sector in relation to the phenomenal growth of exports in Korea. This sector also helped with technological diffusion to other sectors and stepped up the national average growth rate. A recent OECD report (2001) noted that Korean overall productivity growth was largely due to the IT manufacturing

Table 5.13   Rates of TFP growth

Country	Growth of output per worker	Contribution to growth of output per worker		
		Physical capital per worker	*Education per worker*	*TFP growth*
Korea				
1960–73	5.6	3.2	0.9	1.4
1973–84	5.3	3.4	0.8	1.1
1984–94	5.2	3.3	0.6	2.1
Taiwan				
1960–73	6.8	3.9	0.5	2.2
1973–84	4.9	3.0	0.9	0.9
1984–94	5.6	2.3	0.5	2.8
Latin America				
1960–73	3.4	1.3	0.3	1.8
1973–84	0.4	1.1	0.4	–1.1
1984–94	0.1	0.1	0.4	–0.4
OECD (excluding US)				
1960–73	4.8	2.3	0.4	2.2
1973–84	1.8	1.1	0.6	0.2
1984–94	1.7	0.8	0.2	0.7

Source: Collins and Bosworth (1996).

sector. The IT sector also helped other sectors become more IT equipped. This helped the process of spreading the externalities of the IT sector to other sectors and the decentralization effect of market competition thereby improved the productivity of non-IT sectors. Recently Kim (2002) obtained some econometric estimates of the effect of IT capital stock on firm growth through the use of a Cobb–Douglas production function. A total number of 225 manufacturing firms was utilized for the year 1996. His estimate of marginal product of IT capital stock is 0.42, which is eight times higher than the non-IT capital stock. Secondly, the proportion of nonproduction workers (i.e. service oriented labor) increased continuously over the last two decades. While the total employment of all nonproduction workers rose from 35.9% of the industrial labor force in 1981 to 56.2% in 1998, the highly skilled proportion rose from 9.6% in 1981 to 27.7% in 1998. The impact of IT investment on industrial employment at the high skill level was much higher in the 1990s than in the 1980s.

Table 5.14 summarizes the contribution of IT investment in Korean economic growth. Conventional TFP is measured by the standard growth accounting framework from the Cobb–Douglas production function. The revised TFP is the growth rate of conventional TFP plus the growth rates of revised GDP minus the growth rate of conventional revised GDP minus the growth rate of conventional GDP. The growth rate of revised GDP is constructed by assuming the shadow price of IT investment to be six times greater than the acquisition price. The six times rule is adopted from the stock market valuation statistics, which show that the market value of IT fixed capital stock is about 6.8 times the acquisition price.

Table 5.14   Role of IT investment in Korean economic growth

	1981–85		1996–2000	
	Avg. annual growth rate	*Contribution (%)*	*Avg. annual growth rate*	*Contribution (%)*
Conventional GDP	7.525	10.0	4.751	100
IT fixed capital	0.216	3	0.394	8
Non-IT fixed capital	2.313	31	2.599	55
Employment	1.079	14	0.373	8
Conventional TFP	3.917	52	1.385	29
Revised TFP	4.360	55	9.394	74
IT Contribution	0.659	8	8.404	66

Source: Kim (2002).

It is clear that IT sector investment has helped diffuse productivity in other sectors of the Korean economy. This is very similar to the US experience since the 1990s, where the national growth contribution of computer hardware and software has exceeded fourfold according to the estimates by Jorgenson and Stiroh (2000).

The key to long-term sustainable growth in Korea in the new economy phase lies in the contribution of "knowledge" to output growth. The best proxy for this knowledge (capital) is R&D investment. In the "new economy" R&D investment improves domestic innovation and provides important linkages for technology transfer from the US. Two important characteristics of R&D investment in Korea have to be noted. One is the increasing role of the private sector. The second characteristic is that the overall cost elasticity with respect to R&D knowledge capital is positive and lower than unity. This implies that the Korean economy is in a better position to absorb new innovations. The recent econometric estimates by Thangavelu and Heng (2001) show the following trend in the elasticity of cost to R&D capital stock:

	1978–85	*1985–90*	*1990–97*
Korea	0.015	0.042	0.081
Singapore	0.026	0.011	0.021
Taiwan	0.0087	0.0024	0.001

The R&D expenditure in average percentage terms has the following breakdown for 1978–97 between the government and private sector:

		Govt.	*Private*
Korea	1978–85	42.36	57.64
	1985–90	21.79	78.21
	1991–97	19.10	80.90
Taiwan	1978–85	59.18	40.82
	1985–90	54.28	47.72
	1991–97	47.16	52.84

It is clear that in privatization efforts in R&D expenditure Korea has done much better than Taiwan. Note that the basic component for long-term growth in the knowledge-based economy depends on the "absorptive capacity" of the economy and the latter is provided by education and skill formation in the workforce. Thus economic policies need to focus on tertiary education as well as primary and secondary levels. Korea has accepted this challenge and its private sector has stepped up its investment in R&D. This has helped Korean enterprises to translate research and innovations into successful products and IT services. There is some recent evidence as noted by Thangavelu and Heng (2001) that technology cycles are getting shorter in Korea, implying that the benefits of R&D activities are spread more rapidly to different sectors of the economy other than the IT sector.

One major problem in estimating the R&D contributions to output growth is that the effects of technical change are usually not separated. A recent attempt by Nadiri and Kim (1996) has tackled this problem. They estimated a translog cost function that includes separate inputs as labor, materials, physical capital and R&D capital and the output is measured by gross output in the manufacturing sector over the period 1974–90 for three countries: US, Japan and Korea. They estimated that the conventional measure of TFP growth in US manufacturing averaged about 0.51% over 1975–90, while in Japan and Korea the figures were 0.69% and 1.26%. Secondly, the internal rates of return (%) on physical and R&D capital investment were estimated as follows:

	Physical capital			*R&D capital*		
Year	US	Japan	Korea	US	Japan	Korea
1980–90	10.63	7.69	17.84	12.39	11.73	19.42
1985	11.74	7.96	15.06	11.56	12.31	18.94
1990	9.63	9.33	22.78	11.11	15.60	23.88

What is remarkable is that the internal rate of return for both physical and R&D capital in Korea is much higher than in the US and Japan. It is no wonder that factor accumulation in the private sector was significantly stimulated by the prospect of high rates of return on physical R&D capital. Finally, they estimated the five sources of manufacturing output growth over the period 1975–90 as follows:

	Gross output	*Sources of growth (%)*				*Technical change*
		Labor	*Materials*	*Capital*	*R&D*	
		US				
1975–80	1.90	–0.03	0.62	0.34	0.01	0.81
1981–90	2.47	–0.13	1.55	0.18	0.18	0.39
		Japan				
1975–80	3.47	–0.11	2.32	0.30	0.12	0.75
1981–90	4.27	0.15	3.32	0.60	0.21	0.36
		Korea				
1975–80	13.39	0.99	10.47	2.54	0.02	0.46
1981–90	12.66	0.34	9.62	1.58	0.18	0.25

It is clear that the average growth rate of gross output was extremely high for Korea, more than three times higher than that of Japan and six times higher than that of US manufacturing. In terms of the contribution of technical change however the US and Japan performed better. The R&D effect for the period 1981–90 is almost similar for the three countries. It averaged about 0.18%. Their estimates for the overall measure of returns to scale in 1990 were 1.146, 1.137 and 1.020 for the US, Japan and Korea and they are all statistically significant at the 1% level of t-test. Although the economies of scale in Korea is lower than that of the US and Japan, one has to note that the growth of different factors in Korea was remarkable. For instance the average annual growth rates of labor, intermediate input (raw materials), physical capital and R&D capital for the period 1975–90 were 5.0%, 11.9%, 14.3% and 29.9% respectively. The remarkable growth of R&D inputs played a catalytic role in Korea's long run sustained growth.

5.5   Research and technology in India's growth

Research and technology in the context of India's economic growth have to be viewed in the broadest terms such as Schumpeterian innovations. These include R&D in the traditional sense, design, development and business application of new processes of production, skill development in the technology-intensive sector, improving borrowed technology and developing new products and services especially for the world market.

A growth strategy for "the new economy" in India should be based on four core principles. One is to use openness in international trade through the expansion and diversification of the IT sector. The second is to develop innovations in the Schumpeterian sense in sectors which have the highest comparative advantage in international markets. The third is to reorient and restructure the IT operations to exploit new opportunities, new products and new markets through a detailed procedure of market research. Finally, proactive policy should be adopted and implemented toward the diffusion of IT innovations in rural and medium scale enterprises and a sequential plan for training and skill development must be adopted with the private sector playing a more prominent role than the public sector.

Based on this growth strategy we emphasize five rules for the new economy in India comprising the information and knowledge capital oriented sector. First, the rapid growth of the IT sector in India in terms of exports in recent years has opened up new possibilities. India can now compete easily with all the NICs in Southeast Asia. However to succeed in world competition tomorrow India has to look into two basic links: (a) linking trade and productivity, and (b) increasing R&D investment for technology and market enhancement. As Grossman and Helpman (1990) have argued, increased foreign investment and learning best practice technology help to increase productivity, and productivity growth is mainly driven by private sector research and development, which results in new intermediate goods that enhance final good productivity and also contributes to public knowledge. This contribution to public knowledge is an externality benefit which may be spread to other sector of the economy. As opening up provides a larger market, demand rises for any new product or service, so that market size encourages innovation. Recently Tybout (1992) has empirically analyzed the experiences of countries like Chile (1979–85), Columbia (1977–87) and Morocco (1984–87) and found that exposure to increased foreign competition is associated with improvements in the average level of technical efficiency, reduction in the cross-plant dispersion in technical efficiency and reduction in plant size. It is important to note that reduction in plant size has occurred but efficiency is not sacrificed. Taiwan and China have similar experiences. Here the link is technical diffusion through the village and township enterprises in China. India could benefit greatly by enhancing this trade link with productivity growth across medium scale plant sizes, provided efficiency is not sacrificed. A dynamic growth strategy must include efforts and economic policy reforms aimed at expanding the volume of trade from the IT sector and modern manufacturing sector. Total trade (exports plus imports) in India was only 27% of GDP in 1999/2000 accounting for about $2.3 billion, whereas China had FDI of about $45.5 billion, which is about 20 times larger.

Secondly, investment in R&D and knowledge capital needs to be greatly improved if India has to reach the level of the fast growing NICs in Asia. The share of government in total R&D activity is dominant and is not very oriented to changing world market conditions. As Korgaonker (2001) reported, total R&D expenditure in India during 1985–95 averaged about 1% of GNP of which 80% was in the government sector. Private sector accounted for a mere 13% of the total and the industrial R&D expenditure related to industrial goods and services was less than one-third of 13%. Moreover R&D expenditure was mostly concentrated in pharmaceuticals (8.03% of total), electrical equipment (15.74%) and defense (11.86%). The need to diversify is most urgent for India. A recent World Bank study by Goldman and Felker (1997) shows that research institutions in India are not able to provide the information services and product and process engineering R&D in IT products most often requested by the foreign firms in Bangalore, Hyderabad and Chennai. Clearly India needs to improve its research and technological capabilities. The two important components of an optimal research and technology policy for India are: (a) improve quality standards and efficiency, especially for the export market, and (b) improve the diffusion of computer-integrated manufacturing. Korgaonker (2001) has summarized the following results of a survey of 150 manufacturing firms (see Table 5.15) conducted by the Confederation of Indian Industries (CII) on a rating scale of zero to 50, 50 being the highest.

Since these ratings are the averages from the ratings assigned by the individual company respondents, these are likely to have an upward bias. As Korgaonker noted, the firms rated had little experience in the application of advanced technology with a rating of 2.08. As a result the contribution of such applications to the firm's success was very low.

One has to note some encouraging trends in recent years. First of all, India has started development centers, mostly through collaboration with foreign firms catering to packaged software business applications. Offshoring and outsourcing have been used not only for custom application development but also by packaged application software. Several locations exist for application development vendors such as Eastern Europe, China and Vietnam but India is the most popular due to its cost efficiency. For example Oracle's Indian facility is currently responsible for maintenance of all the application software products. Possibilities exist for subcontracting such services to Indian enterprises,

Table 5.15   Manufacturing technologies in India: implementation and success

Technology type	Rating (%)	Technology type	Rating (%)
Information technology		Manufacturing planning &	
integration	2.8	control	
internet use	3.4	predictive maintenance	2.5
networking	3.4	enterprise resource	2.5
		planning	
Product and process design		materials planning	2.7
computer aided design	2.9		
integration	3.8	Total quality management	3.0
internet use	4.1		
networking	3.9		

provided cost efficiency can be sustained. Indian industries have great scope here. Secondly, industries in the private sector in India have slowly awakened to the need for more R&D investment. Forbes (2002) has recently studied this trend. His data cover the period 1996–97, for 990 private firms with R&D units registered with the National Department of Science and Technology. The data show some rise in R&D spending by Indian firms to around 0.64% of total sales in 1996. The following figures (in million rupees) show the growth in R&D expenditure for some of the top 20 firms:

	R&D expenditure		*Growth multiple*
	1998–99	*1992–93*	
Reliance industries	751	24	31
Mahindra & Mahindra	414	33	12
Rambaxy Lab	523	84	6
Eicher Ltd.	222	40	5
Crompton Greaves	217	54	4
Hindustan Lever	373	113	3
Telco	1000	308	3
Bhant Electronics	661	705	0.9

Note the jump in R&D spending for several private sector firms – up 2 to 20 times in six years. The change in R&D investment is most dramatic in the pharmaceutical sector, where India's signing of GATT with the WTO has helped protect Indian project patents to the year 2005. Thus R&D spending by Indian pharmaceutical firms doubled during 1995–2000 to US $70 million and exports tripled to $1.5 billion. Finally, the software sector has grown at a remarkable rate in India with an annual growth rate of 50% over the last decade. But now it needs some restructuring in skills in order to meet future competition from other countries like the NICs in Asia and China.

Thirdly, India has to explore the process of diffusion of innovations much more vigorously than before. The experiences of China, Taiwan and other NICs in Asia have shown alternative paths to achieve this goal. India has all the potential to do it. Political will and private sector initiative are the keys to success. It is useful to note new areas of opportunity here. First of all, India's IT industry grew by 26% in the year 2004. Companies like Infosys recorded a whopping 51.39% jump in net profit during October–December 2004 as against the same period in 2003. This company has set up a subsidiary in Fremont, California to provide business consulting to US corporations. It currently employs 23,000 people, and offers software development and back-office financial transactions for US companies. It surpassed $1 billion in revenue by the end of 2004. Many of the services offered by Infosys and other companies like Wipro Infotech, Tata Infotech, and ICICI Infotech can be easily decentralized to different regions of India besides Bangalore, Hyderabad, Chennai and Kolkata. Secondly, during 2003 Indian IT services grew 15% over 2002 to US $1.66 billion. The market is forecast to grow at a compound annual growth rate of 17.4% through 2008 to $3.7 billion. Since a large share of this industry is held by FDI and foreign subsidiaries of US Infotech firms, it may be easier to implement the decentralization policies by government reforms and incentives. This was done by China and Taiwan. Selected promising areas of growth in innovation diffusion in India are: (1) product support services in the IT sector, (2) development and integration services which currently accounts for 57% of the IT services market in India, (3) process management and IT management services which have a current annual growth rate of 21.9,% and (4) the telecom and financial sector's demand for IT services which is developing at a fast rate exceeding 20% per year. Thirdly, there exist broad-based areas of development that can flow from the growth of information technology in India. Two areas need special mention. One is the private participation and development in information-based projects for rural India. Recently Kaushik and Singh (2003) have discussed the economic role of two ongoing projects called *Drishtee* in Madhya Pradesh and Haryana and *Taarahat* (Technology action for rural advancement) in Punjab. Their long-term strategies include connecting people to markets via an Internet portal. Both experiments suggests that wider delivery of private and public educational services, marketing information and improved access to government services can be of great value in the diffusion of IT technology. There is a need to extend such IT services to other rural enterprises and households in India. A second line of diffusion is to encourage R&D investment in agriculture-based enterprises like plant breeding and seed technology. Thus Rangnekar (2003) has surveyed the performance of private seed companies in India in recent years and found that the total R&D expenditures and the number of scientists employed have increased substantially over the period 1987–95. The current rate of R&D intensity measured by R&D expenditure to sales ratio is about 5.75 for the large entrant firms and 4.12 for small firms. Since much of the R&D benefit in this sector is in the form of externalities and learning by doing, its social return would be much higher than the private return. The application of information technology to other related areas of rural and agricultural development has immense scope in India.

Fourthly, India has to explore the growth of new business and new enterprises in areas where it has comparative advantage. The biotech sector and the pharmaceutical industry come readily to mind. Similarly outsourcing of preclinical, medicinal and process chemistry offers a great opportunity to be exploited. Many engineering experts believe that India should take a lead in developing nanotechnology products. All these opportunities can be economically exploited by developing two types of innovative policies, where the private sector should take the lead. One is to develop an agency for market research which can accurately forecast the current trend in world markets. This would be useful in developing areas of specialization which enjoy the highest comparative advantage. This market forecasting strategy has been implemented very successfully by NICs in Asia such as Taiwan and Korea. Second, the private sector in IT and other related sectors should directly invest in the process of skill development in information technology which reduces the long-run average cost of IT services to other sectors like agriculture and trade. As Singh (2003) has observed, "In the context of complementarities it is important to recognize that these effects of IT are not just in terms of cost savings. IT implementation may enhance the quality of service beyond anything that is feasible through other methods. Furthermore, depending on who the customers are, the benefits may accrue to a broad cross-section of the population." Improved efficiency in the stockmarket as a result of automated trading, improved banking and insurance services through the use of IT, computerized reservation in the railway system, improved system of automated payments of utility bills and improved availability of research results in agriculture are some of the examples of the benefits of IT services adopted in sectors other than the IT sector.

Finally, the skill development policy should be actively followed by both the central and state governments. The experiences of China and Taiwan are very important here. Recently the Indian prime minister proposed the formation of a Knowledge Commission to undertake a major expansion of skilled manpower in India. This is a good start but a close monitoring of the accomplishments and failures has to be adopted. The private sector should take up the responsibility in two directions. One is to help in funding the growth of skills and information technology at primary, secondary and tertiary levels of education. The IT sector industries should adopt specific schools as charter schools and develop the spirit of competition among schools in order to foster the adoption of IT use.

Endowments and contributions would develop this spirit further. It is important to note that Indian subsidiaries of US companies such as Microsoft, Hewlett Packard, Dell and Motorola have already started this process of involvement, but the Indian companies tend to lag behind. The analysis by Dutta (2003) and Venkata Ratnam (2003) analyze India's potential here.

A second direction of involvement of the private sector should be in the area of management. Some experts believe that India has all the potential for rapid growth but the real bottleneck is the scarcity of good managers in IT and other modern technology-based industries. The role of IIMs in India has to be revitalized and this can be done only with the active participation of the private sector. The IIMs lack expertise in several areas such as (1) inadequate R&D and little contact with real-world business in India, (2) inadequate programs for developing entrepreneurship in all areas from small to medium scale, (3) inadequate contact with onsite and offshore development of the IT sector, and (4) inadequate programs for translating basic research into applications in the IT area. Here also endowments and joint ventures could go a long way toward efficient skill development.

Joint sharing of responsibility between the private and public sectors could inject two new elements of synergy. One is to promote the process of learning best practice technology from the world market and improve it for local endowment structures and the second is to foster competition through the monitoring of results achieved. This must be a continuing process and hence there should be a national consensus for adopting the joint responsibility system. So far the Indian government has established a National Renewal Fund with an allocation of Rs. 2 billion to provide for retraining and redeployment of workers displaced by modernization and industrial restructuring, but this is insignificant relative to the need. The private sector should take the major initiative in developing new skills so that the Indian industry can face the world challenge of tomorrow most efficiently.

References

Aoki, M. (1997) Unintended fit: organizational evolution and government design of institutions in Japan. In: M. Aoki, H. Kim and M. Okuna-Fujiwara (eds) *The Role of Government in East Asian Economic Development.* Oxford: Clarendon Press.

China National Statistics Bureau (2001) *Yearbook of Chinese Electronic Industry.* Beijing: China.

Collins, S.M. and Bosworth, B.P. (1996) Economic growth in East Asia: accumulation vs. assimilation. *Brookings Papers on Economic Activity* 2, 135–91.

Corley, M., Michie, J. and Oughton, C. (2002) Technology growth and employment. *International Review of Applied Economics* 16, 265–77.

D'Aveni, R.A. (1994) *Hypercompetition: Managing the Dynamics of Strategic Maneuvering*. New York: Free Press.

Drucker, P. (2000) Interview by James Daily. *Business 2.0*, 22 August 2000.

Dutta, S. (2003) Using offshore software development to drive value: the experience of Motorola in India. In: F. Richter and P. Banerjee (eds) *The Knowledge Economy in India*. New York: Palgrave Macmillan.

Eppinger, S.D. (2001) Innovation at the speed of information. *Harvard Business Review* 61, 149–58.

Fagerberg, J. (1996) Technology and competitiveness. *Oxford Review of Economic Policy* 12, 39–51.

Forbes, N. (2002) Doing business in India: What has liberalization changed? In: Krueger, A. (ed.) *Economic Policy Reforms and the Indian Economy*. Chicago: Chicago University Press.

Goldman, R. and Felker, S. (1997) *Science and Technology Policy in India: A World Bank Study*. New York: Oxford University Press.

Grossman, G. and Helpman, E. (1990) Comparative advantage and long-run growth. *American Economic Review* 80, 796–815.

Harrigan, J. (1995) The volume of trade in differentiated intermediate goods: theory and evidence. *Journal of International Economics* 1, 15–28.

Hayami, Y. (2001) *Development Economics*. Oxford: Oxford University Press.

Hu, S. and Chan, V. (2001) The Taiwanese experience: impact on production and trade. In: P. Drysdale (ed.) *The New Economy in East Asia and the Pacific*. London: Routledge Curzon.

Jefferson, G.H. and Singh, I. (1999) *Enterprise Reform in China*. New York: Oxford University Press for World Bank.

Jorgenson, D.W. and Stiroh, K.J. (2000) Raising the speed limit: US economic growth in the information age. In: W.C. Brainard and G.I. Perry (eds) *Brookings Papers in Economic Activity*. Washington, DC: Brookings Institution.

Kaushik, P. and Singh, N. (2003) Information technology and broad based development: preliminary lessons from North India. *World Development* 31, 591–607.

Kim, J. (2002) Information technology and firm performance in Korea. In: T. Ito and A.K. Rose (eds) *Growth and Productivity in East Asia*. Chicago: University of Chicago Press.

Korgaonker, M.G. (2001) The Indian experience. In: P. Drysdale (ed.) *The New Economy in East Asia and the Pacific*. London: Routledge Curzon.

Leamer, E. and Levinsohn, J. (1995) International trade theory: evidence. In: G.M. Grossman and K. Rogoff *Handbook of International Economics*, Vol. 3. Amsterdam: Elsevier.

Lin, O.C. (1998) Science and technology policy and its influence on economic development in Taiwan. In: H.S. Rowen (ed.) *Behind East Asian Growth*. London: Routledge.

Lipsey, R.G. (2004) The new economy: theory and measurement. In: P. Drysdale (ed.) *The New Economy in East Asia and the Pacific*. London: Routledge Curzon.

Meliciani, V. (2001) *Technology, Trade and Growth in OECD Countries*. London: Routledge.

Nadiri, M. and Kim, S. (1996) R&D, production structure and productivity growth: a comparison of the US, Japanese and Korean manufacturing sectors. Working Paper No. 5506, *National Bureau of Economic Research*, Washington, DC.

Nadiri, M. and Son, W. (1999) Sources of growth in East Asian economies. In: T. Fi., C. Huang and C.A. Lovell (eds) *Economic Efficiency and Productivity Growth in the Asian-Pacific Region*. Cheltenham: Edward Elgar.

Nelson, R.R. (1996) National innovation systems: a retrospective on a study. In: R.R. Nelson (ed.) *The Sources of Economic Growth*. Cambridge: Harvard University Press.

Noland, M. and Pack, H. (2003) *Industrial Policy in an Era of Globalization: Lessons from Asia*. Washington, DC: Institute for International Economics.

OECD (1994) *European Report on Science and Technology Indicator*. Paris: OECD.

Oi, J.C. (1999) *Rural China Takes Off: Institutional Foundations of Economic Reform*. Berkeley: University of California Press.

Porter, M.E. (1990) *The Competitive Advantage of Nations*. New York: Free Press.

Qian, Y. and Weingast, B.R. (1997) Institutions, state activism and economic development: a comparison of state-owned and township-village enterprises in China. In: M. Aoki, H. Kim and M. Okuno-Fujiwara (eds) *The Role of Government in East Asian Economic Development*. Oxford: Clarendon Press.

Rangnekar, D. (2003) Plant breeding in the era of privatization. In: Richter, F. and Banerjee, P. (eds) *The Knowledge Economy in India*. Basingstoke: Palgrave Macmillan.

Singh, N. (2003) Information technology as an engine of broad-based growth in India. In: F. Richter and P. Banerjee (eds) *The Knowledge Economy in India*. New York: Palgrave Macmillan.

Stiglitz, J. (2003) Globalization, technology and Asian development. *Asian Development Review* 20(3), 1–18.

Thangavelu, S.M. and Heng, T.M. (2001) Factors affecting growth in the region: R&D and productivity. In: P. Drysdale (ed.) *The New Economy in East Asia and the Pacific*. London: Routledge Curzon.

Tybout, J.R. (1992) Linking trade and productivity: new research directions. *World Bank Economic Review* 6, 189–211.

Venkata Ratnam, C.S. (2003) Industrial relations and increasing globalization: a case study of India. In: F. Richter and P. Banerjee (eds) *The Knowledge Economy in India*. New York: Palgrave Macmillan.

Wang, J. and Tsai, K. (2002) Productivity growth and R&D expenditure in Taiwan's manufacturing firms. In: T. Ito and A.K. Rose (eds) *Growth and Productivity in East Asia*. Chicago: University of Chicago Press.

World Bank (1994) *China: Internal Market Development*. New York: Oxford University Press.

Yuntin, D. (2004) The Chinese experience. In: P. Drysdale (ed.) *The New Economy in East Asia and the Pacific*. London: Routledge Curzon.

6
India's New Economy: Competition and Decentralization

Three principles are important for India's new economy, the three C's: the principle of Competence, the principle of Competition and the principle of Comparative advantage in trade. Each of these principles emphasizes the role of economic efficiency and productivity improvement in stimulating growth. The first principle deals with organizational efficiency: how to improve economic efficiency through restructuring of organizations and realigning managerial skills. The second emphasizes the efficiency gains from competition through market enhancing and cost effectiveness. Borrowing the best practice technology from abroad and adapting it to the domestic framework are possible strategies by which firms can gain market efficiency here. Finally, the comparative advantage principle emphasizes how to maximize economic gains from international trade by taking advantage of its comparative advantage in some goods and services. For example, India currently has a comparative advantage in IT goods and services such as body shopping and IT consulting, since it is relatively intensive in the supply of skilled IT manpower. However competition from other NICs in Asia is intensifying and there is a great need now for India to restructure its exportable services toward applied business applications and software package development.

6.1   Competence in organizations

Growth and development are sometimes viewed as a problem in the efficient coordination of investment and skill formation activities. Coordination failures may arise in many forms, e.g., lack of interdependence and matching of complementary investment projects, failure of coordination of public sector activities and failure of forward and backward linkages. These coordination failures are accentuated by the presence of strong monopoly elements causing market failure, rent-seeking interests by politicians and bureaucrats and the various forms of market failure causing inefficient utilization of private and social overhead capital.

Huntington (1996) has viewed the growth of the developing economies as a clash of two civilizations: the eastern and the western. The eastern model as exemplified by China selected a new direction in economic policy by the end of the twentieth century: it combined capitalism and the competitive market system with political authoritarianism and recommitment to the traditional Chinese culture of Confucianism. It took Britain and the US 58 and 47 years respectively to double their per capita output, but Japan with an eastern culture did it in 33 years, South Korea in 11 and China in 10.

How did China do it? First, by political will and determination, thanks to the insight of Deng Xiao Ping, who pursued a course of rapid market reforms against the mounting criticism that economic liberalization often hurts the poor and the middle class. Deng's reply was that if all Chinese are going to get rich, someone has to get rich first. Secondly, one has to note that for the 18 years 1960–78 Chinese investment had to use capital equipments manufactured either by Chinese domestic firms or by USSR and Eastern Europe. After 1978, China was increasingly able to import most up-to-date best-practice capital equipment produced in Japan, the US and Europe. The increase in the quality of capital along with the increase in capital accumulation helped to increase productivity and efficiency. Thirdly, the increasing availability of foreign capital and foreign exchange help break the bottlenecks of key intermediate inputs such as steel and IT technology. This generated competitive pressure to export more and more manufactured goods and led the Chinese industrial enterprises in these sectors to rapidly upgrade quality and efficiency and thereby reduce unit costs. What is remarkable is that these improvements spread quickly to the manufacture of goods for both domestic and foreign consumption. Thus the major contribution of market reforms in China was not to the large state-owned sector. It was the small and medium scaled enterprises owned collectively or privately that benefited most. New township and village enterprises sprang up by the thousands. While the primary (mainly agriculture), secondary (manufactures and construction) and tertiary (mainly services and trade) sectors contributed 28.1, 48.1 and 23.7% to GDP respectively in 1978, the figures in 1998 were 18.4, 48.7 and 32.9. Since 1998 the share of the services sector exceeded 39% of GDP. Finally, Chinese government policy has systematically sustained a philosophy of business clusters by various means, e.g. promoting collaboration with multinational companies in the design and manufacture of electronic products, wireless technologies, e-commerce platforms and R&D centers. Microsoft, Intel, IBM, Bell, Lucent and Ericsson have established their own R&D centers in Beijing and Shanghai. This has helped China's R&D capability to grow at a fast rate.

It is important to emphasize the role of *clusters* in improving the economic environment. It enhances competitive markets and improves overall economic efficiency by spreading and utilizing the externality effects of knowledge capital. Clusters are geographically proximate groups of companies, suppliers, service providers and associated institutions and enterprises in a particular field such as IT services linked by many common goals and complementarities. Thus the electronics industry in Beijing and Shanghai and the software industry in Bangalore (India) are examples of business clusters located in specific towns, though clusters can be concentrated in a region comprising several towns and cities. Porter (2004) has shown that clusters improve competitiveness in three broad ways. First, they increase the productivity of constituent firms or industries. The presence of a full range of inputs, skills and knowledge promotes greater efficiency and flexibility than vertical integration. Secondly, the clusters increase the capacity and capability for innovation and productivity growth. Thirdly, the clusters enable new businesses and ventures that support innovations and expand the cluster. Usually there is an array of clusters in different locations with different levels of sophistication and specialization. The clusters help to decentralize competitive efficiency across other regions and areas and China used its village and township enterprises to exploit this array of business clusters which spread across coastal and inland areas. The lessons of China are useful for India for two reasons. With a large population India needs to decentralize the competitive model and adopt a method of business clusters to effect technology diffusion on a large scale. Secondly, the technology base in Bangalore must diversify and spread to other regions of India. A proactive government policy like China and Taiwan with incentives and R&D support is urgently needed. The IIMs and other managerial training centers have a significant role to play here. The private sector also has to undertake its own responsibility for spreading the network of technology.

The resource advantage that India has today in the IT sector ought to be exploited in three profitable ways. First, a restructuring of IT industries in response to changes in world markets has to be fostered in the private sector. Two types of innovative activities have to be distinguished: proactive and reactive. Reactive policies arise when firms discover their competitive disadvantage and plan for restructuring response. Proactive policies involve discovering a new product, new software, or a new market niche in the biochemical field. Both are needed, though the proactive front needs much more attention by the private sector today.

Secondly, Indian enterprises have to realize the gains from managerial efficiency by adopting optimal decision rules for firm expansion. As a firm expands, it balances two types of costs and benefits: one is the net advantage over costs of internal coordination and the other is the transaction costs due to competitive markets. The optimal decision rule for a competitive firm under expansion is to equate the marginal return from internal coordination with the marginal cost. Growth of the IT service providers in India has not always maintained this optimal decision rule. Other countries like Russia in recent times have failed in this respone in market reforms. As Herbert Simon (1997) noted, failures in organizing skills played a big role in the current development by Russia in its effort to pursue a market model.

Thirdly, it is essential for both government policymakers and private entrepreneurs in India to understand that true competitiveness is measured by productivity. The national productivity of a country is ultimately determined by the productivity of its enterprises. Thus companies must directly attempt to shift from competing on endowments like low-cost labor services in the IT sector to competing on dynamic comparative advantages arising from superior products, services or processes. From body shopping to process development, from managing agency to package development and R&D should be the goal. One of the major unexploited sources of productivity growth in India is the managerial excellence which may be summed up by the concept of *core competence* developed by Prahalad and Hamel (1990). This is collective learning in the organization, especially coordinating diverse production and marketing skills and integrating multiple technologies. Firms in India need to emphasize competence-enhancing strategies in their investment and network policies. The state should also adopt a proactive policy towards enhancing competence and efficiency in several forms, e.g., cooperation in research, collaboration in technology transfer and the smooth transfer of best practice technology in the world. The Asian NIC experiences show very clearly that only a country with a high technology absorption capacity can make the best use of foreign capital and knowhow and can thereby promote export-oriented industrialization. It is useful to refer to the Japanese model of technology transfer in this connection. It consists of two shapes. At the first stage of direct Japanese investment in a foreign country, technical advisors from the parent company train domestic employees. There is no difference here from the Euro-American style. But in the second stage of technology transfer most of the Euro-American companies withdraw their technical advisors when the factory is running well, however in Japanese companies the technical advisors stay and continue to train the workers step by step in maintenance and repair, quality control and R&D innovations and so on. India should develop this two-tier policy for improving its core competence, first in the IT sector and then in manufacturing where the penetration of IT services is almost negligible.

6.2   Improving competitiveness

An industry's competitiveness may be measured in several ways. Two measures are often used. The most frequently used measure is the index I_c

$$I_c = E \cdot (p_f/p_d) \tag{1}$$

of competitiveness based on consumer prices. It is the nominal exchange rate (E) measured in units of domestic currency for one unit of foreign currency multiplied by the ratio of foreign (p_f) to domestic (p_d) price index. Thus a rise in the domestic price index relative to the foreign consumer price index would translate into an appreciation of the real exchange rate and hence a fall in the competitiveness index I_c. On replacing the two price indices by the respective unit labor cost u_f and u_d respectively we get the second measure

$$I_c = E \cdot (u_f/u_d) \tag{2}$$

This index is particularly useful as an indicator of competitiveness, when wage costs are higher relative to capital costs. It becomes less useful where a variety of intermediate inputs are used in its production process and where capital costs are high. A better measure considers the overall productivity ratio (π_d/π_f) rather than the labor productivity ratio in order to define an international competitiveness index

$$I_c = E \cdot (\pi_d/\pi_f) \tag{3}$$

Thus if domestic productivity index (π_d) improves relative to the world, productivity (π_f), competitiveness improves. Porter (2004) has used this measure to build a business competitiveness index (BCI). Also a growth played competitiveness index (GCI) has been developed by Blanke, Pana and Sala-i-Martin (2004) in their Global Competitiveness Report for 2003–04 prepared by the World Economic Forum. The BCI is constructed from the survey of 7,707 senior business leaders in 101 countries in 2003. Here the aim is to rank competitiveness across countries, identify countries' competitive strengths and weaknesses and reveal the trends in competitiveness in the global economy. Bivariate regressions on GDP per capita are run with two groups of explanatory variables which are the sources of competitiveness. These two groups comprise (1) company operations and strategy comprising for example production process sophistication, a capacity to innovate and a prevalence of foreign technology licensing, and (2) a national business environment comprising overall physical infrastructure, administrative infrastructure, quality of human resources in public schools and management institutes and financial market sophistication. To derive an overall BCI, sub-indexes are first computed measuring the sophistication of company operations and strategy and the quality of the national business environment. The weighted average of the two sub-indexes is defined as the BCI. The weights are determined from the coefficients of a multiple regression of the sub-indexes on per capita GDP. This method resulted in a weight of 0.66 for the national business environment and 0.34 for company operations and strategy. Some important points are borne out from these estimates of BCI discussed by Porter (2004). First of all, India's BCI ranking has improved from 44 in 1998 to 37 in 2002 and 2004. It is better than China and Indonesia. Table 6.1 presents selected estimates of ranks for 2003 with its two components: company operations and strategy (A) and quality of national business environment (B). The

Table 6.1 The BCI for selected countries (2003)

	BCI	(A)	(B)	Real GDP per capita (2002 $)
Finland	1	4	1	25,859
US	2	2	2	35,158
Singapore	8	12	4	23,393
S. Korea	23	19	25	16,465
Malaysia	26	26	24	8,922
Thailand	31	31	32	6,788
India	37	40	36	2,571
China	46	42	44	4,475
Hong Kong SAR	19	22	15	26,235
Indonesia	60	62	61	3,138
Taiwan	16	16	16	23,420
Japan	13	6	20	25,650

highest rank is one and the lowest is 101. Note however that the NICs in Asia are far better in business competitiveness. Company operations and strategy offer a competitive comparative advantage for their success. Secondly, this Global Competitiveness Report also explored the ranking estimates of innovative capacity by a national innovative capacity index (NICI). This innovation capacity index is found to be highly correlated with BCI with a correlation of just over 0.9. Innovative capacity and competitiveness are found to be highly correlated even for low income countries. Technology absorptive capacity is also highly dependent on the NICI. Table 6.2 provides ranking estimates for the 2002 NICI for selected countries.

Here higher ranks indicate better innovative capacity. Clearly India is closely following China and Malaysia. Since technology absorptive capacity is highly and positively correlated with the NICI, it is clear that India has a high growth potential in terms of technology absorptive capacity. Among low income countries Thailand and India register the highest absorptive capacity scores but a more modest level of innovative capacity, while China scores relatively high on innovative relative to absorptive capacity. As Porter and Stern (2004) have observed: India's positioning is based more on *exploiting* global technology while China is making systematic investments relative to its level of development in *developing* global technology.

The growth competitiveness index (GCI) is a more general concept than the BCI. It is based on three broad mechanisms: the macroeconomic environment (X_1), the quality of public institutions (X_2) and technology (X_3). These three are what Sachs and McArthur called the

Table 6.2 National innovative capacity index

	2002	*2003*	*Change*
US	37.21	36.60	–0.61
Singapore	32.45	34.19	1.74
Taiwan	32.34	32.84	0.50
S. Korea	30.59	31.13	0.54
China	26.06	25.86	0.20
Hong Kong SAR	28.73	28.57	–0.16
Malaysia	26.20	26.85	0.65
Thailand	25.16	24.74	–0.42
India	25.24	25.52	0.28
Indonesia	22.09	24.04	1.95
Japan	33.98	34.62	0.64

"three pillars" on which the process of economic growth rests. One central idea underlying the GCI is that this competitiveness varies for core and non-core innovators. A central role is played by innovating economies in today's world markets: this is the basic idea. Thus, core GCI = ½ technology index + ¼ public institutions index + ¼ macroeconomic environment. For non-core GCI an equal weight of 1/3 is assigned for each component. Table 6.3 provides selected ranking comparisons. When one compares the change in technology ranking over 2002–2003 Malaysia and India are found to derive significant gains. Malaysia posted the second largest increase in technology ranks to 20th position due mainly to the highest jumps in tertiary education enrollment rates, and India scored the highest improvement in the perception of the country's sophistication in the IT sector. It is important to note however that India does not figure in the list of 25 core innovating economies in 2002 as measured by the average annual US patents granted per million population. Table 6.4 reports a selected list of these 25 economies.

Porter (2004) discussed an important point as regards the growth potential of the 101 countries surveyed: which countries have an upside potential? He prepared three groups of countries: (A) for upside potential, (B) for neutral and (C) for current over-achievers. For (A) the microeconomic business competitiveness would support higher per capita real income, for (B) competitiveness and income are balanced and for

Table 6.3   GCI rankings (2003) and the component rankings

	GCI		x_1		x_2		x_3	
	Rank	*Score*	*Rank*	*Score*	*Rank*	*Score*	*Rank*	*Score*
US	2	5.81	14	4.94	17	5.71	1	6.30
Taiwan	5	5.58	18	4.82	21	5.55	3	5.97
Singapore	6	5.54	1	5.69	6	6.28	12	5.09
Japan	11	5.25	24	4.57	30	5.30	5	5.56
S. Korea	18	5.07	23	4.67	36	5.03	6	5.28
Hong Kong	24	4.93	15	4.91	10	6.03	37	4.40
China	44	4.19	25	4.56	52	4.33	65	3.67
Malaysia	29	4.83	27	4.49	34	5.12	20	4.89
Thailand	32	4.63	26	4.54	37	4.97	39	4.37
India	56	3.90	52	3.75	55	4.26	64	3.68
Indonesia	72	3.43	64	3.37	76	3.63	78	3.25

Table 6.4 Average annual US patents per million people

		Rank
US	301.48	1
Japan	273.40	2
Taiwan	241.38	3
Singapore	97.62	10
S. Korea	79.87	14
New Zealand	36.84	22
Hong Hong SAR	33.29	24
Italy	30.49	25

(C) per capita income is high relative to microeconomic competitiveness. Table 6.5 presents a selected list of countries.

The regression estimates reported by Porter show that more than 80% of the variation in GDP per capita across 101 countries is accounted for by the microeconomic fundamentals captured by the BCI index. This shows that competitive efficiency and core competence is deeply rooted in a country's microeconomic fundamentals reflected in the sophistication of its business enterprises and the quality of its microeconomic business environment.

Table 6.5 GDP per capita relative to business competitiveness

	High income countries	*Middle income countries*	*Low income countries*
(A)	Finland	Malaysia	India
	Singapore	Thailand	Vietnam
	UK	China	Indonesia
	Germany	Brazil	Pakistan
(B)	New Zealand	S. Korea	Bangladesh
	Taiwan	Philippines	Ethiopia
	Japan	Mexico	Honduras
	US	Russian Federation	
	Australia		
(C)	Spain	Hungary	Ecuador
	Canada	Argentina	Bolivia
	Hong Kong	Czech Republic	
	Greece		

6.3   Models and methods of decentralization

The economic theory of competitive equilibrium implies a Pareto optimal state of the economy as regards resource allocation. It also possesses a unique feature of a decentralized decision making process. This decentralized process has a number of optimizing features that are absent in a centralized decision-making system. First of all, total equilibrium output which maximizes total consumers' and producers' surplus at the equilibrium price may be simply obtained by summing over all firms the individual outputs of each firm which maximizes its profits. Similarly total equilibrium output may be decomposed into the sum of individual demands for each consumer, which maximizes his utility. This decentralization process allows the incentives of private producers and consumers to act on generating competitive efficiency with lowest prices and costs. Secondly, it does not involve the almost impossible tasks of collecting all the relevant data on each consumer's tastes, each firm's production set, the resource availability and so on, so that the center may aggregate all these data to obtain an optimal decision. Finally, one of the best methods of achieving this Pareto optimum in resource and output allocation is through a proper price guided allocation as illustrated by the Walrasian adjustment process. The delegation models of Koopmans and the Arrow–Hurwicz model of decomposition have developed such adjustment models of an efficient decentralized system of resource allocation, where the shadow prices could be compared with market prices. Thus the implicit costs of the two sets of prices could be considered as a broad measure of market distortion in the sense of deviation from a purely competitive framework.

Two practical methods of achieving an efficient decentralization system are: how to reduce market distortions of all sorts and how to develop market enhancing institutions and strategies. The NICs in Asia have achieved stellar success in both respects. Some examples would provide useful lessons for India. Consider the case of China's growth. A World Bank Study *The Chinese Economy* (1996) stressed some of the key elements in Chinese growth during 1985–94 when average GDP growth was 10.2%. First were economic reforms comprising substantial liberalization of domestic prices, internal and international trade and significant freedoms to agricultural households, non-state enterprises and local authorities through a gradual process of dissemination of best practice technology and knowledge. Secondly, large scale reform of state owned public enterprises by altering the policy environment, e.g., by reducing subsidies and also promoting competition through increased trade, foreign investment and low barriers to entry. The state also followed a proactive strategy of altering incentives within public enterprises by making management more autonomous and accountable, restructuring operations and reforming corporate governance. Thirdly, a network of 18 cities were been chosen under the Ninth five-year plan for comprehensive enterprise reform, where additional capital was provided by the center to increase production capacity, upgrade technology and run more than 2,600 retraining programs to upgrade the skills of laid-off workers. The latest five-year plan has adopted proactive strategies to improve the efficiency of over 14,000 large and medium sized state enterprises by diversifying ownership, encouraging mergers and consolidation and if all else fails, by liquidating. For some important cities like Shanghai promising state owned industries like the chemical and radio plants have been drastically reorganized so that the message gets through to other cities. The reorganizations and reforms include (a) establishment of a variety of commercial incentive-building relationships with township and village enterprises in rural and suburban areas through joint ventures and subcontracting, (b) exploration of joint venture arrangements with foreign firms from Singapore and the US, and (c) implementing a systematic program of enterprise restructuring at the local level. Fourthly, the Ninth and Tenth five-year plans have stressed strategies to develop and systematically implement an industrial restructuring program so as to transfer all 90,000 small industrial enterprises to the non-state sector through sales, leases or mergers. Finally, the years since 1990 have seen more and more large and medium sized electronic enterprises establish their own R&D centers and step up their capital investment. Current statistics show that every year China attains about 2,000 major research achievements, which have brought about breakthroughs in fields as diverse as local area digital switching, Galaxy large scale computing, a Chinese electronic publication system, a large scale software development platform, an air traffic control system and the thin film transistor industrial manufacturing technology. Since 1996 the number of Internet users has grown exponentially, doubling every six months. By the end of June 2001 there were 26.5 million Internet users, a figure exceeded only by the US and Japan but accounting for only 2% of China's population. Clearly the scope of developing e-commerce in China is enormous and the important point to note is that the rapid growth of the IT industry in China has been mainly due to strong emphasis by the government and private business sector on technology innovation.

The emphasis on technology innovation and large investment in the IT industry by China has helped the process of diffusion from large cities to suburban areas and from large to medium enterprises. This type of diffusion also creates jobs and skill development. Two aspects of the IT sector's product and process innovations, which helped the rapid growth of IT goods and services in both China and Taiwan are important for countries like India, which has a rich potential in IT skills. First, in this age of fierce world competition and technological and market uncertainties the traditional R&D policy which targets specific outputs and processes needs to be replaced by a new type of R&D policy involving not just basic and applied research but also commercialization of the knowledge resulting from that research. Taiwan has exploited this new R&D strategy to its fullest extent for developing its computer industry. One major channel in Taiwan, that of technology diffusion, are government affiliated laboratories and research institutions such as the Institute for Technological and Industrial Research which develops new technologies and then transfer them along with their skilled personnel to the private sector. This channel has been critically important for the start-up of Taiwan's major integrated circuit firms such as United Microelectronics Corporation and the Taiwan Semiconductor Manufacturing Corporation.

Secondly, the IT sector has profitably exploited the linkages with other sectors like manufacturing, trade and marketing. Both China and Taiwan realized very early that there exists a broad range of institutions at local and suburban areas that are complementary to the R&D activities in the IT sector with its technological capabilities and productivity. As Nelson (1995) has argued, such institutions combine to constitute what he terms a *National System of Innovations*. Thus the system of finance, marketing and distribution and managerial training in technology management are all institutions that are complementary to R&D investment in the IT sector. Their interaction in software development improves the efficacy of mutual investment.

One major source of linkage of IT sector growth with the growth of other complementary sectors is the "cluster effect." This effect emphasizes the point that the technological performance of a specific region may be the more superior, the larger the existing stock of skilled human capital in that region. Positive externalities play a critical role here. This cluster effect reminds us of the large economies of scope along with the economies of scale, which would generate the concentration phenomenon and its positive feedback effects. Thus Krugman (1991) has cited an example of productive linkage between Stanford University and IT development in Silicon Valley in California:

> There was a noticeable cumulative process operating through university itself. The revenues from the research park helped to finance Stanford's ascent to world class status in science and engineering and the university's rise helped make Silicon Valley an attractive place for high-tech business. Perhaps the most important thing to emphasize in these high-technology stories is the importance of non-high-technology factors in the agglomeration process. Both in Silicon Valley and around routes I-28, the main advantage is the existence of a pool of people with certain skills. (Krugman 1991: 64)

Thus India needs to develop a proactive policy of interregional decentralization through competition. The state and local governments have to be given support for developing competitive efficiency through attracting knowledge capital. As in China, Taiwan and South Korea the competition of regions will become the competition to accumulate, attract and build human capital locally. If a region is successful in competing for human capital, the general economic situation will improve and a process of acceleration and catching up will take place. Human capital accumulated today determines the opportunities for the future. This is as much true for an individual, as for the country.

Recently the prime minister of India proposed the setting up of rural business and information technology hubs across rural India on the lines of China and Taiwan to enhance gains for the rural and agricultural sectors. In China the local and state governments enjoy autonomy to invite FDI in information technology and thereby engage in healthy competition which improves efficiency all around. India has every reason to adopt such a policy. Note that India received about $4 billion in 2003 in FDI from OECD countries as against China's $53 billion. This superior record for China is largely due to competition and experimentation by the state, local and village and township enterprises.

It is useful to emphasize here the role of biotechnology and biochemical industries in enhancing the process of decentralization of IT and its complementary sectors in India. These enterprises are defined by their skilled scientists. One has to note that many of these scientists do not work for the company full-time but instead are members of university facilities and research institutes. These university-based scientists fulfill a variety of roles within biotechnology and biochemical companies, e.g., founders, members of a specialized team, etc. In order to gain access to this knowledge foreign enterprises interested in biotechnology rely on a strategy of outward foreign direct investment in the geographic areas where the latest technical knowledge is most heavily located. There are numerous examples of European computer companies which have established affiliates in Silicon Valley in California, so that the new knowledge can be most easily transferred back to the home country. India should adopt a similar strategy to invest in the US for gaining access to the latest knowledge available in biotechnology and IT fields. The aim should not be to penetrate the US market but rather to access valuable economic knowledge and then transfer it back to India in order to increase market share in India, Asia and the world. This knowledge will subsequently enhance the competitiveness and productivity of the Indian economy. From "brain drain" to "brain gain": the way is clear.

6.4   Strategy for structural transformation

India's new economy need three types of structural transformations: to shift from the primary to secondary and tertiary sectors, to build infrastructure framework and the quality of public institutions and to adopt the best practice technology of the world to enhance global competitiveness. These three mechanisms have been called the "three pillars" of the concept of the growth competitiveness index (GCI) developed by Sachs and McArthur and surveyed in the Global Competitiveness Report 2003–2004 by the World Economic Forum. In terms of GCI the rankings among 80 selected countries are reported in Table 6.6, where

Table 6.6   GCI rankings and comparisons

Country	2002 rank	2003 rank
Finland	1	1
US	2	2
Taiwan	6	5
Singapore	7	6
Japan	16	11
S. Korea	25	18
Hong Kong	22	22
Malaysia	30	27
Thailand	37	30
India	54	53
China	38	42

one indicates the highest in terms of global competitiveness and 80 means the lowest. Note the changes in South Korea, Malaysia and Thailand over the period 2002–03. India's position is worse than China's. Taiwan's ascent to fifth place in 2003 is mainly due to higher scores in the quality of public institutions, e.g., less favoritism in the decisions of government officials, better control of corruption and greater public trust of politicians. Taiwan received a very high rank (No. 3) in the technology index and increased volume of patents.

Two sub-indexes: the public institutions index and the technology index provide the two basic elements of the growth competitiveness index. Table 6.7 presents selected estimates from 80 countries. Note that India's position in the corruption index is the worst (No. 80), while China has rank 65. Since corruption increases transactions costs and rent-seeking attitudes, it discourages efficiency and productivity. More transparency is urgently needed here. In technology scores China does much better than India and Taiwan where economic growth reducing inequality of income distribution holds third rank after the US and Finland. Some US estimates in March 2005 showed that the US does not hold the leading position in information technology anymore. Singapore is on top followed by Finland and Iceland, and Taiwan holds the largest number of US patents per million people.

The poor record of India's performance in the technology sector may be mainly attributed to three factors. One is the failure to restructure the IT sector services as the world market changes. The second is the

Table 6.7 Three sub-indexes: public institutions, corruption and technology (2003)

	Public institutions		Corruption		Technology	
	Rank	*Score*	*Rank*	*Score*	*Rank*	*Score*
Finland	2	6.52	4	6.68	2	600
US	17	5.71	17	5.71	1	6.30
Taiwan	21	5.55	19	6.08	3	5.97
Singapore	6	6.28	5	6.68	12	5.09
Japan	20	5.58			5	5.56
S. Korea	36	5.03	38	5.34	6	5.28
Hong Kong	10	6.30	9	6.42	37	4.40
China	52	4.33	50	4.84	65	3.67
India	55	4.26	80	3.86	64	3.68
Malaysia	34	5.12	39	5.28	20	4.89
Thailand	37	4.97	45	5.06	39	4.37

lack of decentralization in other sectors, due to the failure of the manufacturing and agricultural sectors to utilize modern IT services to enhance competitive markets and their efficiency. The third factor is inadequate participation by the private sector in R&D projects and skill development in colleges and technical institutions. India's role in the world economy has not grown as fast as China's. But India has a distinct comparative advantage in computer services generating business offshore (e.g., call centers, back office work for banking and insurance, printing and distribution and so on). India has to realize that the information system of a society is crucial for innovation as well as the diffusion process. With advanced communication work and computer use new global opportunities have opened up for learning new information technology, integrating IT knowledge and disseminating knowhow. Now innovation cycles are shortening and Schumpeterian rents from first-mover advantages are declining for firms in regional markets. Welfens et al. (1999) have recently discussed the growth performance of the IT sector in OECD countries and found that about 50% of total OECD spending on R&D is in the private sector and about 67% of R&D investment is performed in the private business sector. European Union countries compares very well with the US in this respect. India's IT sector is still bogged down to offshore body shopping and outsourcing; it is still some distance away from developing software and applied package development. R&D investment in the private business sector is miniscule and there is little or no collaboration between the private and public sectors in research or consulting or commercialization of research products. India's share of US patents is nonexistent, whereas Taiwan is at the top. Two encouraging signs emerged in 2005. One was increased interest by NICs in Asia to invest in IT and its complementary sectors in India. Thus South Korea announced in March 2005 that it would invest in India's semiconductor development. LG of Korea decided to invest $105 million in consumer electronics in India. Taiwan also announced its intention to collaborate with India's technology sector in the field of designing system-on-chips. The second is the slow trend by Indian entrepreneurs to collaborate with universities and technology institutes in R&D, patenting and commercialization of research products. The Indian government announced plans to create special economic zones to develop biotechnology parks and free trade warehouses with 100% FDI participation. This follows the Taiwan model of dissemination of information technology toward small and medium enterprises in suburban areas.

In order to restructure IT and related sectors in India for facing current world competition in international trade India needs to adopt two dynamic strategies. One is the managerial strategy based on the concept of "core competence" mentioned before. It involves three steps: learn the best practice information technology, coordinate and integrate. Improvement in competence would then follow automatically. The second is the marketing challenge, where economists can contribute a great deal through applied market research and distributive supply chain analysis. India's export policy ought to be based on optimal lines of specialization based on the dynamic comparative advantage principle. It is useful in this connection to refer to the empirical research for OECD countries, which include countries like Finland and Iceland which are among the top five world leaders in information technology, and above the US. Meliciani (2001) has recently estimated for 13 OECD countries (Australia, Canada, Denmark, Finland, France, Germany, Italy, Japan, Netherlands, Norway, Sweden, UK and US) over the period 1973–92 the significance of the elasticity of price and non-price competition variables in explaining exports in different sectors. Table 6.8 reports selected estimates for selected sectors and shows two points very clearly. One is the dominant role of income elasticity. The other is the role of patents among factors of non-price competitiveness in almost all high-tech and medium-high technology sectors. Note that world income elasticity is highest for office and computer machinery (3.79) and next for professional

Table 6.8 Impact of price and non-price variables on export elasticities of OECD countries (1973–92) by sectors

Sector	Relative unit labor cost	Relative no. of patents	Relative investment	World income
Office & computer machinery	−0.28***	0.19***	0.10***	3.79***
Professional goods	−0.56***	0.11	0.09	2.61***
Radio, TV & commercial equipment	−0.41***	0.21***	0.10	2.54***
Electrical machines	−0.20***	0.38***	0.11*	2.33***
Drugs & medicines	−0.29***	0.11*	0.09	2.07***
Rubber & plastic goods	−0.042***	0.04	0.30***	1.96***
Chemical goods excluding drugs	−0.36***	0.30***	−0.01	1.81***
Transport equipment	−0.428**	0.17**	0.03	1.23***
Basic metal industries	−0.63***	0.07	0.10	1.11***
Textiles & leather	−0.76***	−0.01	0.14**	0.79***

Note: One, two and three asterisks denote significant t-values at 10, 5 and 1% respectively.
Source: Meliciani (2001).

services (2.61). These professional services include outsourcing of jobs and India has a high degree of comparative advantages as evidenced by the rapid growth of IT services in Bangalore, Hyderabad and Delhi.

Two new points emerge from the estimates of Table 6.9. In general the price competition based income elasticities are lower than the other measure based on both price and non-price elements of world competition. One finds a high positive correlation (0.762) between these two measures of income elasticity. Secondly, specialization measured by comparative advantage in the top five elastic sectors is highly positively correlated with income elasticities (0.678 for price based and 0.655 for combined measures). Meliciani (2001) has observed three interesting points. First, Japan shows the larger values of comparative advantage in both above-average and top five elasticity sub-sectors and at the same time has experienced larger increases in technology shares. Secondly, among variables that capture technological competitiveness, relative numbers of patents have a strong positive and significant effect on exports. Thirdly, there is empirical support for the view that the "quality" of trade specialization positively and significantly affects the export elasticities of income. Countries which are able to produce high-income

Table 6.9   Export elasticity and country's specialization for OECD countries (1973–92)

Country	Export elasticity		Comparative advantage in top 5 elastic sectors (3)
	Price-based variables of competition (1)	*Both price & non-price variables (2)*	
Australia	0.374	−0.21	0.152
Canada	1.524	1.432	0.378
Denmark	1.218	1.229	0.798
Finland	1.548	0.804	0.472
Germany	1.618	1.527	1.133
Italy	1.528	1.319	0.753
Japan	2.098	1.257	2.031
Netherlands	1.217	1.121	0.872
Norway	0.455	0.398	0.245
Sweden	1.034	1.197	1.007
UK	1.048	1.265	1.003
US	1.566	1.756	1.086

Source: Meliciani (2001).

elasticity products can appropriate a much larger share of world income than countries producing only low income elasticity products.

The lesson for India is clear: to develop appropriate strategies mainly by the private sector with proactive support by government policy, which improves technological competitiveness in the form of higher R&D expenditures on the job and in the universities-cum-research institutes, higher patenting activity and a higher rate of human capital accumulation through restructuring of education and skill development policies.

Accelerating the shift from the primary to secondary and tertiary sectors is the second most important step in structural transformation for the Indian economy. In current development theory two paradigms of growth have been characterized. One is the shift of agricultural surplus labor and other resources into the manufacturing and tertiary sectors by the process of industrialization. Arthur Lewis and others emphasized this shift as very crucial to the growth of new industries due to higher profits and induced investment. The second paradigm stresses the role of the IT sector, initially in the form of professional services and then shifting to more income-elastic products in software technology. This rapid export growth in the IT sector pulls up the other sector including manufacturing and the income-elastic products in agricultural and rural industries. This occurs through backward and forward linkages. The second paradigm works much faster than the first. The NICs of Asia provides ample testimony to this conclusion. As we noted before, these NICs in Asia doubled their per capita income in about a decade whereas it took three to four decades for other industrial countries – like the UK and US.

Table 6.10 shows the relative position of India compared to the NICs in Asia as regards the contribution of the three sectors: agriculture, industry and services and the composition of export trade as regards these sectors. Clearly India's performance is far below China's. The export composition in India is much more intensive in primary goods. However in terms of agricultural value added per worker India was equal or better than China in 1998–2000. But this productivity is less than one-tenth of South Korea and Malaysia.

India's share of manufacturing exports in 2001 is much lower compared to South Korea, Singapore and China. Even in high-tech exports where India has distinct comparative advantages (IT services) India lags behind all the successful NICs in Asia. One reason is that capital inflows to India in the form of FDI is very small. For example in 1998 FDI in China was $45.5 billion, or about 20 times larger than

Table 6.10 Shares of agriculture, industry and the services sectors in total GDP (%)

Country	Value added as % of GDP in						Primary exports		Manuf. exports		High tech exports		Agricultural value added per worker ($1995 base year)	
	Agriculture		Industry		Services		(As % of merchandise exports)							
	1991	2001	1991	2001	1991	2001	1990	2001	1990	2001	1990	2001	1988–90	1998–00
Singapore	—	—	38	34	62	66	27	11	72	85	39	60	27,176	49,905
S. Korea	8	21	45	19	47	60	6	9	94	91	18	29	7,159	12,374
Malaysia	—	8	—	50	—	42	46	19	54	80	36	57	5,680	6,519
Hong Kong	—	—	25	14	75	85	4	4	95	95	0	20	—	—
China	26	15	42	52	32	33	27	11	72	89	0	20	227	321
India	31	24	28	27	41	48	28	21	71	77	4	6	343	397
Thailand	12	10	39	40	49	50	36	22	63	74	21	31	778	909
Indonesia	19	24	42	27	39	48	—	—	—	—	—	—	343	397

Notes: (a) The shares of GDP for 1999 are based on production and for 2001 on value added for the three sectors.
(b) Agricultural value added per worker includes rural industries and trade in agricultural goods.
Source: World Bank: *World Development Report* (2003).

for India ($2.3 billion). In order to exploit the benefits of FDI capital inflows India has started reflexing caps on foreign equity participation in Indian ventures such as airport development, power and transport investment, etc. But the pace of reforms is still very slow. And some states like West Bengal and Kerala influenced largely by the communist politicians put up an anti-FDI stance in their public posturing, although they profess to follow the Chinese ideology and Marxist political views.

A second reason following from this double standard in economic policy and reforms in India is the policy of reservation of certain products for exclusive production by small scale industries (SSI reservation). As the government-commissioned Hussain Committee reported in 1997, this SSI reservation policy has crippled the growth of several industrial sectors and restricted exports in many areas including garments, toys, leather goods and agro processing where India has a potential comparative advantage. This is a strange contrast to the record of China and Taiwan, where small and medium enterprises in village and township areas have flourished under conditions of free trade and no reservation. They have improved their efficiency substantially. Incentives in the form of IT support and tax advantages were all that was needed to attract FDI and develop these sectors in China and Taiwan at a high rate!

Table 6.11 shows some broad trends in the sectoral components of growth. It is clear that the contributions of agriculture and industry have been almost static but the services sector has improved its contribution over the years. However the services sector has two components: the traditional and the modern. The traditional sector includes low-income and low productivity occupations which have remained stagnant, but the modern sector which includes professional IT services has been increasing at a fast rate. The ICOR in Table 6.11 is the ratio of the investment rate to the GDP growth rate, where a falling ICOR over time indicates improved productivity of capital. However this capital stock does not include human capital accumulation involving learning by doing and cumulative experience and the policymakers have failed to emphasize this aspect in their reforms strategies. This is a marked contrast from the experience of NICs in Asia.

One important point to note from Table 6.11 is the insignificant role played by net exports to GDP growth. Lack of openness in trade and lack of transparent policy towards FDI have impeded the growth of exports. This poses a stark contrast with NIC experiences in Asia. Also it is very clear that the public sector still plays a very dominant role in the growth process. Indirectly this suggests that economic reforms have not

Table 6.11   Sectoral components of growth in India 1951–52 to 1999–2000 (%)

	Average			
	1951–80	*1980–91*	*1992–97*	*1997–2000*
Real GDP growth	3.7	5.9	6.4	5.9
Real per capita GDP growth	1.5	3.8	4.5	4.3
Contribution to growth by				
new exports	—	0.6	0.2	0.6
public sector	1.1	1.7	1.3	3.9
private sector	2.2	4.2	5.7	2.2
Contribution to growth by				
agriculture	1.0	1.5	1.4	0.6
industry	1.1	1.9	2.1	1.6
services	1.4	2.4	3.2	3.9
ICORs by sectors				
overall	—	4.2	4.1	4.8
agriculture	—	2.0	1.5	2.6
industry	—	5.7	6.8	10.7
services	—	4.0	2.9	2.1

Table 6.12   Growth rates of GDP and exports volume for selected countries

	GDP Growth Rate (%)				*Growth rate of exports (%)*	
	1965–80		*1980–80*		*1965–80*	*1980–90*
	Agriculture	*Industry*	*Agriculture*	*Industry*		
India	2.5	4.2	3.1	6.1	3.0	6.5
China	2.8	10.0	3.1	12.5	4.8	11.0
Indonesia	4.3	11.9	3.2	9.9	9.6	12.8
Thailand	4.6	9.5	4.1	9.0	8.6	13.2
S. Korea	3.0	16.4	2.8	12.2	27.2	12.8

Source: World Bank, *World Development Report* (1992).

yet altered the basic incentive structure of the private sector. Table 6.12 shows the annual percentage growth rates of export volume for selected countries. It is apparent that India's performance during 1980–90 is about half that of other comparable countries including China and South Korea.

Some new steps were undertaken by the Indian government in May 2004. United Progressive Alliance announced that it would adhere to six basic principles of governance. Four of the most important economic principles underlying this Common Minimum Program of governance are as follows:

1   The UPA government will adopt policies to ensure that the economy grows at least 7 to 8% per year in a sustained manner over a decade and more and in a manner that generates employment.
2   The UPA government will ensure that the services industry is given all support to fulfill its true growth and employment potential. This includes software and all IT-enabled services, trade, distribution, transport, telecommunications, finance and tourism.
3   The UPA administration will revamp the functioning of the Khadi and Village Industries Commission and launch new programs for the modernization of the coir, handlooms, power looms, garments, rubber, handicrafts, food processing, sericulture, leather, pottery, toy manufacturing and other rural and cottage industries.
4   Academic excellence and professional competence will be the sole criteria for all appointments to bodies like the ICHR, ICSSR, UGC, NCERT and also IITs and IIMs.

What is essential is not the official announcement but a follow up every six months. A monitoring agency needs to be created to assess the record and adopt appropriate policy reform so that the target is realized. The private sector has to be taken into confidence so that this common program is implemented. So far India's planning exercise has been mainly of the indicative variety with some degree of bureaucratic control. There has been no responsibility system, no accounting for lapses.

As is apparent from the trend in productivity reported in Table 6.13, capital productivity has been negative over the last three decades 1959–89. How can that be in a country where capital is so scarce? It is no wonder that India's investment in the ICT (information and communication technology) sector is still so low compared to other NICs in Asia. Table 6.14 provides some estimates for a comparable set of countries. It is clear that India's share of ICT investment in total GDP is barely 1.9, while for Taiwan and South Korea the figures were 3.3 and 6.1 respectively in 1996.

In terms of total factor productivity growth estimated by subtracting the weighted growth rates of factor inputs from the growth rate of value

Table 6.13 Trends in productivity and growth in manufacturing in India (% per annum)

	1959–80	1959–66	1965–80	1980–89
Value added	5.5	9.1	5.0	7.0
Capital stock	8.6	13.4	7.0	7.5
Employment	3.3	4.0	3.5	–0.5
Total factor productivity	–0.5	0.2	–0.3	2.8
Labor productivity	2.1	4.9	1.4	7.5
Capital productivity	–2.8	–3.8	–1.9	–0.5

Source: Ahluwalia (1995).

Table 6.14 ICT expenditures as a proportion of GDP and investment 1996 (%)

Country	ICT investment as % of GDP	ICT investment as % of gross fixed capital formation
Taiwan	3.3	6.5
S. Korea	6.1	7.7
Singapore	6.1	6.7
Hong Kong	6.1	7.6
India	1.9	2.9
Malaysia	4.7	5.1
Japan	6.4	6.5
US	7.7	20.6

Source: Hu and Chan (2001).

added at constant prices India's productivity growth was 1.04 during 1991–97, compared to 2.32 for South Korea, 3.29 for Singapore and 5.94 for Indonesia. This is reported by Thangavelu and Heng (2001). It is clear that India has to make systematic efforts in improving industrial productivity and attaining core competence in world markets. There is no short cut.

6.5   India's growth: the promise and the potential

India's growth potential can be assessed in three ways. Can it be the leader in information and communications technology (ICT) in the next decade? Can it double its per capita income within the same period? Can it restructure its manufacturing and services sector so that it can successfully compete with the NICs in Asia in the world market? An affirmative answer to each of these questions is based on the core hypothesis that India has high economic potential. Like China it may only be a sleeping giant. Once awakened the giant may leap forward in the ICT market exceeding the NIC record in Asia. What do the empirical records and trend show? Is it a pipe dream?

An industry report by Gartner Dataquest entitled: "Indian IT Services Market Dynamics: 2002, 2003 and Beyond" has studied the market trends of the Indian ICT services marketplace and concluded that its growth prospects are robust in the next five to ten years. Although the Indian ICT industry is one of the largest exporters of offshore IT services, its domestic market has yet to see comparable growth. However things have changed since 2003. Factors such as strong profit growth of Indian IT businesses resulting from restructuring of their operations and broad based economic growth across different sectors have opened up new opportunities in the domestic Indian market. For example a private business in Gujarat has announced that it is bringing out a personal computer model costing 10,000 rupees ($220). International long distance calls are now reduced to 13 cents per minute. Given the high price elasticity of Internet costs it is clear that phone call charges are the main barrier to Internet connection. Table 6.15 shows local call costs in various countries as of 2001.

This shows clearly that India has a huge potential in developing e-trade and e-commerce markets through the Internet. With a huge population base and the rapid spread of mobile phones, the market enhancing power of lowest telephone rates in India is enormous. The risk perception

Table 6.15   Local call costs (US $ per 3 minutes)

Country	Cost (US $)
Indonesia	0.02
India	0.01
Japan	0.08
S. Korea	0.03
Malaysia	0.02
Philippines	0.006
Singapore	0.02
Taiwan	0.05
Thailand	0.07

Source: Aswicahyono et al. (2001).

of Internet commerce and trade in India can be considerably improved by following the Japanese model we discussed before, where the wide network of 7-Eleven Stores provides the clearing houses of such trades. This "network revolution" can work wonders for India's promise for the future. This new network technology can make a substantial contribution to India's economic efficiency and competitiveness. Furthermore it can be used for more efficient and effective education, healthcare and public administration at all levels: the urban and the rural. One may recall how the then Chief Minister Chandra Babu Naidu of Andhra Pradesh revolutionized the monitoring process for public officials who are responsible for timely implementation of development projects and rural enterprises. As yet other states and the center have to adopt such monitoring policies so that bureaucrats can be responsible to the public and accountable to those whom they serve. This transparency is lacking all the way.

Recently Callen et al. (2001) have discussed a number of empirical research studies which concluded that, notwithstanding the large dose of economic liberalization introduced in the mid-1990s, India's GDP growth performance has lagged behind a number of other Asian economies like Taiwan, Singapore and Korea and the benefits of more substantial economic reform could be significant. Bajpai and Sachs (1997) estimated that the annual per capita growth in India could be raised by as much as 3.5 percentage points by adopting more extensive market reforms, greater openness and larger share of FDI and improvement in education at the tertiary and technical levels.

The effect of technology growth in the IT sector on job creation and employment in India has been one-sided, i.e., it has raised the wages and salaries of IT professional workers who have the required technical skills but this benefit has not spread across other industries and rural and village industries as in China and Taiwan. Technology diffusion has been minimal. Why? Two main reasons may be given. One is the lack of development of a system of trust and responsibility between large industry and village enterprises. The story similar is between government and industry. Joint ventures and collaborations are either nonexistent or noncooperative. Not competition, but a game theory model of the noncooperative type is the rule prevalent here. Indian IT sector companies would cooperate more freely in joint ventures with multinational corporations from abroad but stay away from forging alliances with local and suburban area enterprises. This is in striking contrast to the Chinese and Taiwanese experiences. Secondly, Indian enterprises lack initiative in developing new markets in the domestic sector. The IT services sector could easily shift a number of their activities to rural and suburban areas and take advantage of developing new markets but this has not happened on a large scale so far.

Many economic researchers have stressed that the export potential of Indian agriculture, particularly of non-traditional commodities is substantial. For example horticultural exports, exports of jewelry of Indian designs, of toys and leather goods could be increased significantly provided the needed infrastructure is put in place. Two basic elements of this infrastructure needed are: availability of latest designs and trends in world markets today and a good system of market research which predicts the change in price and income elasticities of various exportable goods. Lack of use of this type of research has meant that Indian enterprises are not always aware of new windows opening up and old windows closing down. In today's world competition this knowledge is so critical to the growth of new businesses as emphasized by Schumpeter in the theory of innovation as the main engine of rapid growth.

The promise of India's huge growth potential lies in creativity and core competence. By fostering these it can be a leader in information technology in the world today. Singapore, Finland and Iceland are now at the top in information technology. Even in US patents per million people, countries like Taiwan are in the lead. India has the potential to rise to the top but it needs to restructure and revamp. From body shopping to new product development, from low productivity goods and services to high productivity components and from low income elasticity goods to high income elasticity goods and services: this should be the optimal pattern of shift in the growth of the ICT sector.

That India has the capability in steering this new revolutionary challenge is borne out amply by India's development of a new software product called i-flex, which provides vertical financial services to banks. Initially it developed as Citicorp Information Technology Industries Ltd. (Citil) but in 2000 this was renamed i-flex. This helps banks manage all functions other than dealing directly with customers. Its work is a highly applied kind of packaged development but it does not concentrate on the fundamental systems software development like Microsoft. I-flex is at the higher end of the value chain, e.g., it has embedded Oracle's database management system in its own applications. It has attained fairly impressive financial results. It has recorded a compound annual growth rate of 70.17% in revenue. Its profit before taxes grew by an average of 69% from 1995 to 2000. In 2000 the operating revenue was 50% in outsourced software development services and 50% in packaged products such as Flexcube, the latter moving above 55% since the end of 2001. Baba and Tschang (2001) have studied the growth of i-flex and compared it with Sony's TV game industry products like Play Station. They have broken down i-flex's growth in three phases. The first phase involved a relatively simple product called Microbanker, which targeted customers in new emerging markets in India and Southeast Asia. The second phase started in 1997 with a sophisticated new product, flexcube, which was modular and more advanced than its competitors' products. The third phase starting in 1999 broadened its offerings in the financial sector to include consulting and a full contracted systems solution to its consumers.

The new strategies continually developed and applied by i-flex emphasize three new areas. One is the incubation and establishment of new businesses, e.g., it has set up business Internet portals (dot.com companies) offering a full range of services and products, which brings investors, brokers, banks and depositors into one portal. The second strategy is to build joint ventures in vertical business-to-customer (B to C) and business-to-business (B to B) financial "infomediary" portals. The third and the most important strategy is that i-flex has subscribed to international software engineering quality standards. As measured by the capability maturity model of the international Software Engineering Institute (SIE) i-flex is ranked at the highest level of software engineering competence. The principle of core competence is at the heart of growth of i-flex.

It is instructive here to compare the growth strategies of Sony which developed Play Station during 1994–99 in the TV game industry, combining both hardware and software. In 2000 Sony upgraded its TV game business strategy by releasing a new game platform, Play Station 2. It established in 2000 the company Play Station.com (Japan) Inc. and began to use the Internet for direct sales of Play Station 2 software, DVD-video software and related products. The most important strategy followed by Sony since the middle 1990s is to encourage its autonomous business units and internal companies to form "offspring ventures." Thus Sony has used *soft alliances* to decentralize its product platform management. This management style is flexible and based on the concept of "integrated decentralized management."

The lessons for developing software packages in different fields and sectors in India are threefold. The first is to sustain core competence, as Sony did in traditional business by continuing its inhouse development of hardware and advanced semiconductors. The second is to stay on the latest technology frontier by continually investing in R&D. Thus Sony has embraced the latest modular technology and open networks, which helped it to make use of complementary modules from other companies positioning themselves in each of the industrial activities comprising the product. This is the most efficient use of research spillover emphasized by new-growth theorists like Romer and Lucas. Finally, Sony has followed an efficient process of decentralization by forming strategic alliances with a number of key players such as Cisco Systems, AOL (America Online) and Micromedia Inc.

Sony's strategy choice has been adopted by i-flex as regards strategic alliances. Currently the company has strategic alliances with different technology suppliers like Oracle, Microsoft, Sun, HP and Compaq. Also through these alliances i-flex can improve its technological competence by being a part of modular technology which is at the leading edge of the technology frontier.

Many small and medium-scale software development companies have been started in Mumbai, Bangalore, Hyderabad and other cities in India and they are trying to tap into international markets in the UK, US and Europe. But their success rate is very low for two reasons. Firstly, they find increasing difficulty in forming "soft alliances" with other Indian companies like i-flex. There is an acute shortage of the spirit of technological diffusion. Second, the marketing and distribution network is very ill-developed in India. Unlike Taiwan, China and Singapore the leading enterprises in information technology in India have yet to realize the benefit of tapping research externalities. Management institutes, business schools and IITs have a new role for them in developing this information infrastructure. This process of decentralization would help create new jobs and thereby step up the growth of other sectors. At present many sectors other than the financial and IT services fail to use information technology to improve their productivity and hence core competence. This poses a challenge for IT sector entrepreneurs: how to decentralize venture capital and knowhow to all other sectors and thereby improve the linkages to overall growth.

Some of the new areas of growth where new products and hence new businesses can be launched in India include the following:

1 Develop "business process services" (BPO) further in other sectors of the Indian economy such as nontraditional lines of agriculture (horticulture) and subcontracting of government enterprises.
2 Target new types of software development such as antivirus and antitheft and also software to improve trade by e-commerce.

3 Emphasize R&D and quality improvement in every modern industry in India. The responsibility of the private sector is paramount here.
4 New lines of product development by utilizing solar energy must be emphasized. Again the private sector has a dominant role to play.
5 Develop a skill development fund for fostering the growth of information-based knowledge capital. Such funds are widely used in Singapore and Malaysia and were successful because they were a part of institutional context where several different institutions and agencies joined together. What is needed here is a close monitoring of the effectiveness of the program which should be mainly directed to the electronics and export-sensitive goods.

It is clear that to be successful, these strategies need a new orientation for the company policy and structure in India. In addition to creating a greater commitment to human capital accumulation and learning by doing and adopting global strategies and alliances with the best practice technology firms in the world, Indian companies need to strive for the three Cs: core competence, competitive advantage through productivity improvement, and comparative advantage, which facilitates market enhancing and exploitation of scale economies.

How does learning by doing help the growth process? We quote from Helpman (2004) who stressed that increasing interdependence between sectors and also through international trade provides the key to growth.

> To see how learning-by-doing affects specialization, trade and growth, imagine a country that produces two products, with learning-by-doing taking place in each of them. The available resources cannot be expanded, implying that productivity is the only variable source of growth. Also suppose that initially the country does not trade with the outside world. Then total factor productivity (TFP) rises in every sector at a rate that depends on the sector's output level and the sector-specific speed of learning. A sector with faster learning experiences faster growth of its stock of knowledge and faster TFP growth. (61)

This is also the message of "core competence," which is described by Prahalad and Hamel (1990) as the collective learning in the organization, especially in how to coordinate diverse production skills and integrate multiple streams of technology.

India has all the capability to fulfill this promise.

References

Ahluwalia, I.J. (1995) New economic policies, enterprises and privatization in India. In: R. Cassen and V. Joshi (eds) *India: the Future of Economic Reform.* Delhi: Oxford University Press.

Aswicahyono, H., Anas, T. and Ardiyanto, D. (2001) Internet providers: an industry study. In: P. Drysdale (ed.) *The New Economy in East Asia and the Pacific.* London: Routledge Curzon.

Baba, Y. and Tschang, F.T. (2001) Corporate strategies in information technology firms. In: P. Drysdale (ed.) *The New Economy in East Asia and the Pacific.* London: Routledge Curzon.

Bajpai, N. and Sachs, J.D. (1997) India's economic reforms: some lessons from East Asia. *Journal of International Trade and Economic Development 6*, 135–64.

Blanke, S., Pana, T. and Sala-i-Martin (2004) *Global Competitiveness Report.* New York: World Economic Forum.

Callen, T., Reyonds, P. and Towe, C. (eds) (2001) *India at the Crossroads: Sustaining Growth and Reducing Poverty.* Washington, DC: International Monetary Fund.

Helpman, E. (2004) *The Mystery of Economic Growth.* Cambridge: Harvard University Press.

Hu, S. and Chan, V. (2001) The Taiwanese experience: impact on production and trade. In: P. Drysdale, (ed.) *The New Economy in East Asia and the Pacific.* London: Routledge-Curzon.

Huntington, S.P. (1996) *The Clash of Civilizations and the Remaking of World Order.* New York: Simon and Schuster.

Krugman, P. (1991) *Geography and Trade.* Cambridge: MIT Press.

Meliciani, V. (2001) *Technology, Trade and Growth in OECD Countries.* London: Routledge.

Nelson, R. (1995) *National Systems of Innovation.* Oxford: Oxford University Press.

Porter, M. (2004) Building the microeconomic foundation of prosperity: findings from the business competitiveness index. In: X. Sala-i-Martin, (ed.) *The Global Competitiveness Report.* Oxford: Oxford University Press.

Porter, M. and Stern, I. (2004) A report on global competitiveness. In: Porter, M. (ed.) *Global Competitiveness Report.* New York: World Economic Forum.

Prahalad, C.K. and Hamel, G. (1990) The core competence of the corporation. *Harvard Business Review, 66,* 79–91.

Sala-i-Martin, X. (2004) *The Global Competitiveness Report 2003–2004.* New York: Oxford University Press.

Simon, H. (1997) *An Empirically Based Microeconomics.* New York: Cambridge University Press.

Thangavelu, S.M. and Heng, T.M. (2001) Factors affecting growth in the region: R&D and productivity. In: P. Drysdale, (ed.) *The New Economy in East Asia and the Pacific.* London: Routledge Curzon.

Welfens, W. and Warner, A. (1999) *Globalization, Economic Growth and Innovation Dynamics.* Berlin: Springer.

World Bank (1992) *World Development Report.* New York: Oxford University Press.

World Bank (1996) *The Chinese Economy.* Washington, DC: World Bank.

World Bank (2003) *World Development Report.* New York: Oxford University Press.

Index

Printed in the United States
70302LV00001B/172-231